WITHDRAWN

Basic concepts
of rural sociology

Boguslaw Galeski

Professor of Sociology
Institute of Philosophy and Sociology
Polish Academy of Sciences

Basic concepts
of rural sociology

translated by H. C. Stevens
edited by Teodor Shanin and Peter Worsley
with the assistance of Ann Allen

Manchester University Press

Socjologia wsi: pojecia podstawowe
© Panstwowe Wydawnictwo Naukowe, Warsaw

This translation © 1972 MANCHESTER UNIVERSITY PRESS

Published by the University of Manchester at

THE UNIVERSITY PRESS

316–324 Oxford Road, Manchester M13 9NR

ISBN: 0 7190 0432 2

Made and printed in Great Britain by
William Clowes & Sons, Limited
London, Beccles and Colchester

Contents

Editors' preface

Considering that the majority of the world's population are peasants, the under-development of rural sociology in the West is as remarkable as it is depressing. In the last two decades there has only been one sociological textbook which has attempted the systematic conceptualization of the peasantry as a social phenomenon (though the tradition in anthropology has been much richer).[1] The reasons are not far to seek. The social sciences have grown up mainly in countries rich enough to support elaborate educational, research and other intellectual institutions and milieux. Such countries have been both urbanized and industrialized; hence they have not been very interested in rural life, which is increasingly and rapidly ceasing to exist as a distinctive, separate 'peasant culture' or peasant social structure. Even the very work of farming now takes place under conditions more analogous to those under which townspeople work, and general life styles have become shared as modern communications and mass media bridge town and country. In these countries, moreover, the peasantry has ceased to be the majority of the nation; agriculture has assumed a secondary place within the economy. Though a peasantry often persists, it has now become, to use Wolf's terms, 'secondary' rather than 'primary'. Increasingly, what happens in the countryside is determined by what happens in the towns. The most advanced industrial countries, therefore, have also been the most advanced agricultural countries. A developed engineering, chemical and biological technology, plus rationalized management techniques, have brought about agricultural modernization. Traditional social barriers between town and country have become so broken

1   Eric Wolf, *Peasants*, Prentice-Hall, New Jersey, 1966. A few recent 'readers' have attempted to start filling the gap: J. Potter, G. N. Foster and M. M. Diaz (eds.), *Peasant society: a reader*, Little Brown, Boston, Mass., 1967, and T. Shanin (ed.), *Peasants and peasant societies*, Penguin, Harmondsworth, 1971.

down in the process that the very existence of a distinctive rural life, in countries like Britain or Belgium, has become a 'world we have lost'.

The general process can be observed in other parts of the world, even in less developed countries. In Latin America, for instance, 57 per cent of the population of Argentine, Uruguay and Chile live in urban places of 20,000 people or more, and 29 per cent of the remainder of Latin America.[2]

The explosion of cities and towns is, indeed, a universal phenomenon, by no means confined to the industrialized West or to Latin America, though industrialization in under-developed countries proceeds at a pace quite inadequate to absorb these migrants into regular employment—particularly into industrial employment of a kind that leads to economic and general social modernization. For this kind of 'neo-colonial' urbanization is 'implosive' or 'involutionary' rather than development. It may well also be politically explosive.

Despite this growth of cities, half the total population of India still live in communities of 999 inhabitants or less: a quarter of them are landless; another quarter own less than one acre. And 85 per cent of China's population are peasants.

Anyone wishing to understand the nature of the changes going on in rural life in these regions will get little help from established sociology. Rural sociology, in particular, has been, for the most part, theoretically anaemic, descriptive and focused on the problems of North American Middle Western plains and prairies and on the South. Though a gold-mine-full of data has been accumulated over decades, it has virtually been ignored by those who specialize in sociological theorizing—with rare exceptions, such as Pitirim Sorokin and Carl Zimmerman.[3] Usually, those who did show an interest in rural sociology themselves came from countries with a strong peasantry, Florian Znaniecki being the outstanding example.

2   See Gerald Breese, *Urbanization in developing countries,* Prentice-Hall, Englewood Cliffs, N.J., 1966; also P. Worsley, 'Problems of the have-not world', in *The Times history of our times,* 1945-70, ed. Marcus Cunliffe, Weidenfeld & Nicolson, London, 1971.
3   P. A. Sorokin and C. C. Zimmerman, *Principles of rural–urban sociology,* Holt, New York, 1929; also P. Sorokin, C. C. Zimmerman and C. J. Galpin, *A systematic source book of rural sociology,* University of Minnesota, 1932, 3 vols,

Today, the exodus from the countryside has been going on so long in North America and Western Europe that peasant–workers, 'factory farms' and farmers living in the town and commuters in the village, are common. But the process was centuries in the making. The revolution in 'relations of production', for example, began centuries ago in Britain with the enclosure movement, though it reached its height in the eighteenth century with the expulsion of tens of thousands who became the kernel of the modern agricultural as well as industrial proletariat. The breakthrough to modern capitalist agriculture in the eighteenth century also involved a revolution in production techniques, though the greatest scientific advances here occurred a century later. In North America this capitalist and technological transformation of agriculture also went hand in hand with the advance of the frontier westwards. The problems generated by such a rapidly changing rural society were, therefore, much more large-scale, novel and difficult than they are now, and much more important, too, for the whole economy and polity. In the United States, consequently, a whole network of 'land grant' colleges was called into existence to service this technological transformation as science was harnessed to aid the farmer, by carrying out research into soil types, crop rotations, seed selections, and the like, and by educating his son in the colleges' Agriculture Schools. It was in this context that the scientific study of the social problems of the changing countryside also came into being, and gave inter-war rural sociology its distinctive character.

Today this is a dying tradition. Some of its leading figures have turned their attention to the parallel problems of modernization in the contemporary under-developed world, in the understanding of which this kind of rural sociology is by no means entirely irrelevant. But much American rural sociology is parochially concerned with studying its own national variant of rural life, and where American ideas have been applied to the under-developed world—in forms ranging from enthusiasm for capital-intensive, mechanized farming to populist 'community development' work (as American as cherry pie)—they have proved singularly irrelevant or inadequate.

Equally, collectivization on the Soviet model has been mechanistically tried and inevitably found wanting in many countries to which it has been introduced, most of them but by no means all

of them under-developed, even if primarily agrarian. But the
Soviet impact has not been limited to the negative experience of
collectivization. Its more positive aspects remain relevant for
under-developed countries seeking to modernize both their agriculture and their rural society. Two particular traditions of
thought and practice stand out. These are the tradition of Russian
agrarian research (which long antedates the revolution of 1917),
and specifically Marxist—and Leninist—theories about the peasantry. However much these may have been applied with utter
lack of flexibility and imagination in past practice, Galeski's later
chapters in the present work show that the abundance of vitality
and potential contained in these traditions is by no means
exhausted.

Even before 1917 both the radical intelligentsia (too often dis-
missed simply as idealistic, and basically silly, utopians), and
Tsarist governments, had long been preoccupied, inevitably, with
'the peasant question'. The so-called 'Zemstvo statisticians', for
example, collected enormous amounts of data—no less than
4,000 volumes—which constitute an incomparable treasury.[4] These
were widely used by researchers, by administrators and by opponents of the government, who used official data to develop their
own radical and revolutionary critiques of the political economy
of Russia. The best known of these was Lenin.[5] Yet he was, in his
time, only one of a large number of writers concerned with the
problem of modernizing a country in which the backward smallholder family farm was the typical economic and social unit. To
some, communitarian traditions, notably the institution of communal land-holding in the form of the *mir*, were admired in that
they were non-capitalist (more exactly, pre-capitalist) and might,
therefore, be preserved long enough to prevent capitalism developing in the countryside, or might be transformed into an insti-

4   Teodor Shanin, *The awkward class*, Part II, Clarendon Press,
Oxford, 1971. See also the essay by B. Kerblay in *Peasants and peasant
societies* (ed. T. Shanin), pp. 150-160.
5   V. I. Lenin, 'The development of capitalism in Russia', *Selected
works*, vol. 1, Lawrence & Wishart, 1936, pp. 219-385; 'The agrarian–
peasant question in the revolution of 1905-1907', *Selected works*, vol. 3,
1936, pp. 139–286; 'Theory of the agrarian question', *Selected works*,
vol. 12, 1939.

tutional base for modern co-operative farming.[6] Whether this
should be based on peasant smallholder co-operatives or large-
scale collectives was a matter of virulent debate, and, later, not
merely of abstract discussion. Lenin believed that the village was
too far gone in a capitalist direction, and that class polarization
there would lead to a polarization in the villages every bit as
marked as that of the polarization between proletariat and bourgeoisie in the towns. The relationship between the peasantry and
the urban world and the machinery of the socialist State remained, both theoretically and practically, extremely problematic
even after the revolution. In particular, the strategy of accumu-
lating capital with which to finance industrialization advocated
by Preobrazhensky[7] was attacked as involving a tightrope-walking
act, since it depended upon a flourishing peasant agriculture,
which could easily lead to the restoration (or consolidation) of
capitalism in the countryside. His opponents advocated the radical rationalization of agriculture in large-scale collective units.
Chayanov,[8] who more than anyone else pointed to the *diseco*-
nomies of scale, at least in agriculture, was silenced when he
disappeared, with Preobrazhensky, during the Stalin era.

Anyone familiar with the literature of development will in-
stantly recognize that these struggles are by no means purely of
interest to sociologists. They are the very stuff of debate and political struggle in the contemporary Third World. Many of the
problems of the under-developed world are, of course, new ones,
generated by the conditions of neo-colonialism, and hence differ
in important ways from the problems of earlier eras. But many
agrarian problems have been familiar for decades, allowing for
differences of history and culture. The great debate about the fate
of the *mir*, for example, is paralleled in much of President

6   Karl Marx, *Pre-capitalist economic formations* (ed. E. J. Hobs-
bawm), Lawrence & Wishart, London, 1964; F. Venturi, *Roots of revolution: a history of the Populist and Socialist movements in nineteenth century Russia*, Weidenfeld & Nicolson, London, 1960.
7   E. Preobrazhensky, *The new economics* (trans. B. Pearce), Clarendon Press, Oxford, 1965 (first published in Russian, 1924).
8   A. V. Chayanov, *The theory of peasant economy* (ed. D. B.
Thorner, B. Kerblay and R. Smith), American Economic Association's
Transaction series, Irwin, 1967.

Nyerere's thinking about Ujamaa villages in contemporary Tanzania.[9]

In the West most discussion of Communist agricultural development and theory tends to stop with the historically ever more remote period of collectivization. It is one of the merits of Galeski's work that it deals with post-war experience in Poland, a country with a different culture and historical heritage, and whose smallholding agriculture is much more akin to that to be found in most under-developed countries than to Soviet collectivized agriculture.

In calling attention to this Russian and Marxist writing, then, and to its influence upon Polish rural sociology, we by no means wish to imply that Poland had no traditions of her own to draw upon in this field of research. Indeed, the opposite is the case, for sociology has long been established academically—at least as long as in Western countries, where it later developed more speedily and uninterruptedly. Polish social science was already richly developed and theoretically advanced even before world war II, as the names of Znaniecki and Malinowski remind us. Rural sociology, in particular, was well established at the beginning of the century, though not translated. As befits a predominantly agrarian society, studies of the peasantry were plentiful and of high quality, because for Polish intellectuals and social reformers the peasantry constituted a problem. From the nineteenth century onwards the Polish 'Westernizing' intelligentsia, in its desperate search for independence, for national reunification, modernization and justice, had to face the fact that the peasantry, the largest segment of the nation, and the poorest and most oppressed, was also the most inert; yet it was precisely this mass of the peasantry that would have to be infused with nationalist sentiment. In order to mobilize the peasantry it was first necessary to analyse them. The tendency of many peasants and impoverished noblemen to avoid partitioning the land by sending their sons to the towns for education added to the ranks of the intelligentsia many people of peasant, or at least rural, origins and connections. The marginal position of the Polish intelligentsia, too, standing at the intellectual cross-roads between Russia

9   Julius Nyerere, *Ujamaa: essays on socialism,* Oxford University Press, Dar es Salaam, 1968.

and Western Europe, facilitated a flourishing and original intellectual life. For example, Galeski shows below how modern rural sociology developed in the USA in the inter-world war period made its mark upon Polish research. German research was a further influence. It is, therefore, hardly surprising to find that the first, still unsurpassed, major sociological study of the peasantry to be published in English was devoted to the Polish peasantry and was mainly the work of a Pole, Znaniecki,[10] nor—to take another indicator of the importance of the peasantry in Polish life —that the Polish peasant movement became a major political force.

Hence, in spite of ups and downs, dictatorships and occupations, a recent bibliography of Polish rural sociology published between 1918 and 1965 could mention 710 titles, more than 500 of them published since 1945.[11]

The name of Boguslaw Galeski, the head of the rural sociology section of the Polish Academy of Sciences, is probably the single most important name amongst a remarkably advanced group of contemporary Polish sociologists. He has to his personal credit more than seventy scholarly publications, and at the same time has played an important part in theoretical analysis and conceptualization as well as in the gathering of research data, in teaching, in the organization of research, and in advising on State planning. His book is an attempt to draw together the experience of Polish rural sociology and to present a systematic discussion of the position of a peasantry in a rapidly industrializing and urbanizing society.

The society is, of course, a socialist society, and for this reason Polish experience cannot be mechanically transferred holus-bolus to other societies. But it is a socialist society that still depends on that majority of the population which lives on smallholdings worked by family labour. The experience of Poland is thus invaluable for all faced with working out how such an agriculture can be modernized, how archaic and undesirable features of traditional rural life can be dissolved without alienating the peasantry, how the complex interpenetration of town and country can be resolved—all these, though in many respects problems peculiar

10   W. I. Thomas and F. Znaniecki, *The Polish peasant in Europe and America*, Gotham Press, Boston, Mass., 1919.
11   *Bibliografia sociologii wsi polsciej, 1918-65*, Warsaw, 1967.

to Poland and to a socialist Poland, are nevertheless of much
wider relevance. They are obviously relevant to similar socialist
societies in particular, but many of the new States which are by
no means socialist in their general physiognomy have adopted
socialist models of development in agriculture at least, if only in
part or on an experimental basis; this varies greatly in scale, and
from country to country. Thus State Farms and co-operatives
(production, credit, and marketing co-operatives as well as consumer co-operatives) are all experimented with very widely.[12]

The crucial relevance of Polish experience for under-developed
societies, then, stems from the fact that, as in so many African,
Asian and Latin American societies, it is the State which is the
dominant agency of modernization of a predominantly peasant
agriculture. In this sense Poland, too, is a 'developing society'
moving out of a predominantly agrarian economy. Similar developments are occurring even in capitalist societies—notably in
Italy—where the under-developed rural parts are also being subjected to State intervention. And those who think that the USSR's
demonstration effort as a model for agricultural development is
limited to the negative experience of collectivization will be sur-
prised to note the emphasis Galeski places on the State Farm (not
the *kholkoz*) as a possibly more viable development strategy for
the future.

The classical pre-revolutionary debates about the future of the
mir, then; the policies, so hotly debated in the USSR in the
1920s and 1930s, of 'horizontal' integration (increase in size of
the farming unit) versus 'vertical' integration (modernization of
agriculture via the incorporation of smallholdings within a national network of markets, machinery services, co-operatives, etc.);
the debates about the respective merits and demerits of State
Farms, collectives, co-operatives, or of entrepreneurial farming,
both small-scale and business-scale—all are live issues across the
contemporary world. Now, too, peasant revolutions have made the
urban-industrial world conscious not merely of the problems of
agricultural development, but of the peasants of the under-developed world as historical actors. For the twentieth century peasant
has been no inert spectator in a world dominated by industry and
town. Since world war II the cosy small 'world' of 'Western

12   See P. Worsley (ed.), *Two blades of grass: rural co-operatives in
agricultural modernization*, Manchester University Press, 1971.

civilization' has been exploded. The under-privileged majority of mankind has emerged and made its presence felt in the battle-fields of Vietnam, in China's 'cultural revolution', and through our nagging consciousness of India's hunger. In this unified world, peasants represent not simply the numerical majority of mankind but also one of the major social and political forces which are shaping the future of the world.

This is why the 'West' has begun to rediscover the peasantry, and why long-neglected classics such as the writings of Chayanov and Preobrazhensky are now being published in English. Because of this rediscovery it is no longer possible, today, to categorize the peasantry, with Marx, as 'a cleverly stupid anachronism . . . an undecipherable hieroglyphic for the understanding of the civilized . . . the class that represents barbarism within civiliza-tion' or, with Plekhanov, as 'non-existent, historically speaking'.[13]

Nor is it possible, any longer, to affect a general understanding of the substantive problems of society that is innocent of any reference to the life of the majority of mankind. The vulner-ability of social science theories which assume a model of man based on assumptions developed about human behaviour in a few recently industrialized Western societies has long been dem-onstrated by anthropologists. Galeski's discussion of peasant motivation similarly reveals the limitations of most orthodox eco-nomic thinking about peasant agriculture, and his wider discus-sion of the values and social control asserted by family and community, and the disjunction between these and formal edu-cational institutions, reinforces the anthropologists' points. All these, however, are simply partial manifestations of the most general contradictions Galeski points to: the tension generated in peasant life by virtue of the dual character of the peasant farm as both an enterprise and a unit of domestic economy.

In chapter 1 we start with a discussion of these basic charac-teristics of peasant farming, followed by an outline of the main types of farming to be found in contemporary Poland. In chapter 2 the occupational activity of the peasant farmer is examined, whilst chapter 3 looks at the peasant family and chapter 4 at the village community.

The interrelations between farm, family and village, and the

13   See T. Shanin, 'The peasantry as a political factor', *Sociological Review*, 1966, vol. 14, No. 1, pp. 5–27.

wider question of whether the peasantry is to be thought of as a 'class' or a 'stratum', are discussed in chapter 5, whilst changes in rural society, both in terms of new forms of agricultural specialization and in terms of the growth in numbers of people following agricultural occupations in the rural areas, occupy chapter 6. Chapter 7 examines the emergence of new attitudes to farming, the rationalization of the agricultural enterprise, and the new patterns of 'social forces' in a countryside where the influence of the industrial towns and the socialist State are pre-eminent. The book concludes with an examination of the adequacy of traditional Marxist theory for an understanding of contemporary Polish rural society, and an evaluation of the relative merits of the various strategies for the replacement of peasant farming by a modernized agriculture and a modernized rural society.

As a discussion of the peasantry as a general social type, then, this book goes far beyond a parochial codification of Polish experience. It both fills an existing gap in the literature of general sociology and at the same time stands as a representative of an important sociological tradition too little known in the West, the quality of which needs no praise from ourselves.

Finally, we must record that our own joint role has been that of interpreters rather than translators. The text was initially translated by Mr H. C. Stevens, F.I.L. It was then reworked so as to infuse the text with the necessary vocabulary of agricultural economics and rural sociology, and of Marxism, by the two editors, with Miss Allen's assistance, a process that was a lengthy and arduous one, but, we hope, as rewarding to others as it has been to ourselves.

Manchester   Teodor Shanin
January 1971   Peter Worsley

Introduction

Rural sociology, as a distinct scientific discipline, had its beginnings in the United States at the start of the twentieth century. By that time, the main schools of thought concerning social systems and trends of historical development had already been formulated, and a tendency towards specialization and detailed research was beginning to develop. Rural sociology, indeed, had become a separate field of study in the curriculum of Chicago University even earlier (from 1892 onwards), but the first textbook was not issued till 1913.[1] In 1916 the Congress of the American Sociological Society devoted its discussions to rural research. The rapid development of sociological research after 1920 was stimulated by the considerable financial support provided by the government[2] and other organizations which were particularly alarmed at the rapid exodus of population from the rural areas and the growing difference in living standards between village and town. During this period several basic manuals of rural sociology were issued,[3] as well as studies which outlined its main trends and concepts.[4] By the 'thirties American rural sociology was fully developed, and research was being conducted on a large scale.[5] New textbooks were issued as well as many new editions of works published earlier; specialized subjects within the general field were now being isolated and treated independently, while statistical analysis was being applied on a wide scale. 1935 saw the formation of the American Rural Sociological Society, which in the same year started publication of its journal *Rural Sociology*, a publication which continues to make a significant contribution to the area of study. These trends towards the treatment of specialized subjects as independent fields of inquiry, towards grappling with concepts and applying statistical and mathematical methods, were now strongly marked. And the positive knowledge accumulated in the course of research justified the expectation of an imminent return to an overall theoretical perspective based on sounder empirical foundations.

In comparison with the United States, Europe was late in commencing the study of rural sociology. In Poland the *Roczniki socjologii wsi* (*Annals of Rural Sociology*) began publication in 1936, but only three numbers appeared before the war. This journal printed Grabski's sketch (a theoretical outline), which initiated the Polish approach to rural sociological problems, and the first research centres in this field were founded at this time.[6] Sociological emphases became noticeable in much writing in the field of other longer-established social sciences concerned with the village and with agriculture. During the same period, or shortly afterwards, the earliest publications bearing the title 'Rural Sociology' began to appear in other European countries.[7] It was only after the second world war, however, that rural sociology came to occupy a permanent place in European universities and research centres.[8] The European Society for Rural Sociology was founded in 1957, and in 1960 the Society began publication of its journal *Sociologia ruralis*. August 1964 saw the first world congress on rural sociology, at Dijon, organized by the joint efforts of the American and European societies. Today, research centres dealing with problems of rural sociology exist in most European countries, and special periodicals devoted to studies in this field are published.[9]

In Poland, studies in rural sociology were renewed almost immediately after the war. In 1947 systematic research, originally initiated in 1934 under L. Krzywicki, was re-started, and is now carried on by the Zaklad Spolecznej Struktury Wsi (the Workshop on Rural Social Structure) attached to the Instytut Ekonomiki Rolnej (Institute of Agricultural Economics—IER). In 1961 the Zaklad Socjologii Wsi (Workshop for Rural Sociology), attached to the Institute of Philosophy and Sociology of the Polish Academy of Sciences, was founded—the only body which incorporates the name of this discipline in its title. These two centres (which in fact constitute a single working team) are the headquarters of Polish rural sociology. The *Annals of Rural Sociology* has been restored; annual conferences are held which cover the whole country and which bring together the leading specialists in this field and related disciplines; and international research has been initiated.

Comparison of the points in time at which rural sociology as a separate scientific discipline came into being in the United States and in Europe can be misleading, however. Many subjects—agrarian structure, regionalization of the country, demographic changes, the socio-occupational structure of the rural population, etc.—which in American conditions traditionally fall within the sphere of rural sociology, in Europe fell instead within the bounds of agricultural economics, or related disciplines, such as 'social agronomy', which flourished for short periods. If we take the contents pages of textbooks as broadly indicating the sphere of interests of rural sociologists, we can confidently assert that many of these have been subjects of research for many years in Europe, possibly even earlier than in the United States.

Inter-disciplinary boundary lines do not greatly concern us. The essential fact is that in Europe the greatest emphasis is generally laid upon questions of stratification (or classes) and peasant culture. This is undoubtedly why rural sociology, in Europe, is the sociology of peasant strata, with a long history behind it, whereas in the United States it is rather a sociology of agriculture—undoubtedly a peasant agriculture in the beginning, but one which developed comparatively recently, and under different conditions. Thus, in so far as some problems are concerned, European rural sociology is closer to American ethnography, or 'cultural' anthropology. But the differences between sociology and ethnography (or cultural anthropology) are indefinite, to say the least, and it would possibly be better if these two sciences were considered jointly.

Apart from ethnography the subject matter of rural sociology comes closest to that of agricultural economics. Both in the United States and in Europe, rural sociology has developed in close association with this discipline, and economic and demographic problems, such as the agrarian structure or socio-economic regions, are, as a rule, dealt with by both sciences. Moreover, since the field of economic activity, and, above all, the study of how people earn a living, are much more closely linked with the whole of family life in rural than in urban areas, it is not possible for studies in rural sociology to ignore these matters. To put it more strongly, it would be difficult to say anything about rural life without taking these areas as the starting point. The agricultural economy determines the characteristics of rural life as a whole to such a great extent that an understanding of the manner of its functioning is the basis for an understanding of social phenomena. On the other hand, it must be recognized that the farm is a particular kind of production unit (as will be seen later), and that for the agricultural economist, too, rural sociology is indispensable if he is to be able to make valid generalizations.

Rural sociology began by describing rural life: agricultural regions, types of farms, the family and the village, the living standards of the population and its demographic and socio-occupational structure, rural institutions, and the customs and norms prevailing in village communities. This purely descriptive approach, whether concerned with all rural regions of the country or with only one village or group of villages (monographs of villages or counties), very soon proved unsatisfactory. The primary consideration for rural sociology became that of the nature of the differences between village and town. When it was discovered that the differences were many, and that they could not be measured on the various urban–rural scales in use, the question began to lose its significance. This was especially the case since in many respects these differences, until recently very marked, have been steadily diminishing. These attempts to view the subject as a unified whole, examining rural life speculatively (often developing general theoretical propositions *a priori*, without any reference to empirical facts), and—conversely—to explaining differences between town and country described without any theoretical analysis, were followed by recognition of the need for a more thorough study of specific problems. However, the search for a theoretically integrated conception and clearly systematized analytical model of the special features of rural life, and of patterns of change, still continues. More recent attempts, however, have perhaps been less intuitive and based more often on detailed research findings, which make use of empirical data within the widest possible internally coherent general framework.

The present work also attempts to unify the separate specialisms of rural sociology. Indeed, the very term 'rural sociology' assumes exactly such a viewpoint. For when we isolate a given set of problems within the framework of one or another branch of sociology, we do so with regard to the connection between these problems which makes it necessary to consider them together. The sociology of the family investigates the various types of family, their characteristics, changes in their functioning and the factors causing those changes. Research aims at establishing the common elements in these changes, at eliciting the regularities to be found in all families, and at making the qualifications needed in moving from families in general to particular kinds of family. Industrial sociology, the sociology of occupations, the sociology of class and of social strata, as well as other specific branches of sociology, proceed in the same manner. Almost every one of these divisions of sociology embraces (or at least can embrace) village and rural life within its range of interests. Thus the sociology of the family investigates rural as well as urban families; the sociology of class cannot omit the peasantry, nor can the sociology of occupations omit the occupation of farmer. The sphere of interests of rural sociology intersects with that of all these specialized branches of sociology. Each of them amply confirms the distinctiveness of the peasant farm as a place of work, the distinctiveness of the farmer's occupation, of the peasant family, of the village as a local community, of the peasant class, and so on. The need therefore arises for a specialized perspective: one which can gather all these special features together, and elucidate whether, and to what extent, they are interconnected or mutually condition one another; and further, whether they can be regarded as the manifestation of a different, 'rural', system of life and, if so, what this different system consists in.

The author is convinced that this is the field covered by rural sociology, the basic concepts of which this book aims to elucidate.

The chapters which follow discuss the characteristics of peasant farming and its mode of operation, the peasant family and the local community; the specific characteristics of the farmer's vocation, as defined in relation to other occupations; the special features of the peasant stratum (or class) in comparison with other social classes and strata. These basic concepts constitute the basic elements of rural life; it is the functional connection between these elements that constitutes village life as a system. Even in outlining what rural sociology is about, then, we find it necessary to introduce the term 'system'. For if it can be demonstrated that (a) the specific features of the peasant family (as compared with other types of family) are connected with specific traits of peasant farming which distinguish the peasant family's work from other kinds of work, and (b) that these elements are so interrelated that changes occurring in one of them will affect the operation of the other—in other words, that they can be treated as a coherent whole—then the use of the word 'system' is justified, as well as the need for a unified theoretical approach of this kind.

The term 'system' has to be used with one major reservation. None of the elements of this system—the farm, the family or the village—exists in isolation. The characteristics which distinguish peasant farming from other kinds of work, the peasant family from other types of family, and so on, are declining in strength. This means that it becomes ever less justifiable to speak of a specifically 'rural' system of life. Nevertheless, basic differences between village and town still persist everywhere in the world; rural life remains distinctive. The gradual elimination of basic social differences between village and town, and the assimilation of the village and of agriculture within contemporary industrial society, are, however, marked features of our time. In describing village life, particular attention has to be devoted to these processes. But it must be borne in mind that what is involved here is not a series of separate institutions or spheres of life but a totality in which these are constituent elements. This enables us to comprehend both the resistance of the village to certain changes proposed by reformers, and the amazing speed with which, in other respects, the village undergoes transformations which no one has planned.

The present study is no more than an outline of the problems of rural sociology. Therefore, of necessity, the issues dealt with are only those the author regards as fundamental, those most relevant to the assumption that village life constitutes a specialized phenomenon, both in its functioning and transformation. Each chapter is concerned with village life as a whole, but takes one or another element as its point of departure. Other elements could, of course, have been selected. In the approach we adopt, we do not provide a separate chapter on the specific set of norms and values which arise out of the system of village life and which contribute to the preservation of that system. But every chapter leads up to this, and in the author's view the characterization of the objective factors determining recognized norms and values provides a basis for such a study at some future date. So far, however, the empirical knowledge available on this subject is insufficient to enable us to go beyond speculative or intuitive conjecture. This time, empirical research now being carried out in rural areas will make it possible to analyse this problem systematically.

The general conceptual scheme presented here, constructed on the basis of ideas and findings drawn from sociological and other kinds of social research in rural areas, does not mean that the interpretations offered need be accepted as the only correct ones. The findings of all research can be differently interpreted according to varied theoretical perspectives. For instance, the results of research into the diffusion of agricultural innovation[10] can be interpreted within the framework of behaviour theory or information theory, i.e. within the context of social psychology. But they can also be analysed with reference to the process of the specialization of farming in the sense used in this book. The choice of a theoretical perspective, which affects the research findings, depends on the author's training, interests and general hypotheses. The present book takes the principles and field of interest of Marxist sociology as its point of departure. Its focus of interest is the direction of social change, and we accept as the fundamental factor in that change, the transformation of the objective structure of the conditions of existence, in particular of production relations. We assume this factor to be basic to social life as a whole (an approach expressed in this work by giving the peasant farm pride of place). This does not imply a lack of recognition of the significance of other factors (which are in fact considered in later chapters) or of the need for research into these areas.

It would be desirable, too, to look at the socio-economic problems of rural areas from a more general viewpoint. Changes in rural society are not only an indispensable part of any wider analysis of the direction of contemporary social change but are also a sphere in which assumptions derived from general theory have proved to be most misleading. Rural society is still the weak point of general social theory. This is not because too little attention has been devoted to it. On the contrary, socio-economic literature on the village and agriculture is very rich. Nevertheless, a satisfactory synthesizing theoretical approach to the subject as a whole is still lacking. This book, of course, does not fill that need either. It grew out of the need to systematize concepts used in the field of rural sociology during seminar work which the author conducted in the Department of Philosophy and Sociology of Warsaw University; some of the chapters have been previously published in *Roczniki socjologii wsi* or in *Studia socjologiczne* but have been revised and partly rewritten. But if the present work does help to meet that need in some degree, it will have accomplished all that the author could wish.

Notes

1   J. M. Gillette, *Constructive rural sociology*, New York, 1913.
2   Especially through the 'Purnell funds' (the Purnell Act, passed by Congress in 1925).
3   J. M. Gillette, *Rural sociology*, New York, 1922; C. C. Taylor, *Rural sociology in its economic, historical and psychological aspects*, New York and London, 1926; N. Le Roy Sims, *Elements of rural sociology*, New York, 1928; P. Sorokin and C. C. Zimmerman, *Principles of rural–urban sociology*, New York, 1929.
4   C. J. Galpin, *Rural life*, New York, 1920; J. H. Kolb, *Rural primary groups: a study of agricultural neighborhoods*, Madison, 1921; E. C. Young, *The movement of farm population*, New York, 1924; J. M. Williams, *Our rural heritage: the social psychology of rural development*, New York, 1925; E. de S. Brunner, *Village communities*, New York, 1927.
5   E. G. Brunner and I. Lorge, *Rural trends in depression years: a survey of village-centred agricultural communities, 1930–36*, New York, 1937. This publication analysed the results of three studies carried out in 140 villages in 1933 by E. Brunner and J. H. Kolb (see *Rural social trends*, New York, 1933).
6   Instytut Gospodarstwa Spolecznego, Instytut Socjologii Wsi, SGGW, Panstwowy Instytut Kultury Wsi.
7   A. Blaha, *Sociologie sedlaka*, Prague, 1937.
8   For a discussion of European sociology see H. Mendras, 'Les Etudes de sociologie rurale en Europe', *Sociologia ruralis*, 1960, No. 1.
9   E.g. in Yugoslavia, *Sociologija sela*; in Czechoslovakia, *Sociologie a historie zemedelstvi*; in Italy, *Quaderni di sociologia rurale* and, more recently, *Societa rurale*; in France, *Etudes rurales*.
10   E. M. Rogers, *The diffusion of innovations*, New York, 1962.

1 Peasant farming

Peasant farming is of interest both to rural sociology and to other social sciences (notably agricultural economics), as well as those who shape and execute government agricultural policy. It would be difficult to isolate the field covered by rural sociology or even to define its specific components exactly. Both the economist and the sociologist are interested in defining the main characteristics of peasant farming and the changes that occur in it. The economist may use findings in this sphere as a basis for the analysis of problems of the agricultural market, whereas the sociologist may move from propositions concerning peasant farming to observations about the peasant family. In both cases, however, the observations and generalizations may be identical, since they pertain to the farm, and we will take these as the starting-point for our thinking. Discussion as to whether the description and clarification of the principles of peasant farming are part of rural sociology or of agricultural economics would seem to be of no scientific value, and it is probably wiser to regard these problems as common to both sciences. But these problems are *not* identical with those the sociologist studies in industrial plants.

The sociological problems of the farm, like those of a non-agricultural enterprise, are more clearly visible when considering large production units. True, the large farm also has a number of peculiarities deriving from its own special type of agricultural production and the relations this imposes upon the producers. There is no doubt that here too various kinds of differences will emerge, according to (1) the nature of the particular conditions of agricultural production and the nature of relations between producers this entails; (2) the conditions of life in a small, relatively isolated community, inhabited by workers from a single enterprise; (3) the special characteristics of different groups of agricultural workers, each of which has evolved its separate identity. Nevertheless, the large farm exhibits basic attributes of the sociology of the enterprise as formulated by specialists in this field.[1]

Large agricultural units (estates or State Farms) are of only marginal interest to rural sociologists unless they are farms of a specifically peasant character (collective farms, and, in Poland, certain production co-operatives), where there is a more or less definite, but always visible and distinctive, mode of life, the characteristics of which will be examined more closely later. But the problems associated with the 'sociology of the enterprise' are hardly ever found in relation to peasant farms, or prove to be identical with the study of the peasant family, the village community, the peasant stratum (class), or the collectivity of farmers as an occupational category.

The special features of the peasant farm as a production unit

Family labour is commonly held to be the chief feature of the peasant farm, a feature which determines its functioning and distinguishes it from other production units. If we confine ourselves to this characteristic, however, it could be said that this is an attribute of small commodity production generally, and not only of peasant farming. But the peasant family produces articles of food which are or may be—at least to a considerable extent—consumed by the family. This phenomenon is not found in handicraft production, where the production function is also performed by the family. Hence it is not enough to state that the family is the production group on the peasant farm. We need to emphasize that the family produces *food*, to one extent or another, directly for its own consumption[2] on a disproportionately larger scale than do non-agricultural small commodity producers. A handicraftsman may indeed also produce certain articles for his own use, but this is of no great importance to his productive activity. The farmer, however, even a farmer working a quite specialized farm, usually produces a number of basic products which are consumed within his own domestic unit. We must therefore further extend our definition of the special characteristics of the peasant farm as a production unit: its basic characteristic is *the fusion or (more exactly) the identification of the enterprise (i.e. the commodity-producing establishment) with the domestic economy of the family household.*

This fusion has major consequences for the whole of village life. It gives the farmer's occupation its own characteristic quality, for this occupation is less bound up with the social division of labour than are other occupations, and is much more closely bound up with the family, whose production activity is particularly central on the peasant farm (of which more later). It is this fusion, above all, which determines the special characteristics of the peasant farm as a production unit. For the functioning principles of the *enterprise* differ from those of the *domestic economy*. The *enterprise* produces exchange values, which necessarily involve the evaluation of all operations from the point of view of the relation of output to input, as well as of profitability, whereas the *domestic economy* has to do primarily with use values which are measured according to the needs they satisfy and the extent to which they do so.

Since the peasant farm is at one and the same time both an enterprise *and* a domestic economy, its economic activity is based on two different, and sometimes contradictory, principles. The producer (the peasant family) can treat the products either as exchange values or as use values depending on their destination—what he intends to do with them. This is most often determined only *after* the completion of the production process. In this respect the production patterns of the peasant farms are determined not only by considerations of profit but also by the needs of the family. The amount of labour input, equally, can be evaluated in respect of either the profitability of expenditure or the hierarchy of family needs (not to mention the frequent lack of any alternative use of reserves of labour). Nor is the organization of labour necessarily carried out according to economically rational methods. The producer may assess production equipment according to either economic criteria or other criteria, such as convenience, prestige, etc. A farmer buying a tractor, for instance, does not have to give any more consideration to its profitability or amortization than does a family acquiring some durable good (a refrigerator, for example) for the home. Thus the farmer does not necessarily have to assess capital investment in terms of increasing production or enlarging family income, nor

does his productive activity have to be related to such considerations.

Nevertheless, the peasant farm is—as shown above—both a
domestic economy, in which use values—determined by need—
are produced and consumed, and an enterprise. In the latter case
the farmer can be, and to a large extent is, guided in both his
exchange and production decisions by his estimate of the market
situation, of profitability, etc.[3] But even in the market the farmer's
behaviour is determined by the dual nature of the peasant farm.
And many phenomena noted by economists—for example, the
agricultural producer's lack of reaction to cyclical fluctuations[4]—
are explicable when we take all the characteristics of peasant
farming into consideration. To say that the family farm is both
an 'enterprise' and a family production unit is not a very happy
use of language, since we tend to associate the word 'enterprise'
with the capitalist economy, for it is usually associated with establishments of a capitalist type, i.e. with a production unit whose
aim is profit (that part of surplus value accruing from the productive function of capital). There is a controversy among agricultural economists whether or not the profit category, like that
of ground rent, is to be found at all in peasant farming.[5] The
view may indeed be correct that the objective of this kind of
farming is not entrepreneurial profit but family income. But we
must distinguish two separate issues: the economic analysis of
peasant farming on the one hand, and the motivation of the
producer, or the categories in which he thinks of his farm, on the
other. In the first instance the question is whether the characteristics of peasant farming justify applying to it concepts used in
analysing capitalistic enterprise (interest, ground rent, production
and trading profit), and whether these concepts lend themselves
to analysing the way it functions. In the second instance it is a
matter of analysing the producer's attitude to his farm, of defining the motives which guide him in taking production decisions and in his calculations about the outcome of his labour.
These two approaches are closely connected, for both arise from
the producer's actual behaviour. They are, however, different
approaches serving different cognitive ends.

In the light of what has been said, the agricultural producer
may in some cases think within categories of the domestic
economy; in others, within the categories of the enterprise, here

understood as a commodity-producing establishment. But thinking in 'enterprise' categories (i.e. when thinking about the products of his labour in terms of exchange values) he may or may not, under capitalist conditions, be induced to try to realize also those values accruing from the ownership of capital (interest) and of land (rent), as well as those he would be entitled to as a capitalist producer (profit) or as a capitalist seller (trading profit). That the majority of farmers do not realize these values does not mean that they do not attempt to do so. This suggests that the definition of the basic characteristic of peasant farming as the fusion of the domestic economy and of the enterprise makes it necessary to determine the variety of types of peasant farm in which the dual principles of peasant farming operate (generally) in different ways.

Types of peasant farming in contemporary Poland: large-scale farming

In the light of the above, the most appropriate criterion for defining the various types of peasant farm should be the extent to which a farm possesses the features of an enterprise or of a domestic economy. The nature of the interconnection of these two features and their relative proportions determine the sources of the peasant family's maintenance, and therefore (following the assumptions adopted here) constitute the most important elements which determine its overall social character. The elements which delimit the differentiation of the types of peasant farm are in turn determined by the general socio-economic conditions within which the farm operates, the stock of productive equipment it possesses, the skills of the head of the farm, his ability to adapt his activities to the conditions within which he has to operate, and the manner in which he achieves this end. It follows that in the various socio-economic systems recorded in history, peasant farms will be distinguished by many features and classified according to diverse principles. The processes shaping the transformation and differentiation of peasant farms will be considered later. The classification into types presented below relates to the socio-economic conditions existing in modern Poland, for the following reasons. In the first place, the socio-economic system within which Polish State policy operates is based on the socialization of the means of production. This also finds expression in agricultural policy. Second, in agriculture the means of production have been only partially socialized. Hence it is necessary to distinguish two basic types: agricultural economies peculiar to systems based on the private ownership of the means of production, and those appropriate to systems based on the socialization of production units. Of course, the existence in Poland of socialist relations in the basic sectors of the national economy also fundamentally determines the conditions under which individual peasant farming functions and the transformations it undergoes.

The simplest classification, which reveals most vividly the degree of intensity of the element of enterprise in peasant farming, is the proportion of the product (as measured by the proportion of commodity production to total output) which is marketed. However, this classification—basic to both sociological and economic analysis—is still not adequate. For questions immediately arise as to the level of production at which this marketable portion emerges, the size and the technical equipment of the farm, the degree and direction of specialization, and finally the extent to which it is the source of the family's maintenance. For these reasons, in order to characterize the differentiation of peasant farms, we have to take not one but several parallel and complementary divisions into account. Though one division might be adopted as the most important or most convenient, the others also constitute basic elements in the characterization of types of farm.

The most basic sociological classification of rural social relations looks at the farm in terms of its role as the family's source of maintenance and place of work. On the basis of research findings, the Workshop on Rural Social Structure of the IER[6] classifies farms under six categories: five types of peasant farm and one type of large farm.

1. *Farms constituting a secondary or additional source of family support.* Here the value of net output (gross production after deducting material investments) is lower than family income from other sources. In Poland there are approximately one million such farms (27·3 per cent of the total);[7] but if we include as

'farms' only those with an area above 0·5 hectares (according to the IER classification) then there are approximately 700,000.[8] The great majority of these are small farms (80 per cent of them up to two hectares). More detailed analysis breaks this group down into:

(a) *Residential farms used as family dwelling and place of rest.* These are mainly concentrated close to towns or in tourist districts, and are owned by urban inhabitants with high earnings, or by rural intelligentsia (veterinary surgeons, directors of small factories, some teachers, and so on).

(b) *Homesteads with low production intended exclusively or almost exclusively for meeting family needs.* These, as a rule, are run by the families of industrial workers living in the countryside, handicraft workers, shopkeepers, assistants, pensioners, etc.

(c) *Smallholdings belonging to agricultural workers who live in the country* (as well as plots which parents retain for themselves after transferring their farm to the children). These are usually distinguished by higher marketable production than the farms in the previous groups.

(d) *Small-scale enterprises (market gardens, orchards, etc.) which bring the family a supplementary monetary income.*[9] Like the first group, these are located close to towns.

It is difficult to establish figures for these four groups. The IER does not undertake research in suburban areas, where they are most frequently to be found and are most evident, nor do data held by the Central Statistical Office (GUS) contain the necessary information. On the basis of IER research we can deal only with farms in groups (b) and (c).[10] (Those in the other groups do not have the characteristics of the peasant farm.) In most cases they have no horses or agricultural implements, and no cows—or only one—and a pig or two. Vegetable production is limited almost exclusively to the needs of the farm (food and fodder). Monetary income is derived from animal products (milk, poultry). The value of their total output does not exceed 25,000 zlotys.[11] The marketable proportion of their produce may be as high as 20 per cent of the value of the farm's total production, and up to 30 per cent or more on farms belonging to agricultural workers.

2. *Farms which provide the main, though inadequate, source of family support.* Income from other sources here does not exceed the value of net output, but is a constant and important item constituting over 10 per cent of the family's total income. In Poland such farms number a little over 700,000 (about 20 per cent of the total).[12] This group mainly includes farms with an area of 2–5 hectares. These farm families draw additional means of subsistence from labour (commonly manual labour) in industry, transport, building construction, etc., or from work in agriculture, on State farms, or for neighbours. In these cases it is usually not the head of the family who is the wage-earner but rather sons and daughters. As a rule those gainfully employed outside also participate in farm work. Although this type possesses less livestock and fewer implements, buildings, etc., than farms of the same size which provide the *sole* source of family subsistence, the total value of their production does not differ much and generally reaches the level of 25,000–35,000 zlotys. But there is a distinct difference in the volume of marketable production, which in this group is decidedly lower than in other farms of the same size. There are no farms in this group with a definite tendency towards specialization. This indicates that 'enterprise' features are still comparatively weak here and that the farms are really extended domestic economic units mainly intended to satisfy family needs. Detailed analysis reveals two contradictory tendencies within this group. The first is the reduced importance of the farm as a source of family maintenance, with cash income, both from outside earnings and from the farm, directed primarily towards the satisfaction of consumption needs. Family aspirations tend in the direction of making these earnings permanent. The other tendency is for monetary income derived from outside employment to be largely invested in the farm for its intensification, or even for the purchase of more land. In this way the family aims to make the farm the permanent main, and, in the future, exclusive, source of maintenance.[13] Hence a detailed classification of this group of farms can be made with the aid of precise indicators of the degree to which the characteristics of an enterprise are present. In sociological studies classification according to the place of work off the farm is also especially valuable. In farms belonging to agricultural workers 'enterprise' features are usually more prominent, and the marketable level of pro-

duction is notably higher. This is particularly the case with farms whose owner works part-time for neighbours. But generally these are people who are unqualified to get work elsewhere, or who cannot find other possibilities in the vicinity. They are, moreover, usually older persons, with smaller families. When the farm does not provide an adequate means of subsistence for the family, and for various reasons work in industry, handicrafts or services is difficult to obtain, these farm owners, or their children, take up low-paid work for neighbours, which is felt to be humiliating. The money income, moreover, is small. Therefore the family sells farm produce to satisfy its most urgent needs, to the detriment of its own living standards and the level of its farming (livestock feeding). Hence this is a 'hunger' type of commodity production. IER studies of villages composed of families working farms of this type usually distinguish them as a separate group of 'peasant–workers'. In Poland the number of such farms is very small—less than 10 per cent of all farms up to four hectares.

3. *Farms which are the sole source of family support and are based solely on family labour* (with possibly a small number of hired labourers at the height of seasonal activity) constitute slightly more than 80 per cent of the total of individual farms in Poland. Here the features of peasant farming are most clearly expressed. The proportion of commodity production amounts on average to over 50 per cent of the total; about half the finished production consists of articles intended for consumption, the rest being utilized on the farm as means of production (seed, fodder, etc.). Therefore the 'enterprise' features of commodity production and the traits of domestic economy are both clearly observable. More detailed classification is essential, for the investigation of trends within this type of farm group is based primarily on size (the majority being of 5–15 or 7–20 hectares according to the region), the equipment and means of production they possess, the size of family, the number of days worked by day labourers (according to the classification adopted), the use of regular hired labour, the level of production, and the direction of the intensification and marketability of production. It would occupy too much space to provide a fuller characterization of this group, and in any case this can easily be found in detailed studies.[14] Another important indicator of the intensity of 'enterprise'

elements in the peasant farm is the degree to which the farmers
are market-orientated and their ability to estimate the profitability
of production. One estimate, based on the questionnaire issued
by the Osrodek Badania Opinii Publicznej (OBOP) (Public
Opinion Poll Centre) attached to Polish Radio[15] shows that some
60 per cent of Polish farmers are guided by market stimuli.[16]
Another indicator of dominant trends in this group is the
measurement of the possibility of increasing farm output, e.g. by
determining whether the family aims at enlarging the farm or
rather at increasing investment per unit of area, the extent to
which it bases its production on the services of specialized enterprises (e.g. machinery suppliers), how it organizes its market
contacts (whether on a permanent or casual basis), etc.

4. *There are not many farms based on hired labour in Poland
today.* They certainly do not number more than 50,000 (precise
data are difficult to obtain, as the Central Statistical Office does
not collect the necessary information) and are concentrated in
certain areas only, mainly the central regions. Most often they are
holdings of over 20 hectares, based on family labour plus hired
labourers employed permanently or by the day, to an extent
which corresponds with that of permanently employed workers
(i.e. about 200 days in the year). Hired labour is a definite indicator of an enterprise, and of a capitalistic type of enterprise at
that. There are also other indicators, including the high value of
output (averaging 130,000 zlotys) and a high level of production
sent to the market (over 60 per cent), high levels of productive
equipment, of permanent and organized market contacts, of
frequency of specialization, extensive rationalization of the production process, etc. The IER distinguishes two types of capitalist
farm:[17]

(a)   Those with a relatively large area (partially concealed by
      fictitious family allocations) yet with poor technique and
      low commodity production, with labour hired rather by the
      day or based on the payment of debt by poor neighbours in
      the form of labour (the neighbour borrows horses or
      machinery, or rents land, and pays the debt off through
      labour). These farms are typical of the less developed
      market–monetary relations in the eastern part of Poland.

(b)   Intensively worked farms with considerable commodity production, based on regular wage labour (often landless and
living on the farm) or on day labourers receiving money
wages.

It is easy to see that these express differing degrees of the 'enterprise' type of development, and of money–commodity relationships in the rural areas. Under Polish conditions the capitalist
peasant farm, especially the second type, faces a number of difficulties in its development, both of an economic nature (lack of
labourers and the high cost of day labour) and of a general social
nature (in the village it is considered humiliating to work for
neighbours). These difficulties flow from the general pattern of
relations in Polish society.

5. *Multi-family peasant farms*[18]—*production co-operatives*. At the
end of 1962 Poland had 1,342 production co-operatives embracing
26,000 families.[19] We include this type as 'peasant' farms not only
because they have come into existence as the result of joining
together separate peasant farms, but above all because they
preserve their basic features. For production co-operatives are
based on family labour, and a considerable part of the output is
distributed among the families, which, within the co-operative,
run small individual holdings (kitchen-garden plots). These resemble extended domestic economic units or small-scale enterprises organized primarily for animal rearing. Two main types of
production co-operative can be distinguished:

(a)   *That of a definitely entrepreneurial nature.* This type carries
on specialized farming geared to the market (for instance,
vegetable cultivation, animal husbandry); the share-out of
the income is primarily in money; advances are made regularly to members according to the work done—a pattern
resembling the remuneration of industrial workers; the
private plots are able to satisfy most of the families' consumption needs.
(b)   *Co-operative farms which are aggregates of small farms.*
These are geared to grain crop production, above all fodder;
income division is based on produce in kind; the produce
obtained from farming in common makes it possible to

achieve high animal production on the private plots, and thus further raises productivity. Thus the produce of these holdings is destined for the market, and this supplies the families' basic monetary income.[20]

The numerical strength of these two types of production co-operative is shown to some extent by the fact that towards the end of 1961 only 568 of the 1,534 co-operatives sharing out income did not engage in stock rearing.[21] This, however, is a very inadequate indication, since non-stock-breeding production co-operatives may definitely be organized as an enterprise (e.g. a co-operative specializing in vegetable production), while co-operatives engaged in livestock breeding can possess distinctive features of a multi-family domestic husbandry. Consequently the classification of co-operatives according to the intensiveness of entrepreneurial features needs to be supplemented by other indicators. In addition to this classification, another—equally interesting to sociology—should be mentioned, namely distinction according to the social origin of the co-operative's members. Co-operatives of former agricultural workers who obtained land as a result of the agrarian reform introduced by the Polish Committee of National Liberation of 1944 (but who usually proved unable to cope with an independent farm and returned to working in a larger group) should be included in this group. This type of co-operative mainly preserves the old pattern of farming characteristic of an estate before being divided up under agrarian reform. It is also necessary to distinguish these co-operatives from co-operatives founded by farmers with small land-holdings. Here the large number of families and the small size of the co-operative precludes the full employment of its members, and this type of farm is mainly of an agricultural–handicraft or agricultural–industrial nature. It is, finally, worth distinguishing production co-operatives founded by groups of settlers linked together by some special bond, for instance co-operatives or re-emigrants from France, or soldiers of some particular military unit who jointly decided to settle and run a farm, etc. All these co-operatives, to a smaller extent and in a rather different way, maintain the chief characteristics of the peasant farm, i.e., the fusion of an enterprise and a domestic economy.

6. *Large farms without the characteristics of peasant farming.* In this group should be included the pre-war large landed estates and farms run by various institutions, including Church institutions, schools, etc. At present non-peasant farms in Poland are almost exclusively State farms[22] (both the State Farms as such, and the experimental farms run by scientific agricultural institutions, the Centre for Horticultural and Nursery Seed Farming, the Plant and Seed Cultivation Association, by industrial plants, etc.). There are over 8,000 of these farms in Poland, with an aggregate area of more than three million hectares and employing some 370,000 workers. The most numerous of them (6,000 farms, aggregating 250,000 hectares and employing 320,000 workers) are the State Farms run by the General Inspectorate for State Farms attached to the Ministry for Agriculture.[23] They differ from the others enumerated above, which usually serve specific ends (educational, scientific, etc.) or constitute auxiliary holdings of non-agricultural establishments and are most usually organized on industrial lines. Just as the production co-operatives retain many of the features of peasant farming, so the State Farms have retained many features characteristic of former landed estates. Of course, these features are now of small importance, but they do hamper the State Farms' evolution towards the rationalization of the enterprise: production is greatly diversified in a way which is not in accordance with the needs of agricultural production, and labour is remunerated partly by payment in kind (sometimes, part of the worker's reward for the work he does consists of a plot put at his disposal). At other times, though rather exceptionally, the worker's family is obliged to make a contribution in labour to the estate. These are undoubtedly vestiges of the former organization of labour on landed estates. Nonetheless, as far as its social character is concerned, the State Farm is closer to the industrial production enterprise than to the peasant farm. It is distinguished from the small holding only by the particular technical and economic requirements of large-scale agricultural production. The sociological problems of the State Farm, to a large extent, coincide with those of the non-agricultural production plant.

As follows from the above, there is a strong correlation between the general character of the farming unit and the various economic traits which characterize the farm as a type of production unit. This makes it possible to use data concerning peasant farms in sociological analysis of data collected by economists, grouping farms according to size, level of production, etc. Obviously, the correlations noted here should be understood as statistical ones. A detailed subdivision of each of the groups of farms distinguished here would show that deviations are by no means rare (e.g. small farms with a high level of production), and would establish within each group a greater or lesser variety of social types. In other words, the classification adopted is largely conventional, and in particular cases, or for other analytical purposes, may be modified considerably.

The classification of farms by socio-economic types, as noted, is of essential importance for the analysis of the basic subjects of rural sociology: the peasant family, the village community, class and socio-occupational differentiation of the rural population, etc. But such a classification is of special importance in illuminating transformations occuring in peasant farming and thus in the entire system of village life.

Peasant farming: change and the future

In economic terminology there is a well-known term, *subsumption*, which signifies the subordination of some forms of economic activity in the economic system to principles determining the functioning of the economy as a whole. The peasant farm, under the conditions of the capitalist economic order, is usually cited as an example of a subsumed system.[24] This implies that (1) the peasant farm lacks the basic characteristics of a capitalist enterprise, (2) changes in the mode of peasant farming are determined by the laws governing the functioning of the capitalist economic system as a whole, and (3) the peasant farm is acquiring certain features specific to the capitalist enterprise.

If it is accepted that under capitalism (whose basic feature is private enterprise based on hired wage labour) the peasant farm constitutes a subsumed system, a 'medieval relic', as some say, it then becomes important to establish whether this can be conceived as a phase in a certain course of evolution, and to estimate how its further transformation will presumably proceed. Domestic husbandry, which produces everything or almost everything necessary to the family's existence, appears of course not only in Europe in the Middle Ages. It is the oldest and most universal mode of production known to history, to be found in all socio-economic systems so far investigated. If we allow for changed proportions, it is also found in modern times both under capitalism and under socialism (perhaps with the exception of the Chinese communes and the Israeli *kibbutzim*) if production co-operatives are regarded as multi-family peasant farms.

Obviously, the family farm is never found in isolation; it always inheres in some larger or smaller society with a more or less developed division of labour and circulation of products. The variety of types of society, with their corresponding family systems, the organization of distribution, the structure of authority, and so on, is very considerable and, as studies of non-European countries have shown, sometimes highly complicated.[25] An analysis of the features of the family farm and of its transformations in the course of history would go beyond the objectives of this book, which does not aim at elucidating history but only at constructing a simplified and ideal model of evolution. It suffices, for this purpose, to turn to comparatively recent European history, to the period when the peasant family farm was the dominant type. In the medieval economic system the peasant–manor relationship determined the manner of functioning of the economy as a whole. The peasant families, conducting self-sufficient economies and concentrated in small local communities, the villages, were under obligation to render services to the manor house. These feudal dues or tithes, at first mainly in the form of agricultural produce, were the basis for providing the whole of society, not only peasant families, with the means of existence. The peasant's produce passed by way of the manor, through the medium of further obligatory services, from the lower to the higher overlords. This was simply a system for distributing the surplus produced on the peasant farms.

Side by side with this relationship, which dominated the economic system of the Middle Ages, was the non-agricultural production of small, independent craftsmen concentrated in the towns. Since only a small part of this non-agricultural production could be utilized to satisfy the immediate needs of the producer himself, the bulk of it had to be transferred to society by way of some form or other of exchange, which at this period in Europe was based on money. Exchange proceeded mainly between the craftsman and the manor (or demesne) on a local and general European scale. Contacts between town craftsmen and peasant farmers were rare, except in areas where free peasant families had survived who were not bound by feudal obligations, e.g. in Tuscany.

The medieval economic system hence contained (if we may simplify) two types of relationship: (1) the village–manor, based mainly on socage, and (2) manor–town, based mainly on exchange. The second type existed not only between town and manor, but also, or even primarily, within the town (or towns). The division of labour created the basis for exchange, so that production could develop to a certain extent on the basis of exchange among non-agricultural producers.

Non-agricultural production based on exchange creates a dynamic situation in which a number of additional positive correlations are observable, where the growth of one factor leads to the growth of another. One such factor, for instance, is the character of the production–market link, for extension of the market stimulates expanded production, while an increase in production leads to a search for markets. The same applies to the links between market and demand, market and division of labour, division of labour and production technique, and so on. Of course, these symptoms function if one of the important aims (direct or indirect) of human activity is the accumulation of values, but they also signify a situation in which this particular activity and its corresponding aims acquire importance. In Europe the development of non-agricultural production—whose model contained within itself internal growth stimuli—was accelerated by a succession of historical events, but above all by geographical discoveries, by an expanded market and by the accumulation of considerable resources which made possible the extension of production. As a result of this evolution, a non-family type of production took shape in the non-agricultural sphere and gradually gained predominance. This was the commodity-producing enterprise based on an advanced division of labour and on mechanization.

This system also existed in agriculture, above all through the manor. The growth in its share of exchange occurred by way of an increase in the peasants' dues, and changes in their nature.

Services in kind were supplemented by monetary contributions (rent), and labour services (socage). On this basis the manors undertook agricultural production on a large scale, partially or wholly enclosing the land the peasant families had been cultivating. The principle of obligatory services, however, hampered the stimulating activity of the market. Their increase did not lead to the growth of production on the peasant farms (although the peasant families attempted to meet these services by an increased input of labour). It resulted rather in peasant resistance, mass flights, etc. The manorial farm based on the *corvée* could achieve higher production results only to a small extent, although the better organization of labour and the application of more advanced technique made it possible. Consequently the growth of the market had a disorganizing influence on the village–manor relationship. The emergent economic system based on non-agricultural production and the market broke up the former system of bondage and laid the foundation for mass social conflicts which resulted, among other things, in the transformation of agriculture so as to correspond with the dominant type of production. The nature of services (and the peasant serfdom which conditioned them) changed, the peasant farm lost its autarchic character and became linked with the market.

Gradually certain activities were removed from the range of tasks performed by the family, which originally produced all its needs. These activities were usually easier to break down into operations fully under human control, thus providing a basis for non-agricultural economy. The division of labour thus established, and the consequent necessity for exchange, effected the emergence of a dynamic order which in turn led to the formation of a system of enterprises resting on the labour of specialized producers, namely those who sold their labour-power in exchange for the means of existence. Consequently the industrial model came to dominate non-agricultural production, which to a great extent ruined the guild crafts. In terms of society as a whole, this transformation can be regarded—with considerable simplification—as a transition from a society in which each family produces all its needs (the family model of production) to a system in which the producers, concentrated in specialized workshops, carry out specific production operations allotted to them, while society as a whole may be regarded as a production–consumption unit based on the complex organization of the division of labour.

The system of commodity economy, based on private ownership of the means of production, created the foundation for the concentration of production in large factories. The extension of the market initiated the expansion of production by way of the organization of new enterprises, and above all by enlarging the size of enterprises to their rational limits. A rise in the supply of goods and a fall in their prices led to a search for possible ways of reducing production costs and therefore to technical change and a further rationalization of the production process. This is easier to accomplish in a large enterprise in which internal organization renders it possible to exploit all equipment to the limits of its technical efficiency.

The concentration of production creates a new socio-occupational structure and, under the conditions of private ownership of the means of production, a new class structure. At the same time, inherent in the chain of transformations outlined above, whose principal element is the concentration of production, is a 'compulsion to rationalize'. This results not only in the alienation of the producer from the product of his labour (if it is still possible to distinguish the product of the individual producer's direct labour from that of others in the production unit) but also in the restriction of the role of the small—above all, of family— forms of production in the economic system.

The superiority of large over small enterprise is not as obvious in agriculture as it is in industry. A large farm which replaces several or a dozen and more small ones does not result in increased production (unless new land is brought under cultivation), but it can reduce the cost of production per unit of product, since it may make it possible to apply new labour-saving techniques. To a certain extent techniques increasing output may also be applied; for instance, on certain soils tractor ploughing may not only save labour but also effect an increase in the yield. But, generally speaking, techniques which increase output can be applied on a small farm too. Of course, on a small farm there is a greater waste of labour-power (if it is not also employed outside the farm), as well as a smaller exploitation of equipment. But a unit of 20–30 hectares does not suffer from these defects. Moreover, in all specialized agriculture there is a limit to the rational size of the farm,[26] beyond which a further enlargement of area with a given level of technique yields no benefits whatever in the form of a reduction in costs.

The view has been expressed that in agriculture, unlike industry, small units are more rational than large ones,[27] and the argument has been adduced that as a rule the output value per unit of area is higher in smaller farms. But this may be achieved by the small farm through an increased application of labour, which is effective where technique has not made much progress, as in livestock breeding,[28] in vegetable production and other types of labour-absorbing cultivation. Labour expenditure on a small farm can prove unprofitable as compared with a large one, where the labour is subject to calculation. But peasant farming is not only an enterprise, and unprofitable labour expenditure does not lead to bankruptcy.

In agriculture there are thus bases for the preservation of the family model of production. Nonetheless, an industrial type of production emerges even in this model. In many countries there remained, first of all, large non-peasant agricultural enterprises— the former feudal *latifundia*—which are now operated as large private or State enterprises. Elsewhere large farms have arisen on lands newly brought under cultivation. These enterprises emerged from the beginning, and remain on a different basis from that of peasant farms. But if the latter are privately owned they also tend to enlarge their property holdings, which leads to the formation of large farms. Because of its basic characteristics, growth in relation to the peasant farm is of a different kind from that in the non-agricultural enterprise, where the urge to increase profit is the sole and all-sufficient stimulus. In the peasant farm the need for modernization emerges as a necessity for the family which desires a better life, lighter work, and wishes to avail itself of the conveniences enjoyed by other families. Industry and mass communications media create new peasant needs, and contacts with the market must therefore expand.

This in turn impels economic rationalization of farm management and the use of cost accounting. The market also stimulates a desire to increase production, above all to increase the farm area. Given a low level of technique, high cost of machinery, and low labour costs (in conditions of over-population), any increase in production entails the hire of labourers. It is in this manner

that the capitalist agricultural enterprise comes into being. The
farm loses its peasant character if the family no longer partici-
pates in the labour and if specialization restricts the family's own
consumption of the produce, or even renders it impossible. The
growth of entrepreneurial features and even an increase in the
size of the peasant farm do not, however, lead necessarily to its
becoming a capitalist farm. Present-day technique makes possible
the existence of large farms of several dozen hectares based on
family labour, and in many countries it is cheaper to apply this
technique than to hire labourers.

Capitalistic farms never developed anywhere on a mass scale.
A number of factors were responsible: the low prices for agricultural produce conditioned by the dispersed character of
peasant production, the difficulties and risks of specialization,
and the troubles and uncertainties connected with the farm's
complete dependence on market mechanisms, etc. This tendency
is nevertheless present, and it is illustrated in Poland by the
existence of that group of farms which was earlier defined as
capitalist, although they still retain definite features of peasant
farming. Of course, in capitalist conditions only a few peasant
families succeed in gaining the status of large farm owners. The
majority have difficulty maintaining their existing position and
are constantly threatened with the danger of a diminution in area
(mainly because of the necessity to divide the farm up in the
course of changing generations, land parcellation, or because of
the burdens connected with the necessity for family share payments).

In socialist countries large farms come into being by the joining together of peasant farms in the course of agricultural
collectivization. The resulting production co-operatives to a large
extent continue the production pattern, which must be regarded
as that of multi-family peasant farming. Undoubtedly the entrepreneurial features involved in the operation of production co-
operatives will steadily increase, and in the long term only the
form of ownership will differentiate this type of co-operative from
the State Farms established on the terrain of former estates.

As against the above described manner of emergence of agricultural enterprise through the creation of large farms (often
called the 'horizontal' consolidation of agricultural production),
there is another way, defined as 'vertical' consolidation. In this

case a trading (or a trading-cum-industrial) firm concludes a contract for the farmer's produce. The enterprise supplies the farmer
with the raw materials (fodder, breeding stock, etc.) and sometimes with credit; it even builds the necessary installations on the
farm. In return it takes the finished produce from the farmer,
processes or prepares it, and sells it. It is not necessary of course,
for all the links in this chain to be controlled by a single enterprise; there may be several different, associated enterprises involved. The point is that the contract and the guarantee of
constant prices, as well as the restriction of the farmer's labour to
a single production phase, create an 'agrobusiness', within which
the farmer is subject to definite controls. In this case, the
peasant farm too becomes a specialized production establishment,
separated from the domestic economy. But this establishment is
only one element in a larger production aggregate in which the
farmer's role is that of an employee.

The increasing concentration of production in large units is a
rule applying to all economic spheres. The division of labour laid
the basis for this trend, and the market provided its mechanism.
In agriculture the concentration of production has encountered
a number of restrictions deriving from its specific characteristics.
Nonetheless, here too the process appears with the development
of technology, and takes the forms of horizontal consolidation—
which corresponds to field production—and of vertical consolidation, similar to other branches of production. In agriculture
horizontal consolidation can yield beneficial results only if it is
based on new techniques; its advantage consists rather in the reduction of production costs than in any increase of output.
Obviously, a large enterprise can more easily adopt technical
equipment to achieve higher production, and the reduction of
the costs of production can benefit not only the enterprise, in the
form of profit, but also society as a whole, and, above all, the
farmer, who desires to free himself from the excessive labour
hitherto universal in agriculture. However, the magnitude as well
as the cost of production is important. So far horizontal consolidation has made possible only a slight increase in output per
unit. If introduced without the assurance of appropriate technical
conditions it may even cause a serious decline in production,
since the incentives specific to individual farming cease to operate,

while technique does not compensate for the fall in labour expenditure. In reality, vertical consolidation differs from horizontal only in its more evolutionary and indirect method of bringing about transformation. One way or another, the future of agriculture lies with the large farm. It seems, though, that enterprises which come into existence by way of vertical consolidation do so at a smaller social cost (without causing crises associated with changes in property relations) and develop along lines more akin to the non-agricultural enterprise. Obviously, whether the one or the other method (or a combination of both) is introduced depends on the country's socio-economic conditions (the technical level of agriculture, the labour supply, the level of produce marketed, the extent to which market relationships are organized, society's need for accumulation, etc.). In this respect the attitude of the direct producers is especially important, for this factor will remain of primary significance for the level of agricultural production many years after the transformations have occurred.

Notes

1   The subject of the sociology of the enterprise has been treated, among others, by J. Szczepanski in 'Uwagi o przedmiocie i zadaniach socjologii pracy' ('Remarks on the subject matter and tasks of industrial sociology') in *Jak pracuje czlowiek (How man works)*, Warsaw, 1961, and by A. Sarapata and K. Doktor in *Elementy socjologii przemyslu (Elements of industrial sociology)*, Warsaw, 1962.

2   A. Brzoza, 'Indywidualna gospodarka chlopska jako system gospodarczy' ('Individual peasant farming as an economic system') in *Ekonomika rolnictwa i polityka rolna (Agricultural economics and agrarian policy)*, second edition, vol. ii, Warsaw, 1963, p. 70.

3   M. Pohorille and A. Wos, *Motywy produkcyjnych decyzji chlopow (The motivation of peasants' production decisions)*, Warsaw, 1962.

4   M. Ciepielewska, 'Rynek rolny w Polsce i jego regulowanie' ('The agricultural market in Poland and its regulation') in *Ekonomika rolnictwa i polityka rolna, cit.*, vol. i, Warsaw, 1962, pp. 375 ff.

5   H. Cholaj, *Procent jako kategoria ekonomiczna w gospodarce chlopskiej (Interest as an economic category in the peasant economy)*, Warsaw, 1963.

6   See the symposium *Spoleczno-ekonomiczma struktura wsi w Polsce Ludowej (The socio-economic structure of the village in People's Poland)*, Warsaw, 1961, p. 125, and A. Szemberg, *Przemiany*

struktury agrarnej gospodarstw clopskich w latach, 1952–60, (Changes in the agrarian structure of peasant farms, 1952–60), Warsaw, 1962, p. 77.

7   M. Czerniewska and A. Szemberg, 'Liczba indywidualnych gospodarstw rolnych w Polsce w 1957' ('The number of individual farms in Poland in 1957'), *Zagadnienia ekonomiki rolnej (Problems of Agricultural Economics)*, 1959, No. 2, pp. 82 ff.

8   R. Turski distinguished farms of 0·1–0·5 hectares as tiny plots of 'workers–allotment holders'. The figures he gives are higher, as they are based on the 1962 census. See his *Miedzy miastem a wsia: struktura spoleczna-zawodowa chlopow-robotnikow w Polsce (Between town and village: the socio-occupational structure of peasant–workers in Poland)*, Warsaw, 1965, p. 207.

9   G. Isbary, 'Probleme der Entwicklungsplanung in Verdichtungszonen', *Sociologia ruralis*, 1962, Nos. 1–2, p. 49.

10   M. Dziewicka, *Chlopi-robotnicy: wyniki badan ankietowych przeprowadzonych przez IER (Peasant–workers: results of research by the IER)*, Warsaw, 1962.

11   For methods of calculating production see *Spoleczno-ekonomiczna struktura wsi . . . , cit.*, p. 48.

12   M. Czerniewska and A. Szemberg, *op. cit.*, p. 91.

13   M. Dziewicka, 'Stosunek chlopow-robotnikow do gospodarstwa rolnego' ('The peasant–worker's attitudes to farming'), *Studia socjologiczne (Sociological Studies)*, 1961, No. 1.

14   See *Spoleczno-ekonomiczna struktura wsi . . . , cit.*

15   B. Galeski, 'Rolnicy jaki przedsiebiorcy' ('Farmers as entrepreneurs'), *Wies wspolczesna (The Contemporary Village)*, 1961, No. 6, pp. 70 ff.

16   M. Pohorille and A. Wos give more weight to this factor (*op. cit.*, pp. 113 ff.).

17   J. Tepicht, 'O calosci prac nad spoleczno-ekonomiczna struktura wsi w Polsce Ludowej' ('Work on the socio-economic structure of the village in People's Poland') in *Spoleczno-ekonomiczna struktura wsi . . . , cit.*, p. vi.

18   J. Tepicht, *Doswiadczenia i perspektywy rolnictwa (The experience of and outlook for agriculture)*, Warsaw, 1961, p. 103.

19   These data relate to production co-operatives sharing their income in 1962. Towards the end of that year 1,515 production co-operatives with 28,000 members were registered (*Rocznik statystyczny—Statistical yearbook*, 1963, p. 237).

20   In addition to production co-operatives, certain common holdings run by Agricultural Circles ought to be included here.

21   For a broader discussion of this set of problems see J. Czyszkowska and K. Dabrowski, 'Rolnicze spodzielnie produkcyjne: przeglad kierunkow, zmian organizacyjnych i gospodarczych' ('Agricultural production co-operatives: a survey of trends, organizational and economic changes') in *Ekonomika rolnictwa i polityka rolna, cit.*, vol. II, pp. 229 ff.

22   In addition to the farms operated by the State, there are a few
run by dairy or horticultural co-operatives and by certain Agricultural
Circles which in their organizational pattern are closer to State Farms
than to production co-operatives.
23   For fuller information concerning State Farms see M.
Kosteradzki and T. Rychlik, 'Aktualne i perspektywiczne problemy
ekonomiki i organizacji PGR' ('Present and future economic and
organizational problems of State Farms') in *Ekonomika rolnictwa i
polityka rolna, cit.*, vol. ii, pp. 283–386.
24   H. Cholaj, *op. cit.*, pp. 16 ff.
25   See B. Malinowski, *The sexual life of savages*, Warsaw, 1967.
26   There are many studies on the optimal size of a farm with a
particular specialization. For instance, in a study carried out in Iowa
the optimal area of a farm devoted to grain production was found to
be about 200 acres of better-class land. See E. M. Rogers, *Social change
in rural society*, New York, 1960, p. 202.
27   For a criticism of this view see V. I. Lenin, 'The agrarian question and Marx's critics', *Works*, vol. 5, Warsaw, 1951, pp. 112 ff.
28   In livestock breeding, small farms can achieve even lower production costs per unit of product. See A. Brzoza, *op. cit.*, p. 80.

2   Farming as an occupation

As part of a research inquiry villagers were asked whether one could say of a farmer working a medium-sized farm that he was 'pursuing the occupation of "farmer" '. The question clearly caused them some difficulty. They found it hard to give any reasons why the term 'occupation' seemed inappropriate, yet they were clearly of the opinion that it *was* out of place. When similar questions were asked about agronomists or veterinary experts, about agricultural labourers on State Farms, cattlemen, production employees or technicians or engineers on livestock farms, and other such categories, the term 'occupation' caused no difficulties; yet its use in connection with the term 'farmer' did. For employees in socialized agriculture are such a large and differentiated category that the term 'farmer' is too general to be applied to them, and does not therefore constitute a useful classification. Naturally, however, the question then arises: to what occupational category should one allocate cattlemen or tractor drivers? In agriculture, as in industry, differentiation in the allocation of labour, differences of work specialization or differences of social position cause many difficulties in classifying work roles. These difficulties can be resolved, however, by adopting an appropriate convention, and while one recognizes that such differences are greater in agriculture, it is still only a question of degree.

The difficulties that one comes up against in applying the term 'occupation' to the work carried out by families working individual farms are of a different kind. In this case, though it is a general term, the term 'farmer' does not arouse any reservations. Of course, owners of individual farms can be classified as gardeners or pig rearers, bee-keepers, tobacco growers, etc. But the majority of peasant families are engaged in such a variety of production tasks that the general term 'farmer' is appropriate, though it is, perhaps, erroneous and unsuitable for other categories of workers in agriculture. However, the statement that a family working its own farm is following the 'occupation' of

farmer raises further difficulties. The first has already been indicated by the necessity of saying 'family' and not 'person'. Unless
we are prepared to renounce the application of the term 'occupation' for families working small farms, we shall have to recognize that it is an occupation fundamentally different from all
others, i.e. different in respect of the features normally connoted
by the term 'occupation'.

Definition of the term 'occupation'

The term 'occupation' is normally used to denote a complex of
activities which:

(1)   is differentiated from other complexes of activity and is
      performed regularly;
(2)   provides services to other persons in the society;[1]
(3)   constitutes a regular means of support;
(4)   requires appropriate training, entitling the individual to
      pursue the occupation specifically as an occupation, i.e. to
      perform its functions regularly for the benefit of others in
      exchange for the means of support.

None of these four features (the last of which is consequential on
the others) is sufficient, taken by itself, to establish any particular
complex of activities. As J. Szczepanski remarks,[2] no one would
describe as specialized work, for instance, the work of a woman
preparing food for her family, although in other circumstances
these same activities could quite permissibly be described as those
of a specialized work role (for instance, a cook working in a food
processing factory). Equally, one can think of many people who
possess permanent means of support (for instance, individuals
'supported by their family' or who possess an appropriate bank
account) but who have no defined work role.

One can also point to activities requiring special training which
confers the right to perform those activities—driving a car, for
instance—which yet do not constitute occupational skills except
when they are performed for pay and as a service to others (for
instance, a taxi driver). On the other hand, there are many
activities—e.g. those performed by workers engaged in land improvement work—which do not require special training or

qualifications, yet *are* recognized as specialized activities. Finally, one can think of people who perform a certain activity disinterestedly—which shows that work for the service of others is not an adequate criterion of the definition of an occupation either although undoubtedly it is the most important one. So the basic distinction of an occupation is the simultaneous presence of certain features. We can therefore define an occupation as a group of activities regularly performed for the service of others in exchange for the means of support, or—to put it differently—as a group of activities performed regularly, and dependent upon the exchange of the individual's labour for that of the community. This definition of 'occupation' has been adopted in the present work.

In passing, it needs to be added that the term 'profession' is often used in the literature to denote a collectivity of persons, for instance 'the medical profession', which connotes the *whole body* of doctors. We shall indicate this meaning by using the term 'professional or occupational category', signifying the whole body of individuals following the one profession.[3]

In the light of the definition we have adopted, lists of occupations mention many categories which we would find it difficult to accept as examples of *work* roles. For instance, we would find it difficult to designate owners (of land, buildings or capital) as an occupational category if their activity is directed solely to the extraction of profit and not towards directing an enterprise.[4] On the other hand, one must now recognize the majority of social workers as an occupational category, since the functions they perform provide them with their means of support. But under certain circumstances we have to accept that a particular set of activities sometimes has the character of an occupation—and that people performing these activities can therefore be defined as belonging to a single occupational category—while, in other contexts, these very same activities are not of this nature. This applies, for instance, to the examples already cited (the housewife, the car driver and, sometimes, the social worker). In such cases it is essential to determine whether, under modern conditions, these activities are *becoming* distinct occupations. With regard to some of them, it may be possible to give an affirmative answer; in other words, they are passing through a contemporary process of becoming specialized occupations. The features we specified as defining

an occupation can thus serve as criteria for including a certain
group of activities in a schedule of occupations, and can also act as
indicators of the extent to which the process of occupational
specialization has developed in any particular group of activities.
Accepting the features specified as the criteria of an occupation,
we can determine with greater accuracy the degree to which the
process of specialization of any particular kind of work has developed, and the extent to which it can be defined as an occupation, on the basis of the following considerations:

1.   The extent to which the group of activities under
     consideration is differentiated from other activities, as
     against activities performed within the framework of family
     management.
2.   The extent to which the group of activities is integrated
     into the systematic social division of labour, as against the
     situation where the producer works for himself or his family.
3.   The extent to which the occupation provides the main
     means of support, as against intermittent occupations.
4.   The extent to which the qualifications entitling an indi-
     vidual to perform those activities are formally specified, and
     the absence or presence of specialized institutions in which
     these qualifications can be acquired and appropriate entitle-
     ment obtained, as against work which anyone can perform.

Thus, in view of the contemporary tendency for the economic
functions of the family to become weaker, one might say that the
housewife's work is at present undergoing a process of specialization, and is giving rise to the formation of a differentiated group
of occupations. The same may be said of the activities of social
workers, where the process of occupational specialization is
already well advanced. But the process is equally apparent when
one considers changes occurring amongst families working peasant
farms.

The special characteristics of farming

If we are to apply the term 'occupation' (*zawod**) to the work done

* *Zawod* denotes both 'profession' and 'occupation' in Polish.—*Translator.*

by members of families working on their own farm (and to families in production co-operatives embracing numerous families), we need to ascertain the presence of social features clearly distinguishing these kinds of work from other jobs. A list of these features (confining ourselves only to the most important) would include at least the following:[5]

1. Labour is performed by the family. Moreover, the generally accepted pattern of the organization of labour in peasant farming involves the participation of the family,[6] since otherwise the work will not be fully performed, or will not be performed well, or will be fraught with considerable difficulties. Unlike 'cottage' craft production, which is very often a family activity but in which the family can easily be replaced by another group, in peasant farming the range and variety of activities are closely dependent upon the family as the production team, upon the physical capacities of individual members of the family, and upon the place those individuals occupy in the family.

2. The position of the farming family within this occupational category is determined by their class situation. Any advance in the status of farmer is bound up with a change in the extent to which he owns the means of production. Usually, the class situation is, in general, strongly correlated (at times, e.g. in crafts, very strictly) with the scale of the farmer's operation. In peasant farming the class of 'peasants' are people who perform many different work roles. The 'larger' farmer, however, is much more an organizer and director of labour than its executant, while the farmer owning a small farm works as executant not only for himself but also for his neighbours.

3. A farmer's work is to a large extent autonomous. He produces articles which satisfy his basic needs. Every other occupation can be followed only when other people have other occupations—otherwise the producer could not work or even exist. The modern farmer, too, cannot produce without the work contributed by people in other work roles. But until comparatively recently the peasant family produced almost everything it needed for its existence, and even today produces the basic means of its own support. So the interdependence between the work of the farmer and other occupations is not equally strong for both parties. Society could not exist if the farmer did not pursue his occupation. The farmer's life, equally, would be extremely diffi-

cult if it were not included in the general system of the social division of labour; nonetheless, he *could* keep himself alive.

4. The activities which make up the farmer's labour are not only very wide in range but also basic to the existence of a number of separate specialisms. This by no means implies that the farmer must be knowledgeable on many subjects. One can point to many occupations in which acquaintance with various branches of knowledge is useful or even necessary. Thus, although it may be important for the director of a large enterprise to have, for instance, some knowledge of building construction in order to make informed decisions with regard to investment in buildings in his enterprise, he does not do those jobs which are the speciality of the carpenter or building worker. Many of the jobs which a farmer must do are in themselves occupational categories—above all such agricultural specialisms as breeder, gardener, production organizer—or jobs connected with agriculture (food processing, etc.), or even non-agricultural work (machinery repair, transport, building work to some extent, etc.). With so many tasks to perform, he cannot possess the requisite training for all of them. The most important feature of his work is that he performs these operations in the same manner as someone who, for instance, repairs the electric light in his own home; he performs them as a non-specialist, yet these same activities are still part of the work of farming.

Therefore, when considering the variety of tasks the farmer is involved in, one may conclude that the work of a family running its own farm can be defined as following a specialized occupation only in so far as it occupies a special place as the work of those who produce food in the present-day organization of production, based on the social division of labour. Nevertheless, essentially, this kind of work does not have the characteristics of a specialized occupation and is the legacy of a formerly different social organization of production, in which specialization scarcely existed. The range of activities which make up the labour of a family running a small farm has already become greatly restricted today, and is being further restricted by the existence and development of a social division of labour outside its own area of activity. This suggests that a process is at work of adapting this labour to the specialized pattern of the organization of production obtaining in the wider society.

The process of specialization in farming

The process of specialization in farming can be looked at from several angles. Because of the nature of peasant farming it can be observed in changes both on the farm and in the family; in the way in which the farmer does his work; in the activities which make up that work; in his attitudes towards his farm; and in his attitude to the work he does. This process can also be viewed against the background of general social change expressed in the form of changes in the socio-occupational structure.

We use the term 'socio-occupational structure' because, under the conditions of private ownership of the means of production, there is a clear connection between the place the individual occupies in both class and occupational structures; a connection which, as far as the farmer is concerned, has been defined as 'identification'. Where the family works its own farm the farmer is usually the *owner*, the *entrepreneur*, the *producer* and the *seller* of the product produced. While ownership is exclusively a *class* status, and the status of producer an *occupational* status (though connected with one or another class situation), the positions of entrepreneur and seller can be *both* a matter of class status (if it is bound up with ownership of the means of production) and of occupational status (production organizer, sales organizer, or employee engaged in the preparation of the commodity and in serving customers). Under capitalist conditions the concentration of land-holding (occurring first and foremost in the form of mortgage indebtedness) is particularly important. The concentration of other means of production also occurs, both because of indebtedness and via the operation of enterprises which hire out the means of production or whose special function it is to provide service to peasant farms.[7]

Finally, there also occurs concentration of the processing and sale of agricultural products. Enterprises which buy and process agricultural products gradually organize the market and subordinate it to themselves (mainly by contracting for the peasant farmer's produce). The complete domination of the market leads to a situation in which, under capitalism, in Marx's words, 'the peasant parcel is now only a pretext which allows the capitalist to draw profit, interest and rent from the soil, and leaves to the farmer himself the problem of how to extract from it wages for himself'.[8] Thus, with the development of capitalism, the farmer is reduced to the class position of a worker (though he is left with the illusion of ownership) and to the occupational role of a producer. The process of class polarization is, therefore, at the same time a process of functional specialization in the work of farming.

This process does not abolish peasant farming, nor does it eliminate the presence in the farmer's situation of elements of both class and occupation; the proportions of these elements vary, however, in different types of farming. And although this process does not lead to the abolition of peasant farming, the tendency for this to happen is clearly visible.

Under socialist conditions, both during the period when individual farms continue to exist (or in that kind of socialism which assures their continued existence), as well as during the period when only *multi*-family peasant farms (production co-operatives) remain, the process of specialization—which depends upon the separation of the functions of production organizer, producer, and seller of the produce—does not lead to class polarization. Although the process of formation of agricultural occupations has gone a long way in some countries, it is not possible, so far, to speak of its completion.

The process of separating out the farmer's labour into the functions of organizer and director of production, seller and producer respectively is bound up, under both capitalist and socialist conditions, with the development of large-scale agricultural enterprises, either horizontally or vertically integrated. It is obvious that in a large agricultural enterprise there is not only a separation of functions, as we have already mentioned (above all those of organizer/director and producer), but a separating out, too, of the activities which make up the work of farming into various horizontal occupational specialities (e.g. agricultural accountancy, breeding, gardening, field cultivation), as well as into a vertical hierarchy of positions within these professions (e.g. director of the enterprise, agrotechnician, head of work team,* agricultural labourer). The same process occurs in the enterprise (or system of enterprises) based on vertical integration: in this case, the functions of seller, processer and producer are more clearly dis-

---

* This term, borrowed from Soviet terminology, denotes a position roughly equivalent to foreman—*Translator*.

tinguished (organizing and directing functions are also differentiated) but production decisions are shifted outside the peasant farm and located in the controlling enterprise (the bank or the trading enterprise). The scope of the peasant family's production activities is narrowed down also as a result of the co-operation of agencies which service agriculture, e.g. machinery–tractor stations.

The development of large agricultural enterprises brings about the separation of the domestic economy from farm production. There is, in consequence, a tendency, on the one hand, for those features which distinguish the farmer's work from other occupations to weaken, but the result of this process is also an increase in the division of labour within agriculture, and the formation of a differentiated occupational structure in this sector of the national economy.

However, the peasant farm is not simply an enterprise: it is also a unit of domestic economy. Consequently the process of specialization in farming work proceeds both via a diminution in the scope of the farm family's production activities and via a diminution in the scope of its activities in the domestic economy. With the extension of the general social division of labour, a number of activities traditionally performed by the peasant family (e.g. the making of clothes) are taken over by industrial enterprises. Other economic and educational activities too are increasingly taken away from the family (schools, reading rooms, creches, nursery schools), although this process does not take place as swiftly as it does in the towns and comes up against a number of resistances connected with the existence of the peasant farm and the maintenance of a family pattern subordinated to the functioning of that farm.

The process of specialization involves an increase in the number of owners of small farms who regularly earn wages in non-agricultural enterprises. In this situation the process of specialization occurs not in connection with the formation of an occupational structure for agricultural workers and the development of a network of establishments supplying both production and non-production services to families living in the countryside, but through changes in the nature of the rural settlements, which today, are becoming to a large extent places of residence for people who work in towns and in industry. However, when discussing the transformation of family patterns of production,

which are the basis of peasant farming and of farming as an
occupation, it is necessary to note this trend also, because the
family pattern of production also shrinks as a result—in this case,
through the owner's transfer to work in non-agricultural occupations, so that the peasant farm consequently loses its character as
an enterprise.

Finally, when discussing the process of specialization in farming, one cannot but draw attention to the fact that it begins
outside peasant farming itself. The market and industry create
the basic stimuli for the transformation. State intervention, too,
plays an important role, some of the manifestations of this being
a ban on break-up of the land-holding; social insurance and
retirement pensions; the demand that heirs should receive agricultural education; the extension of agronomic and veterinary
services to agriculture.

On the macro-sociological scale, analysis of the process of
specialization of labour, of its varying rates of change and the
varying forms in which it occurs, and of the difficulties it con-
fronts and itself engenders, all require research into changes in
the socio-occupational structure of the population employed in
agriculture and of the rural population. The process of specialization of farming work can be analysed from yet another angle,
however—namely that of the work of the farmer in relation to
his occupational attitudes.

*Farming as an occupation and the farmer's attitudes to his
work and his farm*

In recent sociological literature, and, more importantly, in public
discussion, the view has been expressed that the chief motive for
the flight of young people from the villages is a reaction against
the general pattern of life involved in individual peasant farming, and not simply a revolt against conditions of work in
agriculture. This view would appear to be over-simplified. Undoubtedly village youth abandon a way of life in which they
cannot obtain the things they desire (above all, a skilled occupation), things which are inherently connected with the town and
with industry and which are impossible to obtain in peasant life.
Nonetheless, the flight from the village is to be observed on an

even greater scale in *large* agricultural enterprises, in which the features of the 'peasant' way of life are not the inevitable result of the method of running the farm. So it would seem that difficult conditions of work in agriculture do play a decisive role, but that in addition there are other factors impelling young people to leave the villages: factors associated with the way of life based on individual peasant farming. There are certain factors which encourage this exodus and yet others which counteract it. This problem will be discussed in the next chapter. Here it is only necessary to state that the situation of the young man who regularly 'helps' in the family, while his brother of the same age or even younger has gone off to town and has already achieved independence,[9] constitutes an adequate reason why young people are reluctant to consider remaining on the farm. On the other hand, the family type of ownership and production simultaneously imposes obligations upon young people in the form of the child's obligation to his parents. Thus the pattern of organization of the peasant family itself contains both stimuli to flight from the village as well as inducements to remain there.

The attitude of young people to the family farm (or, more correctly, to remaining on the family farm) is sometimes considered to express a permanent attitude, and thus provoke fears that the countryside will be depopulated. But when a young man does take over the obligations of a farm his attitude to the farm changes, indeed, is obliged to change. Hence, in thinking about the future of the village we should appreciate that attitudes which arise from the functioning of the farm, and which find expression in the youth's behaviour, are more important than the attitudes he holds before he acquires the farm, which change fundamentally when he himself takes over the running of it.

1. The first sociological problem associated with the relationship between the work farmers do and their attitudes is that of work motivation. When surveying the factors which influence work activity in any particular sphere, economists are inclined to attach decisive importance to the income which the individual obtains as a result of his activity. This is undoubtedly a simplification. Work may be undertaken not only in order to obtain the means of existence; the individual may be engaged in his work irrespective of the income level it assures him. Besides economic stimuli there are the effects of ideological stimuli, of faith in a

mission, satisfactions derived from work well performed, and so on. Non-economic motives for work are particularly strongly connected with certain kinds of situation (war, revolution) or with particular kinds of work environment (that of inventors, artists, scientists, writers, social workers), but their influence on occupational activity generally is also undeniable.

However, the simplification made by economists does have some basis. Thus in both capitalist and socialist systems the individual's income determines his opportunities of access to many generally desired values.[10] Under the conditions of socialist society the operation of income as an incentive is undoubtedly limited because of the considerable narrowing of the range of income levels, the restriction of the supply of goods which can be acquired for money and, finally, because of limits upon the importance of money even in the case of those goods which are acquired with it. Thus the purchase of commodities in scarce supply is not determined solely by the amount of money an individual possesses (for scarcity of goods does not affect their price, which is fixed by the State) but by other factors as well, e.g. the distribution system. Nevertheless, the principle accepted under socialism, 'to each according to his labour', also finds expression in the differentiation of incomes, which would be senseless if such differentiation did not determine the individual's access to goods in general demand. This principle also provides a basis for the statement that under socialism the level of income expresses the society's greater or lesser appreciation of the individual's labour. For these reasons we can see that the one factor which determines occupational activity more than anything else is the attempt to obtain the means of existence and to increase income (leaving out of consideration unusual situations or peculiar social categories).

However, while recognizing the basic role of economic stimuli, we do not confine ourselves exclusively to market stimuli as far as the peasant family is concerned, for the peasant family does not draw its income only from this source; indeed, some families draw it chiefly from other sources.[11] Moreover—and this is most important—it must not be thought that the peasant family treats its farm simply as a means of obtaining income.[12] Such an attitude is more appropriate in the case of farms of a more definitely entrepreneurial nature—for instance, capitalistic peasant farms or certain specialized 'commercial' farms in Western Europe and the

United States.[13] In the first place, the peasant farm is directly geared to the satisfaction of the family's needs, and many of the changes which the family introduces into it have no connection with the market situation. Second, the farm is also the place where the peasant family resides and lives, so that any improvements the family introduces, even larger investments, may simply be aimed at the immediate improvement of the family's living conditions. The income the family earns may, to a large extent, be directed towards improvement of the farm (e.g. erecting new buildings) not necessarily so as to produce more or at a lower cost but simply because, as a result, the family will have a better and more pleasant life. However, in many cases it is impossible to separate the production and the consumption aspects of investment, and it must be recognized that in erecting a new building (which as a rule comes first in investment plans)[14] the family simultaneously improves the farm and raises its standard of living.

Thus the basis of the peasant family's occupational activity is the farm—a farm treated, however, not only as a means of achieving and increasing income but also as the subject of that income's expenditure, as the place where they reside and live. Nor is there any special allocation for the enterprise, in which money is acquired in order to direct it to the maintenance or enrichment of the domestic economy. *For peasant husbandry is both enterprise and domestic economy.*

Thus in the work of farming (on a peasant farm) the problems of motivation to occupational activity, and of economic stimuli in particular, are sociological problems with a special content of their own. The same applies with regard to trends in specialization of the occupation.

2. As we have noted, the situation of the peasant family is based on an identity of class and occupational situation. Therefore occupational activity may be examined from both the one or the other standpoint. The traditional tendency in the village towards maximizing the ownership of land (today, however, in Polish conditions, an unusual phenomenon) is the kind of activity which obviously leads to a change both of class and of occupational activity. By increasing the area of land owned, the farmer avoids the necessity (and even the possibility) of working at other jobs, or of working for neighbours. Sometimes this creates a need to employ labourers; it always changes his status in the farming

community, since there is a change in the proportions of managerial and executive labour he contributes, and the roles of
entrepreneur and of commodity seller acquire greater importance.
   But, confining ourselves to the sphere of occupational activity
(which we consider legitimate, since in Poland and in other
socialist countries the mechanisms of capitalist stratification in
the village are not found, or function only marginally), we must
observe that the combination of the functions of producer, entrepreneur, and seller in farming suggests of itself the need to
examine the farmer's occupational activity against the background
of the formation of various occupations related to agriculture, and
the need to examine the farmer's self-definition within the context
of the developing occupational culture and organization of people
working in agriculture. However, other occupations will continue
to be linked with farming as long as peasant farms exist. It is
difficult to suggest adequate criteria for estimating the degree of
specialization in farming, and it is difficult, too, to quantify it. It
could be measured by labour inputs, by results in the form of
production, by the degree of rational organization of the farm, by
reference to market orientation (and the farmer's efficiency as a
seller), by the extent to which he introduces technical improvements, and so on.
   However, since the time and interest the farmer devotes to his
farm cannot be divided into interest in the production side on
the one hand and interest in the domestic economy on the other,
all general and statistical comparisons of farmers' and non-
farmers' occupational activity are very problematic,[15] and it is
vital to define precisely the problems being studied in such
research: whether the question is one of comparisons between
various *groups* within the rural population,[16] or the link between
the *individual* and the activities of the group.[17] But whatever
approach is used, questions about the farmer's occupational
activity must take into account the fact that we are dealing with
an occupation which combines activities belonging to various
other occupations, and one, too, which is the *basis* of the formation of various other occupations.
   3. This postulate also has to be applied to the notion of the
(so-called) 'good farmer'. This concept, often mentioned in public
speeches, does not by any means always have the same meaning
everywhere in rural areas, as empirical research demonstrates.[18] In

areas of traditional peasant culture, a 'good farmer' is usually, above all, one who possesses a lot of land.[19] Second, even in areas where occupational skills are independently valued the concept of the 'good farmer' varies in content; he may be a good organizer of labour, an industrious man, a man with a good idea of what is profitable to produce, a rationalizer or an innovator in some agricultural speciality, a man of great experience obtained in an agricultural school, or a popularizer of agricultural science. The accepted stereotype of a 'good farmer' may vary from community to community, too, and the descriptions given may thus provide a basis for characterizing more general changes occurring in those communities. This is also important in understanding the diffi-culties encountered when trying to convince farmers of the benefits of this or that activity. For instance, an agronomist's economic arguments aimed at persuading farmers that it is irrational to own a horse can be fallacious if in that community the farmer's prestige is based on property, not on the economic outcome of his labour.[20] Thus both in practical decision-making and in research it is necessary to recognize that there are varying stereotypes of the 'good farmer', and when propagating the idea of the 'good farmer' it is necessary to have a clear idea of the kind of farmer one has in mind.

This leads to a further issue in connection with farming as an occupation: that of avenues of upward mobility within the occu-pation. Built into the nature of the peasant farm is the fact that the hierarchy of positions in the division of labour is bound up with the hierarchy of rank within the family. Gaining the position of head of the family is equivalent to reaching a position of independence in the division of labour. Thus upward mobility in farming depends upon a change of status within the family, not upon the acquisition of greater skills—though, undoubtedly, the process of growing towards maturity does involve the acquisition of experience. Apprenticeship in the occupation of farming, then, is marked by clearly defined rungs on the ladder of the peasant family (from goose-minding to more and more difficult work that calls for greater strength and dexterity).

4. Advancement in the occupation also involves, as we have remarked, class mobility, the movement from being the owner of only a little land to the position of owner of a larger farm. There-fore the place of the individual in the family and the position of

the family in the class hierarchy are the factors determining the
main avenues of advance in this occupation. Undoubtedly, in this
situation, the achievement of mastery in any branch is important,
since it affects access to valued goods, above all esteem in the local
community. Research into farmers' occupational ambitions would
enable us to weight this factor more precisely, but it would seem
that at present the main avenues of advancement are not opened
up by acquiring technical skills. The comparatively minor importance of what is learned at school, and of titles denoting
technical qualifications (for here the supreme 'title' is the ownership of land, so that one must wait for an independent position
irrespective of any technical skills acquired), lead to a situation in
which the connection between the family and work is a consequence of the unique features of this occupation, and one which
induces many young people, therefore, to seek their future outside
peasant farming.

When the process of specialization in agricultural work becomes well advanced, and large agricultural enterprises with
differentiated and specialized structures emerge, new channels of
mobility open up in this kind of work. The tempo of this process,
however, is determined by the totality of changes in the village,
in agriculture and—more widely—in society as a whole.

5. In peasant farming, as a young man grows up he also gains
the general experience necessary for carrying on the operation of
the farm. Distinct functions are linked to different ages, and the
boy or girl performs these functions within the limits of the
family economy, passing in turn through all the stages and preparing him or herself for the future role of farmer or farmer's
wife. Knowledge is passed on by gradually initiating the young-
ster[21] into all the arcana of farming, and the process necessarily
involves the inculcation of specific norms and moral values, beliefs
and habits. Both the content of this knowledge, which is the
accumulated experience of past generations, and the mechanism
by which it is transmitted, attach great weight to tradition, and
constitute the basis of the conservatism of the farmer's method of
working. In this system for transferring knowledge the school, at
first, was a foreign element imposed from outside. It restricted the
family's educational influence, wrested the child away from a har-
monious system of labour and social life, and introduced into his
mind patterns which were not in agreement with that system:

foreign values, even values which could not possibly be realized within its bounds.[22] Hence the opposition which this institution encountered and still encounters in the village today—an opposition which finds its minimal expression in the difficulties the village child has to overcome in combining learning and work. However, the farmer's ever-widening circle of contacts with society outside the village enforces a recognition of the need for this institution and provides a basis for its adoption in the village. But while schools which provide general education have been adopted almost completely in most countries, the specialized agricultural school still meets with a great deal of resistance both to the recognition of its value in preparing the young person for carrying on the farm,[23] and—to an even greater extent—resistance to making practical use of knowledge gained at school in farming.[24] As in the case of schools providing general education, the agricultural school, too, becomes an indispensable element in technical training, usually as the result of State regulations—and thus the result of measures imposed from outside. In addition to such measures, most countries organize the spread of agricultural science in the form of educational propaganda.

6. In most countries the Press and radio and television programmes include articles and talks for farmers as well as practical advice for women, 'do-it-yourself' talks, etc. This is a result of those features peculiar to the occupation of farming, which, although formally recognized as constituting an occupation, in fact is not and cannot be treated as such. No other kind of work is subjected to such wide and all-embracing activity aimed at spreading specialized knowledge. Sociological issues examined as part of this activity are usually of a practical nature, and the aim of research in this field is usually to work out effective principles which should guide farming practice. Consequently the channels through which agricultural science penetrates to the farmer are studied; the effectiveness of advice given by agronomists or suppliers of agricultural machinery and other means of production (fodder, machinery, fertilizers); the actual mechanisms through which new technical information reaches him: how it is communicated from the agronomist or the farmer-innovator to leading farmers, and from them to others; the permanent establishment of particular techniques as the expected norm in the community, etc.[25]

However, the process of making agricultural science generally available is connected to a broader group of sociological problems. There is the question, first, of the nature of the resistance which technical innovations meet with in the village. Often this resistance has an economic content: it is not easy for the small farmer to purchase the requisite equipment, or there is a great risk associated with the introduction of a particular branch of production, or the need to reduce labour inputs is not felt very strongly because of absence of any alternative. However, economic reasons do not generally exhaust the motives which cause a farmer to be slow in introducing improvements. As we have noted, he may not be successfully persuaded by economic arguments, for his activity may be conditioned by other values, such as those of prestige based on property rather than productivity. Moreover, technical improvements change methods of labour long established as the norm through education within the family and thus, as we have already observed, come up against the farmer's conservatism. In changing methods of work, technical improvements also change the allocation of responsibilities in the family, or lead to their inequitable distribution. Finally, they change the existing mode of family life, habits and patterns of activity established over generations. One cannot, therefore, isolate problems deriving from the introduction of improvements into peasant farming from analysis of the entire system of village life based on that kind of agriculture.

Second, technical innovations reach the farmer principally *via* contacts with neighbours, who in turn are units within the structure of the village community. External activities which ignore this structure cause it to change to one degree or another, or to have varying degrees of success. Thus to introduce innovation *via* a family which is low in the village prestige hierarchy rarely leads to success. Respect for a neighbour, and a person's appreciation of his own position within the community, may vitally affect decisions on whether a certain innovation is introduced or not. Finally, the position the person undertaking educational activity in the field of technical knowledge occupies in relation to the farmer is a further essential factor: whether the positions of the educator and the recipient are on an equal footing, and what links bind them together. One example of a situation which is not favourable to the effective spread of agricultural science is that of the agronomist who instructs a farmer, the head of a family, on how to farm, in the presence of his wife and children. The problem of spreading agricultural innovations cannot, then, be considered in isolation from the rural family and the village community.

7. Besides the State, farmers' organizations are also active in spreading agricultural knowledge. Farmers' organizations usually have specific features distinguishing them from other such organizations, features which derive from the peculiar characteristics of the famer's occupation. They have a more or less definite class character, and yet are organizations of representatives of small enterprises and domestic farming. Therefore their functions depend on organizing co-operation among the producers, and simultaneously among sellers and entrepreneurs in fields beneficial to them. Hence economic problems come to the forefront. A farmers' organization must also attend to the affairs of families dwelling within the limits of a certain territorial community, and so has to take up local problems. Consequently a farmers' organization has to possess some of the attributes of a political party, a co-operative, and a territorial self-governing unit. Under socialist conditions, in which there is no basis for class differentiation in the village (because of the socialization of the means of production), nor any conditions making for its intensification, identification of the farmers' organization with the co-operative organization or with local government tends to result. The formation of organizations of agricultural workers does certainly create a basis for the emergence of organizations of the same type as we found in other occupations, but these organizations do not extend their activities to include peasant farms, even when only multi-family peasant husbandries, in the shape of production co-operatives, exist in the particular country.

The problems associated with the occupation of farming which we have discussed above provide at least a preliminary basis for clarifying the farmer's position in a society's occupational structure. Leaving aside the connection between occupational and class structure, which is particularly strong in this case, we must observe that, because of the objective features of the farmer's occupation, he must be regarded as falling outside any specialized occupational category and as falling within that sector of the social organization of labour which has not as yet become com-

pletely dominated by the pattern of specialization, yet is subject
to and affected by the process. As a result, the relatively high
social evaluation of the occupation of farming (in the opinion of
the urban population) does not correspond with its objective
attractiveness, i.e. its attractiveness as measured by the flow of
recruits into the occupation. In discussions on the decline of
farming as an occupation this contradiction between social
evaluation and the actual state of affairs is rarely noted, nor is it
often noticed that the situation cannot change fundamentally so
long as agriculture remains the domain of the family model of
production, which usually means that a farmer is someone who
has been born into a peasant family and who takes over the farm
by right of succession.

Notes

1   The definition of a profession as a 'type of activity possessing
market value' stresses this element. See *Encyclopaedia of social sciences*,
vol. 2, New York, 1931, p. 424.

2   'Czynniki ksztatujace zawod i strukture zawodowa' ('Factors
shaping occupational specialization and occupational culture and
organization'), *Studia socjologiczne* (*Sociological Studies*), 1963, No. 3.

3   J. Szczepanski, *Elementarne pojecia socjologii* (*Elementary concepts of sociology*), Warsaw, 1963, p. 123.

4   For instance, they figure in the so-called North–Hatt scale. See,
for example, L. Kolb, *Sociological analysis*, New York, 1949, p. 464;
National Opinion Research Center, 'Jobs and occupations: a popular
evaluation', *Opinion News*, vol. ix, 1942, No. 3, p. 13.

5   For a broader discussion of this and related problems see B.
Galeski, 'Chlopi i zawod rolnika' ('Peasants and farming as an occupation'), *Studia w socjologii wsi* (*Studies in rural sociology*), Warsaw,
1963, p. 162.

6   If one man or one woman works a farm it is not regarded as
being a proper unit. See, for example, Z. T. Wierzbicki, *Spoleczno-
kulturalne przemiany wsi Malopolskiej* (*Socio-cultural changes in the
villages of Malopolska*), Warsaw, 1963.

7   E.g. A. Romanow, 'Pionowa integracja w rolnictwie amerykan-
skim' ('Vertical integration in American agriculture'), *Wies wspolczesna*
(*The Contemporary Village*), 1963, No. 8.

8   K. Marx. *The 18th Brumaire of Louis-Napoléon*.

9   For a comparison of the occupational situation of sons emigrating
to the town and those remaining in the village see M. Pohoski,
Migracje z wsi do miast (*Migration from village to town*), Warsaw,
1963, p. 168.

10   E. Lipinski, 'Bodzce' ('Stimuli'), *Kultura i spoleczenstwo (Culture and Society)*, 1961, Nos. 1–2.

11   E.g. families of the so-called 'peasant–workers'.

12   E.g. C. Bobrowski, 'Ekonomia na ekranie panoramicznym' ('The economy in broad perspective'), *Przeglad kulturalny (Cultural Survey)*, 1963, No. 45.

13   E.g. E. M. Rogers, *Social change in rural society, cit.*, p. 366.

14   B. Galeski, 'Badania nad aktywnoscia zawodowa rolnikow' ('Studies of farmers' occupational activities'), *Studia socjologiczne*, 1962, No. 1, p. 195.

15   W. Makarczyk, 'Czynniki stabilizacji i aktywnosci zawodowej rolnikow w gospodarstwach indywidualnych' ('Factors in the stability and professional activity of farmers on individual farms'), *Studia socjologiczne*, 1961, No. 2, p. 125.

16   W. F. Mleczko, 'Konceptualizacja badan nad iniciatywa i aktywnoscia zawodowa i spoleczna no wsi' ('The conceptualization of research into occupational and social enterprise and activity in rural areas'), *Studia socjologiczno-polityczne (Politico-sociological Studies)*, 1962, No. 13.

17   D. Galaj, *Aktywnosc spoleczno-gospodarcza chlopow (The socio-economic activity of peasants)*, Warsaw, 1961.

18   J. Marek, 'Z badan nad autorytetem w zawodzie rolnika' ('Aspects of investigations into authority in the farmer profession'), *Roczniki socjologii wsi (Annals of Rural Sociology)*, vol. 1, 1963.

19   During studies carried out by the IER Worshop on Rural Social Structure in 1960, 70 per cent of those who filled in the questionnaires considered that a farmer owing a small piece of land cannot be termed a 'good farmer'.

20   H. Mendras, *Les Paysans et la modernisation de l'agriculture (Peasants and the modernization of agriculture)*, Paris, 1958, p. 40.

21   K. Dobrowolski, 'Chlopska kultura tradycyjna' ('Traditional peasant culture'), *Etnografia polska (Polish Ethnography)*, vol. 1, 1958.

22   J. Chalasinski, *Mlode pokolenie chlopow (The young generation of peasants)*, vol. 1, Warsaw, 1937.

23   In a questionnaire sent out by OBOP 20 per cent of the farmers considered that the agricultural school was not indispensable to the farmer. See B. Galeski, 'Tresci zawodowe w opiniach rolnikow' ('The meaning of occupation in the eyes of farmers'), *Wies wspolczesna*, 1961, No. 7, p. 12.

24   B. Galeski and A. Wyderko, 'Poglady chlopow na przyszlosc wsi' ('Peasants' views on the future of the village'), *Wies wspolczesna*, 1959, No. 4, p. 30.

25   E. M. Rogers, *The diffusion of innovations, cit.*

3 The peasant family

The family occupies an important place in sociological literature. This is evident not only from the numerous works devoted to it[1] but also from the position it holds in most sociological theoretical systems or in general textbooks on sociological and ethnographic problems. The special importance of the subject lies in the significance of the family as a primary institution or group in relation to all others. As with industrial or occupational sociology, the majority of macro-sociological schemas regard the sociology of the family as a separate scientific discipline with its own subject matter, its own terminology and its own methodology. It is, moreover, a sphere which provides an extremely rich comparative–descriptive literature[2] (mainly ethnological) and, in many fields, a well developed and established body of theory and general propositions. Under these circumstances one is inclined to refer the reader to specialized works and, ignoring problems of the family *per se*, to concentrate instead on a detailed study of the nature of the peasant family. However, it is impossible to ignore altogether problems of the family in general, if only because in order to discuss the special features of the peasant family it is necessary to refer to those characteristics common to all families—or at least to those entities which are subsumed under the label 'family'. The point is that the analysis of the peasant family, unlike the analysis of, say, the problems of an enterprise or an occupation, provides a basis for observations about the family in general. And when speaking, for instance, of changes in the present-day family, the majority of authors do in fact take the peasant family as their frame of reference. For this reason it will be valuable to summarize certain general factors that sociologists have established relating to the family.

Preliminary concepts: definition of family types and functions of the family

1. A family is usually defined either as an institution[3] or, more often, as a social group. Whilst there are many variations in these and other definitions, there is general agreement on the fact that the basis of the family is relationship through marriage and kinship, or adoption; and—as is usually added—that the members usually live together and co-operate within the framework of a socially determined and recognized division of roles and tasks.[4] It should be noted that this is not an entirely accurate definition. In everyday speech the word 'family' usually refers to a group of persons linked together by kinship, irrespective of whether or not they live together. For instance, uncles and aunts (and their wives or husbands) are included in the family as a rule, although they do not usually live with the person recognized as the centre of the family circle.[5] Since one can go a long way back in tracing descent (on the father's or mother's side), the word 'family' in its everyday sense cannot be accepted in scientific work; one speaks rather of closer or more distant bonds of kinship (objectively or subjectively conceived), of stronger or weaker family ties, or of a broader or narrower family circle, whether determined on the basis of objective features or by feelings of closeness. In this work the term 'family' covers only persons linked by the closest bonds of consanguinity (parents and children), living together, and as a rule carrying on a common domestic economy.

2. The principle of classifying types of family according to the number of persons living within marriage bonds (monogamous, polygynous or polyandrous marriage), and according to the choice of spouse (endogamy or exogamy), will not be discussed here. Types of marriage can be further classified according to who decides the choice of spouses (the interested parties themselves, or their parents), or according to the motives that are dominant in the contracting of the marriage (economic, prestige, love). The hierarchy of prestige and authority in the family—i.e. patriarchal or matriarchal families, on the one hand, and families based on egalitarian relationships between the marriage partners on the other—is also involved here. The structure of authority in the family usually involves the mode of inheritance (name, property, social position) and the rules governing consanguinity:

patrilineal or matrilineal. With this is also associated the residential principle adopted in the given society: whether the young couple live with the husband's parents (patrilocal marriage) or the wife's parents (matrilocal marriage).

In addition to the principles enumerated, it would seem appropriate to classify families according to the purpose of the marriage: whether it is in the interest of the family (the line), or of the individuals and their desire for personal happiness. This differentiation corresponds to the earlier classification of families according to the motives for choice of a spouse. It would also seem essential to distinguish families according to the kind of relations maintained with distant relatives, which are usually defined by custom.

Many more principles could be cited for classifying family types. These will depend upon one's cognitive purpose: for example, according to class or ethnic affiliation. However, the types cited above are the most important for characterizing the family and the changes it undergoes, and they constitute the most frequently used framework. The elements of such a typology are at the same time the characteristics which distinguish the major differences between the working class and the peasant family, for instance. Apart from ranking the family within the framework of this classification, one important element characterizing the family is the functions it performs.

3. In the literature these functions are also more or less differentiated. The biological function of marriage as a socially approved institution which regulates sexual intercourse and reproduction is usually mentioned. This implies certain economic functions of the family notably that of securing the existence of its members who cannot obtain the means of subsistence from their own resources (above all, small children and old people). A further economic function is that of carrying on the domestic economy. Among the family's other economic, or, more broadly, social, functions should be included, in part at least, the following:

(a)   Insurance (providing material and other kinds of support for the individual in times of failure or crisis—the extended family often performs this function as well).

(b)   The transmission of inheritance (both material and cultural).

(c)   The provision of facilities for the individual's start in life
and the preliminary determination of his position in the
hierarchy of stratification, based on income, prestige, and
authority.

These functions are also performed to some extent by more distant relatives. The family also performs educational functions to
some degree: socializing and controlling the children's education, providing knowledge they will need in life; instilling the
norms and values dominant in the community, and introducing
them into social groups and institutions.

The family's cultural functions are linked to the above. The
domestic economy is not only the place where goods—both
material and cultural—are produced but also the place where
they are consumed. The organization of leisure, amusement, etc.,
for family members within or outside the household is another
aspect of family life. Finally the family gives moral and emotional
support for the individual member, providing his defence against
social isolation and loneliness, as well as satisfying his need for
personal happiness, for recognition, for understanding and for
warmth. These functions are particularly important today, and
are always performed by the family to a greater or lesser degree.

4. A description of the functions of the family also provides a
basis for classifying its types. It also enables us to compare the
characteristics of families in various collectivities, communities,
or cultures, and to disclose changes within these communities or
in society generally.

It may be analytically useful to introduce, among these preliminary concepts, that of the differentiation of the various phases
or cycles of family life. This is the so-called 'little dynamic', distinguished from historical change in society at large. Thus one
can distinguish the early period of matrimony before the arrival
of children, the couple with small children (in this connection it
is necessary to distinguish between the period during which the
children are incapable of working and the period when they help
or perform particular tasks on the farm), and the period when the
children have achieved independence. In each of these stages,
different family functions come to the fore; they are most extensive during the period when the domestic farm unit consists of
parents with children who are still dependent.

The social distinctiveness of the peasant family

Taking into account all these criteria we are using to distinguish the various types of family, or to define their functions, the peasant family appears to be more traditional than others. First of all, it is a larger family. In Poland in 1960 the average number of persons per family was 3·09 in the towns, as against 3·86 in rural areas.[6] In the United States in 1958 the urban family averaged 3·5 persons, the non-agricultural rural family 3·82, and the agricultural family 4·08.[7] Also, the traditional peasant family is generally a three-generation one.[8]

In the parts of Poland less influenced by industrialization a form of the three-generation family still survives. The grandparents control the joint domestic economy (and/or farm), together with the married sons and daughters (at least in principle), in a residence shared with one of the children; or—more strictly speaking—one of the children remains with the parents in the common dwelling. This last phenomenon leads to several different patterns of relationship requiring separate discussion. In Poland the typical marriage in the village is patrilineal, and may be either patrilocal, matrilocal or neolocal, while in town it is on the whole neolocal. In the rural areas the pattern of choice of spouse reveals strong elements of endogamy within the framework of the local village community.[9] In the Polish village, parents still play an important part in choosing the spouse. The economic advantages of the marriage are often taken into consideration, and the principle of endowing the couples entering marriage also persists. The peasant family, again, is distinguished by a higher birth rate. In Poland in 1961 the birth rate per 1,000 was 11·1 in the towns as against 15·1 in the villages.[10] The peasant family is more stable; divorce is rarer amongst the peasantry than in other milieux. The hierarchy of authority and prestige in many peasant families exhibits distinctly patriarchal features. The interests of the family and its farm still play an important part among the objectives of marriage. Ties with more distant relatives are much more significant and more durable, and also often differ from patterns of kinship links in urban environments.

The functions of the peasant family are more diversified and are performed on a broader scale. The peasant family operates a domestic economy which is at the same time an enterprise, thus fulfilling an important production function, but because trade networks are less developed other economic functions cover a wider range than is the case in the towns. The family's cultural functions are of greater importance for the same reasons, with the qualification that the type of cultural entertainment—in the broad sense of the term—is peculiar to the village. Because of the importance of the family's economic functions, less time is available for relaxation of this kind. With the training of children for farm work, the peasant family undertakes more extensive educational functions, which differ in kind from those of the non-peasant family. The question of personal happiness is less important in comparison, because of the high degree of identification of the individual with the family interests.[11] Hence we may make the generalization that the peasant family performs the above-mentioned functions over a wide range of activities, is a more compact group, and determines the life situation and behaviour of the individual in many more situations than other types of family. And, as indicated above, it performs some of its functions in a quite different manner and in different proportions.

The basis for this difference is primarily the peasant family's ties with the farm. This takes the form of an extended domestic economy—one which includes not only the cultivation and processing of agricultural produce but also the production of other basic goods for consumption. As a result, the peasant family is less dependent on the organization of production within society as a whole. It is not, however, as self-sufficient today as it was in pre-industrial society. Today the farm still displays the characteristics of an enterprise, in which the family performs the role of a production team. (This implies the development of a system of relationships appropriate to a production group.) The farmer thus becomes an administrator (organizer) and an executive who evaluates the individual on the basis of his production performance. In short, the farm is drawn into a system of relations determined by the division of labour which occurs in the production process. All the above-mentioned differences between the peasant family and other families have their roots in the farmer's production activities and, more broadly, in his ties with the farm. These ties are the main source of both the significant degree of autonomy and the solidarity of the family, as well as of the multiple nature of the functions it performs.

A second cause of these differences is the peasant family's connection with the local community. A number of its basic functions
—particularly economic, educational and cultural functions—are
supplemented by corresponding activities on the part of the village community. The strong ties of kinship among the families
which make up the community, the firm bonds of neighbourliness,
the ramified system of socio-economic relations, the existence of
many specific village institutions and other features which constitute the village community as a primary group—all these factors
make up the special environmental conditions under which the
peasant family, with its distinctive cultural, educational and
'social insurance' functions, derives its existence and its dura-
bility.

It may be thought that many of the characteristic features of
the peasant family are determined simply by the conditions of
rural life: poorly developed trade and service facilities, poor
communications, and so on. However, these conditions do not
arise solely out of man's difficulty in mastering space in the rural
areas, but are mainly a result of those features of the village community which give rise to a social system different in kind from
that of urban settlements.

To sum up: the basis of the distinctiveness of the peasant
family is its basis in farming. This is the source of its main special
features, which are as follows:

1.   It is the production team of a small enterprise.
2.   It is autonomous to a greater extent than other families as
     far as the satisfaction of its members' needs is concerned.
     This stems from the nature of peasant farming .
3.   The scope of its functions is more comprehensive and they
     are performed in a more permanent manner. The individual
     is consequently more deeply rooted in and subordinated to
     the family, while the family itself is more solidary, and re-
     sists disorganization more effectively.
4.   The peasant family derives support for its functions from
     the village community.

The family and the farm

These somewhat abstract observations on the distinctiveness of the peasant family can be made more concrete if we examine the place the farm occupies in the life of the family. Without making the bonds between the family and the farm absolute, and whilst far from claiming that all the features of the types of family known to history derive from the mode of production (for that would be nonsense), it is still difficult to deny that such characteristics as monogamy or polygamy, patriarchy or matriarchy have their source in the mode of organization of production.

But the question of the relationship between the type of family and the mode of production goes beyond the subject under consideration. To analyse the family farm more thoroughly we need now to consider several problems connected with its genesis and functioning.

1. The first problem is that of choice of spouse. As shown above, a considerable role is played in the peasant family by the views of the parents and by their regard for the interests of the family and the farm. In essence, the formation of a new family involves the problem of ensuring the basis of its continued existence. In village life this means that the new family must be guaranteed land. This involves the necessity of solving the economic problems as to which parent will allocate part of his or her land, and how much land is needed in order to ensure the young couple's basis for existence.

In countries where the principle of the indivisibility of the farm was adhered to before the war (for instance, in Poznan province in Poland), the new family remained on the farm of one of the parents, and the brothers and sisters had to contribute to the dowry. In this case the share which the other party contributed became important. Where the transfer of land has no significance, either because State laws or rights of inheritance restrict the division of the farm, or for other reasons—such as lack of available land—these questions may arise in a different form. For instance, it may then be a question of increasing not the area of the farm but its reserves of labour-power. And in any case, the starting of a new peasant family necessitates some kind of settlement of economic affairs on the part of the families of the persons contracting the marriage. Thus a child's marriage involves the peasant family; the burdens which fall on the family and the eventual benefits it will obtain from the marriage must be considered and decided upon, and the family is involved not only materially but also

with respect to its prestige and position in the community of
which it is a member. In view of the connection between the farm
and the farmer's class position, this in turn depends upon its
material involvement.[12] Thus in the peasant family the choice of
spouse entails a balance between the interests of the two families.[13]

It must be added that the family's main property is the farm.[14]
The married couple received the land from their parents; they
pass it on to their children. Obviously it is desirable to pass it on
with its area as undiminished as possible. The farm is handed
down from generation to generation, while the family—the suc-
cessive usufructuaries—carries a responsibility to its own children (and to village opinion) for the property in its charge. The
starting of a new peasant family, then, involves the interests both
of the farm, as the overriding value, and of the family. Therefore,
as long as the institutions of the peasant farm and peasant family
exist, the choice of spouse has to be looked at from the point of
view of the interests of the family.

In any concrete situation the foregoing schematic outline of the
relationship between family and farm may apply to a greater or
lesser extent. The situation in more affluent families is different
from that in poorer families. The relationship is weaker in the
case of families which draw the main or a subsidiary part of their
means of support from wage labour. The situation is different,
again, in the case of children who leave the farm, although they
too usually obtain part of the family property, a share-payment,
or at least the cost of their education. The situation differs also
in multi-family peasant farming (production co-operatives), although here too the need to divide the private plot with a newly-
married couple involves the interests of the family or even those
of all the families which farm together.

2. The family's links with the farm, which become so visible in
the selection of spouses, have a considerable influence on the
nature of the tasks the newly married couple must undertake. As
stated above, the farm is the key element in the peasant family.
The land handed on by the parents provides the basis of existence for the newly married couple and in turn passes to their
children. When the couple take over the land from their parents
they simultaneously take over responsibility for its transfer to
their children. The amount of land and farm equipment passed
on to the children constitutes the basis for the prestige accorded

by others and for their own assessment of the manner in which they have acquitted themselves of these tasks.

This is the basis for the observed identification of family and farm, and of individual and family interests. Family and farm interests hence help determine the tasks which the new peasant family must undertake.

This links the family's economic functions with its procreative ones. The children are both the heirs of, and workers on, the farm. As heirs they are also co-owners, but because of the patriarchal pattern of the peasant family this is not usually expressed in terms of participation in the hierarchy of authority in the family. The farm must assure the children's maintenance and endowment, while they must guarantee the functioning of the farm. This entails evaluating the children not only from the point of view of their value as workers. In the traditional family the very fact of giving birth to a child is regarded as a fact of significance to the farm as far as its future continuity is concerned. In areas where it is customary for the oldest son to take over the farm from the father he is treated differently; he is made familiar with all the family's affairs and plays a larger part in all family and farm decisions. Customs governing inheritance vary from country to country and from region to region, but in the traditional peasant family, as a rule, the position of the children is determined in accordance with the interests of the farm.

In connection with the above we should bear in mind the question of the birth rate. Thus, according to statistical data[15] more children are born and reared in richer peasant families, or —more strictly—in families which own more land. This phenomenon has various explanations—earlier marriage,[15] the better physical condition of the women, etc. But none of these hypotheses has been confirmed so far. It would seem that this phenomenon (although tending to die out, as might be expected) fundamentally changes the universally accepted view that there is a connection between the birth-rate and wealth. In society generally, the birth rate is lower among the richer categories of the population. The peasantry, however, appear to be an exception to this rule. Since level of income is closely correlated with class divisions, it may be thought that differences in the birth rate occur rather between classes than between income categories.

However, in classes which are cultural entities the dependence

of the birth rate on level of income may vary from the situation
obtaining in the rest of society, and in traditional social groups
may even occur in a reverse manner. Irrespective of how the
differences in the birth rate are explained, they appear to point
to an interesting relationship between size of farm and size of
the family. Any weakening of this relationship would be in harmony with patterns of contemporary rural change.

3. As already mentioned, the peasant family retains patriarchal
features even today in many regions of Poland. The patriarchal
pattern corresponds with its functions. As the production team of
a small enterprise, the members of the family are subject to the
father's authority. He decides on all changes in the farm[16] as well
as on what work is to be done and when. His authority derives
from being not only manager of the farm but also its owner. The
father, and after his death the mother, decides on the children's
dowry, on the transfer to them of the farm and, before that, on
any change in the size of the farm, whether in respect of area or
other means of production. The farm's economic requirements
reinforce the family's solidarity, determine its different production functions—with which the various positions in the family
hierarchy are associated—and the manner in which it disposes
of its income. The break-up of the peasant family is tantamount
to the disintegration of the farm, and is therefore a much more
difficult and more complicated problem than in other kinds of
family.

In considering the connection between the system of relationships, and above all the disposition of authority in the family, as
well as the nature of the peasant farm as a production unit, it is
necessary to take into account the relationship between the size
of the farm and the developmental cycle of the family.[17] Several
phases can be distinguished. The first is entry into marriage; the
married couple usually begin with a small farm (or, in certain
countries, a rented farm). At this stage they do not usually receive
full rights of succession. The youthfulness of the couple and the
woman's comparatively small preoccupation with caring for
the children make possible a considerable input of labour, and the
farm area gradually enlarges. It increases further during the
second phase, when children arrive. The need to support a family
impels the couple to intensive labour, in which the children also

begin to share as time passes. The farm reaches its peak during the third phase, when the children reach the age when they are mature productive workers but not yet married. During the fourth phase the children become independent. Now the ageing of the parents and gradual reduction of their contribution to the work of the family, together with the departure of the children, lead to a diminution in the area of the farm. Even if there is no division of the land within the family, the need to make share-payments may force the family to sell part of it. The land may be reduced to the size of a small plot which the parents retain for life. But even if they remain with a son or daughter, the farm is usually reduced to the size with which the family started. The connection between the size of the farm and the family cycle is evident in the statistically confirmed relationship between farm area and the age of the head of the family. In three-generation families (still common in the rural areas of certain countries, such as Italy) the mechanism described here operates over a longer period of time and in a more complicated manner, but this does not necessitate any fundamental modification of the foregoing observations.

4. The type of production determines the pattern of the educational system. In a peasant family the child is educated in the course of his work. As he matures the child undertakes increasingly difficult and more responsible tasks, and increasingly those traditionally assigned to the appropriate sex. Transfer to new tasks is an expression of the status position the child occupies in the family and indicates the stage he has reached in his social maturity. The child acquires production expertise and patterns of behaviour as well as ethical standards; he learns what has to be done, together with an understanding of his position in the local community. As he reaches maturity and takes over further production tasks the child comes to occupy a place in the village, and acquires knowledge of the outside world. The process of education through the acquisition of greater efficiency in production often finds expression in corresponding rituals. Thus in the peasant family there is a strict correlation between biological and social maturity and maturity as a producer. Biological maturity forms the basis, but the child's assumption of new economic tasks conditioned by age and strength determines his position in the family and in the village community.[18]

5. The child's independence of the family comes about either through marrying and moving to his own farm (in the three-generation type of family not immediately, but after the father's death), or by leaving the family and the local community to work in a non-agricultural occupation or in a large agricultural enterprise.

According to prevailing custom, either the farm is divided among the children, or one heir takes it over and pays off his brothers and sisters. Custom also determines which of the children remains on the paternal farm, and which of them must seek a way out either by marrying and starting their own farms or by changing to another occupation. The mechanism of inheritance, even in the case of the partition of family land, aims at the preservation, or the least possible diminution, of the existing family farm. The child remaining on the farm makes up by marriage for the land handed over to his brothers and sisters or for the losses caused by the shares paid to them. For a time he may manage the farm jointly with his parents, but usually, with the arrival of grandsons, the grandparents retire to the plot of land reserved for them, or arrange an annuity for themselves, in return for handing over the reins. When there is little possibility of leaving the village, rivalry over the inheritance usually develops between the children, and the position of heir is a coveted one. In certain conditions (where the farm cannot be divided) the other brothers and sisters must find work outside if they are not to find themselves without any basis for founding a family.[19]

Partitioning the farm is always the worst solution, and, even in regions where partitioning is permitted, fear of fragmentation, and the consequent prospect of existence on a dwarf plot, is a factor which constantly stimulates migration from village to town, or from areas of parcelized farms to areas of large farming, or to regions of new settlement, if such exist. Under such conditions the interests of the family and of the farm determine the direction of the child's future—whether he follows farming as a profession or has to leave the family and the village.

The situation is different in societies with growing work opportunities outside the village and outside agriculture (and where the town is very attractive). In this situation the rivalry is not over who shall remain on the patrimony, but who is to leave. As a rule, those whom the family considers to have a greater chance of success outside the village are the ones to go. Nevertheless, in general, the peasant farm is not left without a successor[20] as long as there are children in the family. In peasant families, obligations to the farm and to the family are felt very strongly and, as research shows, this is the main motive for a child to remain on the farm even if he does not like farm work and would prefer another occupation.[21] The situation is different again in multi-family farms (production co-operatives) where the feeling of responsibility to the farm and family is incomparably weaker, and the restrictive effects of ownership or inheritance have only a limited influence.[22] In such cases the young generation think of the work only in terms of an occupation and, if there are no special administrative restrictions, consistently abandon agriculture.

In peasant families the forces binding young people to the farm are still very strong today, and in great measure the family decides the fate of the child. Hence it is the rule for the occupation of farmer to pass from father to son. This peculiarity, along with others, is a consequence of the nature of peasant farming.

The phenomena described here—from the starting of a family to the parents' retiring on an annuity—differ in different countries and regions, depending on the type of family, the form of inheritance, the intervention of the State, legal regulations, the influence of industrial society on the village, and so on. Despite the undoubtedly distinctive nature of multi-family farms, i.e. the production co-operatives, even here the family's tie with the farm is the main feature which distinguishes the peasant family from other types. The distinctiveness characterized here pertains to the traditional peasant family, however. Today considerable changes are occurring, as we have seen. But an outline of the features of the traditional family is indispensable in considering these changes.

Changes in the forms of the modern peasant family

Sociologists studying the family are in general agreement on patterns of change in the modern family.[23] They disagree only in their evaluation of these changes: whether they constitute evidence

of the withering away or progressive degeneration of this institution, or evidence only of a change in its content and functions.[24] Leaving the evaluation of the changes to the specialists,
here we need only point to general tendencies in these changes,
about which there is considerable agreement.

There is agreement on the transition from the three-generation
family to the small family consisting of parents and children. In
urban areas it is rather exceptional for married sons and
daughters to live with their parents, and when this occurs it is
dictated by the interests of the younger generation. Most frequently, as soon as the children marry, or even earlier, when
they begin to earn their keep, they leave the family and set up
their own home. Housing difficulties, and the need for women to
take up employment, may delay this process. But aspirations to
set up an independent home are extraordinarily strong and are
realized as soon as the minimum material requirements become
available.

The modern family is smaller not only because of the reduction of the number of generations living together but also as a
result of birth control. With the development of hygiene and
health services, infant mortality has fallen considerably. The
child coming into the world today is more often than not expected and wanted.

The change in the size and pattern of the family, and different
attitudes towards children and better child care, are associated
with changes in the aims of marriage, which today is usually personal happiness. It is not the interests of the family, but those of
the individual, his desire for moral and emotional support and
for assurance against isolation in our atomized society, that is
the most frequent motive. This leads to changes in the choice of
marriage partner, which is more often based on love and mutual
attraction. Today 'romantic choice' is a universal phenomenon,
and is generally recognized as a value to be desired.[25] This increase in the importance of the romantic element in marriage is
associated with changes in the pattern of relations between the
married couple. The universal pattern is the egalitarian family in
which both partners (and increasingly the children too) have an
equal right to personal happiness and an equal share in deci-
ions affecting their common fate. This is the result too of the

economic independence of the woman, who in present-day society more and more frequently follows her own career.

These changes, and particularly the entry of women into the labour market, lead to a diminution of the activities of the family as an economic unit. Domestic obligations are increasingly borne by both partners, and the development of cafes and restaurants, of services and the mechanization and modernization of the home, greatly limit the range of domestic activities. In certain spheres there is also a diminution, or rather a change, in the family's educational role: to a great extent it is replaced by the school and other educational establishments. But in those spheres where the family does still participate in the child's education it performs its functions even more fully than in the past. Its major contribution lies in complementing formal education in the school (which often only crams 'book learning' into the heads of the pupils) by providing emotional support for the child. It thus prepares young people for life in the community as it really is. The family furthermore offers the child, within the limits of the child's own potentialities, a defined social position when it is ready to start an independent life. Social positions, of course, are connected with the organization of society, with the system of stratification specific to the socialist or capitalist system. Nevertheless, the family's influence in assuring the child's future position is undeniable in both systems.

The 'insurance' functions of the family also change. The wide extension of social security more frequently provides people in their old age with the means of an independent existence. The family 'insurance' functions are therefore to a large extent of an emotive–moral nature.

The cultural activities of the modern family are also changing rather than diminishing. True, the existence of specialized cultural centres (the cinema, concert halls and theatres, cafes and places of amusement) restrict the family's cultural role. But television, highly valued in modern society, bonds of friendship and comradeship, as well as contact with distant relatives, maintain the family's cultural role, although its scope and content are changing.

Changes in the pattern of the modern family have seriously weakened its solidarity. Now that personal happiness has become the chief value, the family is subject to disintegration (factual or formal) when one of its members considers that this desired value is not to be found within it. The number of separations and divorces is steadily increasing. The growth in the frequency of divorce reflects the growth in importance of the emotional bonds linking married couples and from this point of view is part and parcel of general social changes occurring in the world today.

These changes in the modern family appear in all societies. They are clearly to be found in a more or less advanced degree according to the general state of development of civilization in particular countries and societies. The greatest differences exist between peasant families and those of other social environments and groups. The modern family pattern—egalitarian, with restricted economic functions and a changed cultural and educational content—is appropriate to industrial society. Historically, it is urban patterns which dominate the occupational organization of society. But the contemporary peasant family also aims at modelling itself to this pattern.[26]

Together with the dominant role of the industrial occupational organization of production or—more broadly—the industrial system of social life, the values and patterns generated by this system also become dominant. They penetrate the village in every possible way: through the mass media of communication, through the rural population's personal contacts with the town, through the contacts which almost every peasant family has with relatives in the urban areas. These patterns begin to appear in the village as one of the ways in which the peasant farm and the farmer's labour adapt themselves to contemporary society.

The directions of change in peasant families coincide with those in society generally. The only difference lies in the degree to which these changes have occurred, since potentiality for change is particularly limited in the life of the peasant family farm. The directions of change can be observed when we begin to find in the countryside the same kind of phenomena that we find in the towns. In both village and town, indeed, the principle of the 'romantic' choice of a mate has become general. Research in Polish villages confirms that land is no longer the main criterion in selecting a marriage partner.[27] Young people's aspirations and images of the kind of family they expect to have correspond with the contemporary pattern of the urban family.[28] However, statistical analysis[29] suggests that these aspirations become realized only when the young person leaves the family farm and the village. If he or she remains in the village the selection of a mate in fact continues to be made as if the size of the farm continued to be the binding principle.[30] But although the principle may no longer be explicitly held by parents, and though they grant the child freedom in the choice of a mate, the circle of social contacts is still determined by the established hierarchy of social status in the village, and this is decisive when it comes to actually choosing. Furthermore, although the parents, when asked their opinion on the subject of their child's marriage, declared themselves to be in favour of complete freedom of choice, under the conditions of peasant farming it is impossible for them to avoid viewing the matter in the light of family and farm interests. Such considerations no longer oblige the child to renounce his personal desires, but they do still have a considerable influence on his conduct. It is irrelevant that in Poland these interests are no longer focused on the land the son or daughter-in-law will contribute; the more essential issue is that of assuring the farm labour-power. Economic considerations continue to play a crucial part in shaping the child's marriage plans, and, although 'romantic choice' is now a recognized value in young people's aspirations, traditional patterns still heavily influence actual behaviour.

Another area where the decision is made by the child and not by the family is the choice of occupation. Although this value also is recognized today in peasant families, nevertheless, as already noted, obligations to the farm and to the family have a deep influence on the behaviour of young people approaching independence. Most young people would like to leave the farm and acquire a trade or skill[31] which would assure them of the same benefits as other occupations. Yet they remain on the farm, and despite fears expressed at times in the Polish Press, a farm with no heir is a rare phenomenon. The peasant family's cultural functions have, in the past, been incomparably less restricted than those of the urban family. In the towns these functions have at least been taken over by a relatively dense network of cultural agencies, which are less common in the villages. The general diffusion of the radio, the Press, television, and more frequent exposure to the cinema have greatly weakened the family's cultural functions. But they have not eliminated them, nor have they succeeded in replacing them to the extent required.

Fundamental changes have also occurred in the pattern of relations within the peasant family. The purely patriarchal family
is dying out. Here, too, individualization in the attitudes of the
members of the family has occurred. The desire of young people
to participate in decisions affecting the family, or at least to ensure that their own personal values are recognized, is now
widespread.[32] Today married couples more frequently make joint
decisions and the older children also participate more often in
decisions concerning the farm and the family.

The peasant family's educational functions have also undergone basic changes. There is greater concern with the general
welfare of the children, and small children attending school are
less burdened with production tasks. However, the necessity imposed by the farm for the performance of these tasks does not allow the child to be completely freed from farm work, although
that work is not of the kind that prepares the child for the life of
a farmer. To a great extent it simply burdens the peasant child
with work which his urban counterpart has not known for a long
time. Just as the authority of the father, who is the farm manager,
cannot be restricted, so the production functions of the peasant
family as a whole cannot be seriously diminished, since this would
be tantamount to neglect of the farm, which remains the basis of
the family's existence.

The decisive cause of the relative slowness of change in family
patterns is the peasant family's production functions. The tendency of the farm increasingly to take on the features of an enterprise[33] comes into conflict with the new aspirations of the family.
This development of the characteristics of an enterprise is usually
accompanied by an increase in labour-saving farm equipment. But
the need for the economic evaluation of these means also increases,
even though the possibility of applying them on a small farm is
limited. Moreover, mechanization does not alter the work load on
the family. It only makes it possible to shift their effort to other
sections of the farm in which inputs of human labour continue to
play a decisive part. In sum, the increase in entrepreneurial
features on the peasant farm is in obvious contradiction to the
general pattern of change in the contemporary family. Instead of
diminishing, the family's economic functions are growing and aspirations towards the extension of cultural and educational
functions, etc., meet with increasing difficulty. Emotional support

provided by the family continues to be subsidiary to economic considerations. Hence the economic demands of the enterprise impose a family pattern which no longer meets the aspirations of its members. As a result, the contemporary peasant family pattern has a disharmonious character resulting from the co-existence of contradictory tendencies: the general increasing dominance of aspirations modelled on urban life styles, on the one hand, and patterns of behaviour imposed by the requirements of the peasant farm on the other.[34] The development of industrial society is intensifying this conflict, and it can be assumed that the peasant family's adaptation to industrial society will proceed even further as industrial forms of production emerge within agriculture itself.

Notes

1   J. Szczepanski, *Socjologia: rozwoj problematyki i metod* (*Sociology: the development of its subject matter and methods*), Warsaw, 1961.

2   G. P. Murdock, *Social structure*, New York, 1949.

3   E.g. in *Dictionary of sociology*, ed. H. Pratt Fairchild, New York, 1943, p. 111.

4   For a definition and broader discussion of the types and functions of the family see, for example, J. Szczepanski, *Elementarne pojecia socjologii, cit.*, p. 149.

5   In everyday speech the word 'family' is sometimes used primarily with reference to distant relatives.

6   *Rocznik statystyczny* (*Statistical yearbook*), 1962, p. 30, table 15.

7   E. M. Rogers, *op. cit.*, p. 173.

8   F. Znaniecki, 'Socjologiczne podstawowy ekologii ludzkiej' ('The sociological bases of human ecology'), *Ruch prawniczy, ekonomiczny i socjologicnze* (*The Juridical, Economic and Sociological Movement*, 1938, No. 1.

9   M. Jarosinka, 'Pozafabryczne srodowisko spoleczne' ('The social milieu outside the factory'), *Studia socjologiczne* (*Sociological Studies*), 1964, No. 1. Research in industrial areas suggests also that migrants from the village usually marry girls from their own village.

10   *Rocznik statystyczny, cit.*, p. 31, table 16.

11   J. Chalasinski, *Mlode pokolenie chlopow, cit.*, p. 133.

12   B. Galeski, 'Socjologiczna problematyka zawodu rolnika' ('Sociological problems of farming as an occupation'), *Roczniki socjologii wsi* (*Annals of Rural Sociology*), vol. 1, 1964.

13   P. Bourdieu, 'Célibat et condition paysanne' ('Celibacy and the peasantry'), *Etudes rurales*, 1962, Nos. 5–6, p. 32.

14   W. L. Thomas and F. Znaniecki, *The Polish peasant in Europe and America*, New York, 1927, p. 169; J. Chalasinski, *op. cit.*, p. 154.
15   W. Stys, *Wspolzaleznosc rozwoju rodziny chlopskiej i jej gospodarstwa (The contemporary development of the peasant family and peasant farming)*, Wroclaw, 1959.
16   The IER questionnaire of 1960 on the modernization of agriculture showed that in principle the farm owner decides on the introduction of improvements in the farm without consulting the rest of the family.
17   T. Lynn Smith, *Sociology of rural life*, New York, 1953, pp. 79, 411 ff.
18   J. Chalasinski, *op. cit.*, p. 125.
19   W. G. Hoffman, *Zur Dynamik der industriellen Gesellschaft, Wirtschaftsoziologische Bemerkungen: Beiträge zur Soziologie der industriellen Gesellschaft (On the dynamics of the industrial company: economic-sociological observations: contributions to the sociology of the industrial company)*, Dortmund, 1952, p. 7.
20   M. Pohoski, *Migracje z wsi do miast, cit.*, pp. 79 ff.
21   A. Sianko, 'Mlodzi rolnicy o swoim zawodzie' ('Young farmers on their occupation'), *Wies wspolczesna (The Contemporary Village)*, 1960, No. 4.
22   In personal accounts sent in to a ZMW (Rural Youth Union) competition announced in 1963, young people frequently expressed themselves quite willing to live in production co-operatives, but only because they were convinced that it would be easier for them to leave the village, as their obligations to the family and farm would be taken over by the co-operative.
23   R. H. McIver and C. H. Page, *Society*, London, 1961, pp. 250 ff.
24   R. Koenig, *Materialen zur Soziologie der Familie (Materials for a sociology of the family)*, Berne, 1946.
25   J. Chalasinski, *Kultura amerykanska (American culture)*, Warsaw, 1962.
26   Personal statements sent in for the ZMW competition, e.g. those by women, Nos. 2951, 3069, 3571 and 4688, and others.
27   Z. T. Wiersbicki, *Zmiaca w pol wieku pozniej (Zmiaca fifty years later)*, Wroclaw, 1963, pp. 255 ff.; F. Jakubczak, 'Ksztaltowanie sie integracyjno-ekspressyjnej funkcji rodziny wiejskiej' ('The formation of the integrative–expressive function of the village family'), *Roczniki socjologii wsi*, vol. II, 1964, p. 82.
28   E. Jagiello-Lysiowa, 'O czym marzy mlodziez' ('What young people dream of'), *Wies wspolczesna*, 1959, No. 12, p. 89.
29   Research carried out by the IER Workshop on Rural Social Structure, e.g. B. Galeski, 'Uwagi o spolecznym zroznicowaniu warstwy chlopskiej' ('Observations on social differentiation among the peasant stratum'), *Wies wspolczesna*, 1958, No. 1, p. 32; J. Przychodzen, 'Dobor terytorialny i spoleczny malzenstw wiejskich' ('Territorial and social choice of rural marriage partners'), *Roczniki socjologii wsi*, vol. II, 1964, p. 119.

30   A. Olszewska-Ladykowa and K. Zygulski, 'Malzenstwa mieszane na Slasku Opolskim' ('Mixed marriages in Opolean Silesia'), *Przeglad socjologiczny* (*Sociological Review*), vol. XII, 1959.

31   A. Sianko, 'Problematyka zawodu w pamietnikach mlodych mieszkancow wsi' ('Problems of occupational choice in the diaries of young village inhabitants'), *Roczniki socjologii wsi*, vol. I, 1963, p. 97.

32   See No. 5303 in the ZMW competition for diaries kept by rural youth.

33   B. Galeski, 'Chlopi i zawod rolnika', *cit.*

34   D. Markowska, *Kierunki przeobrazen wspolczesnej rodziny wiejskiej* (*Patterns of change in the contemporary peasant family*), vol. 2, Warsaw, 1965, pp. 57–81.

4 The village community

In any systematic classification village communities must be grouped with local communities. There are many definitions of the term 'local community', but despite differences in formulation they all have a common content. A 'local community' is understood to mean the totality of inhabitants of a certain territory in so far as they constitute a social group—that is, if they are linked by some system of bonds and relationships; by common interests, shared patterns of accepted norms and values; by consciousness of being distinct from other groups, defined according to the same principle, etc.[1]

The fact that collectivities distinguished according to one or other of these criteria may live together in a given territory is not always a basis for the appearance of bonds creating a social group. Therefore not every collectivity of people inhabiting a particular territory constitutes a local community. However, areas are usually distinguished by reference to important social characteristics, which tend to be cumulative. As a rule, the headquarters of local government constitutes the seat of many other institutions: administrative regions are usually integral units with characteristic economic, cultural and historic features. Hence the collectivity delineated in the course of scientific research, as well as in social life, is usually a local community to one extent or another.

The phrase 'to one extent or another' is used because in reality the distinction between 'collectivity' and 'community' is not dichotomous. All the objective and subjective features of a social group, and consequently of a local community, are graduated. The system of relations linking the members of any group may be more or less extensive, may carry more or less weight, and can create a more or less compact whole. A collectivity distinguished by a single feature (for instance, the families inhabiting the Muranow II district in Warsaw—a housing estate) does not usually constitute a social group. It may become such, if some important question arises which affects that particular collectivity of people.

If, for instance, its inhabitants are threatened by the danger of a shortage of water they will undoubtedly undertake common action, during which time they will function as a social group.

Local communities can therefore be ranked according to the extent of the presence of those features which make them a social group. This makes it possible for us to measure these characteristics, and consequently to determine empirically the changes local communities are exposed to or which occur spontaneously. The local community, like every social group, has a dynamic character; its characteristics are the fortuitous result of the interaction of the individuals composing it, who are involved both in reciprocal relations and in changing ties with their environment.[2]

Of course, local communities can be ranked and divided into types according to various principles (some of which will be discussed below). For the moment we shall consider only one way of classifying local communities: according to their position in a ranking order. Using the definition adopted here, local communities can be settlements or groups of settlements, villages, communes (embracing a number of villages), counties, provinces, or even countries—all are part of a system in which the local community of lower rank forms part of the local community of a higher order. Obviously other features are associated with this, and the district community differs from the village community not only by virtue of its position in the above-mentioned system but with respect to many other features, and indeed one cannot even be certain whether it is legitimate to use the term 'community' at all.

This is one of the reasons why the term 'local rural community' has not been used here. The township as well as the county are local rural communities. But here we shall only consider one particular type of local rural community: the village.

It is strikingly noticeable that all discussions about the differences between town and country in the sociological literature are in fact reduced to a definition of the features which distinguish the village from the urban type of settlement. We shall attempt to demonstrate that the differences most frequently mentioned are of a partial and secondary nature, and furthermore that they are consequences of a difference in the way of life, determined above all by the nature of peasant farming. Although there are many differences between town and country (eight are specified in

Sorokin and Zimmerman's well known textbook),[3] none of them provides an adequate criterion for defining any particular settlement
as a village or a town. One may thus speak rather of the intensity
of rural or urban features: the division into town and country is
not treated as a dichotomous one but denotes ideal types, between
which there is a whole range of intermediate forms.[4] Hence there
is no generally accepted criterion for the administrative definition
of settlements. For instance, in the United States the number of
inhabitants is accepted as the criterion. A settlement of up to 2,500
persons is defined as a village; above this number as a town. But
such a criterion cannot be applied to India, nor even Hungary or
Slovakia, where villages not infrequently have a much larger number of inhabitants. In Poland no single criterion is applied, and
the question as to whether any settlement is regarded as a village
or a town is decided pragmatically by the relevant authorities. Irrespective of whether one or many criteria are taken into account,
administrative decisions are nonetheless always based on some
kind of appraisal of the actual characteristics of the community.

*The basic attributes of the village community: differences
between town and country*

The basic characteristic of the village community is that the
majority of its inhabitants are members of families which operate
peasant farms. To regard peasant farming as the basis of the village community *ipso facto* excludes concentrations of agricultural
workers employed on large farms,[5] as well as settlements of industrial workers (miners, etc.) where these form a separate spatial
unit. This usage resembles those distinctions we draw in everyday
speech in which not only are the village and the mining settlement distinguished but the former is also distinguished clearly
from the manor, the estate, etc. Agricultural workers permanently
employed and living on a large farm are not as a rule considered
to be the inhabitants of a village, even though a village may be
nearby; nor are they counted as peasants,[6] either in their own
opinion or their employer's. One can, of course, include aggregations of agricultural workers among local rural communities,
but then it would be necessary to distinguish between small non-

agricultural settlements, manors (or, in contemporary Poland, State Farms) and villages. This is a further reason why the term 'village community' is used in this book rather than 'local rural community'.

If the peasant farm is regarded as the basis of the village community, then most of the features characterizing this community derive from the definition of peasant farming as a production system based on the identification of the agricultural enterprise with the family. In the very nature of agricultural production—or rather, the role which land plays in such production—it follows that the producers cannot form very large aggregations. This applies both to the village and to the manor (estate). A large agricultural enterprise requires an even smaller number of inhabitants than a group of peasant farms. The size of the village community depends on the agrarian structure and on the type of production with which the farming area is associated. The greater the fragmentation of farms (because migration from the village is not possible, and because of the operation of the principle of allocating shares of land to each member of the family), and the higher the farming intensity, the greater will be the number of inhabitants in the village. In Poland villages are most fragmented in the south of the country and in regions of intensive cultivation, i.e. in the proximity of towns. In the central and western regions, where the farms are larger, the average village numbers 80–150 families.

Thus the smaller number of inhabitants and the lower density of population in the villages as compared with the towns are the result of the characteristics of agricultural production. It can therefore be said (contrary to the views of Sorokin and Zimmerman[7]) that these characteristics are associated not with urbanism—ruralism (the smaller the number of inhabitants in a settlement and the lower the density of the population, the more marked its rural features), but with agricultural production. Moreover, compared with settlements of agricultural workers, villages are decidedly more densely populated. Hence it may be said that rural traits are positively correlated both with the number of inhabitants and with population density among agricultural aggregations.

Another frequently stressed feature of the village community which derives from the nature of agricultural production, is man's close contact with nature. We all know that in a town men are

surrounded by inanimate objects and human products, while in
the villages they live against the backdrop of nature.[8] Perhaps this
alienation from nature has some influence on the individual's personality and on inter-personal relations. It is difficult to make any
definite pronouncement on this, since the number of factors
moulding the human personality is so large that to give priority
to any one of them would be quite unjustified. One might add
that observations about the beneficial influence of nature on man
are also commonly accompanied by notions about the moral
superiority of the farmer over the urban inhabitant.[9] However,
this kind of consideration goes beyond the domain of science.
Undoubtedly close contact with nature has many beneficial effects,
but since it is associated with poorly developed productive forces
in agriculture it is difficult to evaluate these benefits as enthusias-
tically as some authors do—for that matter, they do not meet with
much appreciation from the farmers themselves.

The characteristics so far mentioned relate to the nature of agricultural production, and are appropriate both to aggregations of
peasant farm families and to settlements of agricultural workers
on large farms. One major characteristic of the village is the weak
development of the social division of labour. The very fact that
the settlement is numerically small makes it difficult to achieve a
more developed division of labour. Service centres are located
where there is sufficient demand for services. Local authorities,
churches and schools are located in the larger villages, or in villages which occupy a central position in the district, and this is
usually where shops, handicrafts, restaurants, etc., are also to be
found. But in the majority of villages these amenities do not exist.
However, we are not concerned here with this kind of division of
labour, although its poor development is self-evident. The point
is that families operating peasant farms concentrated in a village
are not linked by a clearly developed division of labour. It is in
this sense that Marx writes: '... the great mass of the French
nation' (the peasants in the village) 'is formed by the simple addition of homologous magnitudes'.[10] A large agricultural enterprise
is *not* an entity of this kind: its workers constitute a production
team, and the labour of each is connected with the labour of the
others, although in general there is no developed social division
of labour in such enterprises. The nature of the peasant farm, the
fact that it is an extended domestic economy, means that the ties

which derive from the division of labour are much weaker in the
village than in the town community.

Nevertheless, such ties do exist in the village. There may not be
any craftsman in the village, but usually one farmer is more expert, for instance, at building houses, at treating sick animals, or
at repairing equipment, than the rest. Hence, even if there are no
representatives of non-agricultural skilled occupations, and even
if such activities are conducted within the limits of the domestic
economy, a certain division of labour associated with special capacities or skills does exist. Division of labour also occurs in the field
of agriculture. The need for joint activity, for instance in land
improvement, in horse breeding or in the joint use of machinery,
militates against the complete isolation of farm families within
the village. Similar interaction occurs because of the tradition of
periodic co-operative labour in house building, since there is usually some degree of specialization in farming, which forms the
basis for the exchange of products within the village, and so on.

The small size of the village community and the marked spatial
stability of its inhabitants give rise to one of its most important
features, namely that the village community is a primary group.[11]
Relationships among the inhabitants are based on personal contacts. Undoubtedly such relationships are less frequent than in
urban areas where the high density of the population and a
highly developed division of labour make constant contact with
other people necessary. But in the village, unlike the town, contacts are of a personal nature: they are not anonymous and they
are multiple; they are persistent rather than sporadic. In the town
a person is regarded as a role occupant, a number and an address
(the post office assistant, one's fellow passenger in train or bus),
but in the village even contacts connected with an occupational
role (the postman, the sales clerk) are of a permanent, personal
nature. They are contacts with acquaintances, neighbours, relations, friends. The personal nature of village contacts creates a
strong social bond among its inhabitants, which either does not
exist or is present only slightly in the town. Hence the village
community is a social group with a preponderance of personal
bonds. Authority in this group is of a personal rather than of an
impersonal functional or specialist nature. The individual's
authority in a village community is determined by many factors—
first and foremost by the size of the farm and position of the

family connected with it. The roles performed by the individual may also add to his authority, but they are always personal, and not functional, as is the case with the urban local community with its characteristic anonymity of roles and functions.

Bound up with the village community's character as a primary group is the much wider influence of group opinion on the behaviour of families and individuals. This influence is also determined by the fact that the personal nature of relationships, the similarity or even identity of the villagers' mode of existence, the prevalence of kinship ties, and the constant mutual interaction, etc., make it impossible for the inhabitants to conceal their lives from their neighbours' gaze and from their moral evaluations.

Another characteristic of the village community is the basically one-way migratory movement from village to town.[12] In consequence, a comparatively large number of people of village origin are met with in the towns, but one never, or hardly ever, meets people from the towns in the villages. This applies not only to the local community but also to the various social classes and strata or occupational categories. In all social classes, except for the peasant stratum, and in all occupational groups outside agriculture, one comes across persons originating from various groups and social milieux. But in the peasant stratum and in farming it is exceptional to find someone who does not come from a peasant family. It is, then, a characteristic of the village community that the persons living in it are connected primarily by social, but also by territorial, origin. They were usually born in the village or in a neighbouring village (in the latter case, entering the village community by marriage or adoption). But even if they do not originate from the immediate neighbourhood they almost certainly come from peasant families.

The uniformity of social, and usually also of territorial, origin is reinforced by the bonds of kinship, which are very strong in the village. There are usually only a few family names in the village community. The village consists of several interrelated large families (or clans). For this reason, a village is sometimes defined as a family neighbour group. While emphasizing the importance of family ties in the village community, it is difficult to accept this as the main feature, or to accept Grabski's views that the family was the beginning of the village.[13] History affords no instance of isolated families (provided the term is not used to denote a clan or tribe). The basis of the one-way migratory movement—and consequently of the identical social origin of village inhabitants and of their stronger family contacts—must be seen to be in the connection between the family and the farm.

Family bonds, kinship, the uniformity of social and territorial origin, and much feebler spatial and class mobility justify the assertion that there is greater homogeneity among village inhabitants in all major respects: physical features, cultural patterns, and social status. The urban community is more differentiated in every respect.

One should add that we are concerned with old villages which have existed for some time. The situation is different in newly settled areas. Nonetheless, there too settlement often has a group character; families from a single village or its immediate environment settle together; quite often families from a particular village establish a village in a newly settled area. Research in villages in the Western Territories restored to Poland after world war II revealed a great variety of patterns in the way new local communities were built up due to differences in the origins of the settlers and in the group or individual form of the settlement.[14]

The one-way migratory movement from village to town also affects the demographic structure of the rural population. Usually the people who leave the village are those nearing the age when they become economically active as workers on the farm,[15] or older youths seeking to make their way in the wider world through schooling. The exodus from the village is reinforced because of the comparatively slow succession of younger farmers to a position of independence. Consequently the age structure of the rural population shows an over-representation of the youngest and oldest groups. Thus the village community usually includes a large number of children (there is a higher rate of natural increase than in urban areas) but disproportionately fewer young people of productive age or young couples. In addition, besides the main trend of migration from the village, a reverse movement is observable, though it is much weaker. This usually consists of old people who left the village earlier and who now return to end their days in their native village on retiring from active life.[16] This movement further increases the disproportion in the age structure of the agricultural population.

In relation to the differences between town and country,

another characteristic must be mentioned among those features
commonly emphasized: the narrower span of social differentiation
in the latter as compared with the former. Extremes of great
wealth and great poverty are peculiar to the capitalist town. In
the village community class differences are relatively small. Here
too, obviously, there is differentiation with respect to the ownership and size of the means of production. There are also differences in income, prestige and power, which under capitalist conditions are connected with differences in the ownership of the
means of production, primarily of the land. But the inhabitants
of the villages are linked together by common membership of the
peasant stratum, which is a formation older than capitalism and
industrial society.

The priest and the teacher, representatives of non-agricultural
occupations, remain not only outside the peasant stratum but also
outside or above the village community.[17] In the past there were
class antagonisms between village and manor. The formation of
contemporary industrial society is eliminating differences between the peasant stratum and other social strata and classes. This
process is accelerated by migration from village to town, which
has proceeded on such a mass scale during recent years, while the
emergence of socialist societies, in which divisions based on differential ownership of the means of production no longer exist, has
created quite new conditions which speed up this process more
intensively. Nevertheless, in the majority of countries—both
socialist and capitalist—the peasant stratum still exists and is
maintained by the social homogeneity of the families which make
up the village community.

These differences between the village community and the urban local community are—as is shown above—the consequence
of a number of differences: (a) between agricultural and industrial production, (b) between the peasant farm and other
kinds of production unit, (c) between the work of the farmer
and that of other occupations, (d) between the peasant family
and other types of family. For this reason, the briefest, but at
the same time the fullest, definition of the village community
is that it is a settlement inhabited (or mainly inhabited) by
families working peasant farms. The size of the population, its
density, and the degree of the social division of labour, can
differ from village to village, but these differences result from

the characteristics of peasant farming in the particular village. One fundamental characteristic of the village community, namely strong social bonds based on personal contacts, reinforced by kinship, common origin and social homogeneity, is also a characteristic feature which derives from peasant farming.

As a primary (family–neighbour) group, the village community is an entity performing definite functions which complement and over-arch those of the families composing it. We therefore need to analyse the village community as a functional whole in order to fill out what has already been said on this subject.

The functions of the village community

The village community has been characterized above as a social group and therefore as a collectivity of families linked by a system of relationships. This very system, though less extensive than those in the towns, fully justifies our speaking of the functions of the village community.

Firstly, economic functions. Although the village is a 'simple addition of homologous magnitudes'—of families cultivating peasant farms—nonetheless, as already indicated, it has elements of the division of labour and a more or less constant exchange of goods and services. Both of these are of secondary importance in the community, however, for in the main every family satisfies its own basic needs within its domestic economy. With the development of industrial society, the division of labour increases within the village, and is associated with the internal shaping of a system of class relations. Territorial proximity furthermore creates a basis for the emergence of a delimited economic unit.

A more traditional type of economic function performed by the village community is mutual aid of various kinds. This may be contingent, as when villagers assist a neighbour whose home has burnt down to build a new one; or seasonal (threshing, for instance), a common kind of mutual aid when there are tasks which require a large number of hands. These traditional forms are often revived when certain kinds of modern agricultural machinery are introduced into the village. In many villages, for instance, the introduction of earth-moving machinery brought about the revival of various types of family and neighbourly

mutual aid. Regular mutual aid, group labour, or common ownership of means of production (machinery-owning groups, teams
of horses using common pastures, etc.) can bring together families
already linked by kinship, neighbourliness or locality (e.g. families owning plots in an area requiring drainage), or may embrace the entire village.

Forms of group labour, joint ownership or mutual aid which
embrace the entire village may be periodic or occur only on a
particular occasion, for instance, road-building, village electrification, etc., or may occur so regularly that they not infrequently
give rise to specialized economic institutions possessing a legal
personality. Among these are trading, service or production co-
operatives. In the case of Poland, the 'Agricultural Circles' should
be included among these forms of village co-operation. Although
they do not possess the legal status of a co-operative, organizations running machine–tractor stations and other production-
service centres are of this kind; they provide land improvement
teams, groups which undertake the cultivation of abandoned or
virgin land, and so on. In organizing such joint activities they
thus perform functions typical of co-operatives. In Poland the
Agricultural Circles are the most developed form of agricultural co-operative; together with trading, service, and savings
and loan co-operatives, etc., they form a system of enterprises
and organizations which service the day-to-day production requirements of families working peasant farms.

Among such permanent forms of joint activity we may distinguish between those whose activities are confined within the
bounds of the village or which entail economic contacts among
its inhabitants, and those which are in some way directed from
outside the village and which channel its inhabitants' contacts
with the outside world. The former are frequently of a traditional kind; they include vestiges of common ownership (common pasturage), or the pre-industrial organization of labour
(sheep grazing in the uplands). However, alongside them are
forms of village co-operation closely associated with modern
techniques (machinery stations). The second group arises as a
result of the penetration of industrial society into the village,
and includes a number of ways in which the village community
adapts to that society.

The village community's most developed economic function is

to be found in the co-operative organization of production. The joining together of individual peasant farms so as to form multi-family farms turns the village community into a compact production unit. To the extent that the production co-operative develops features characteristic of an enterprise, and takes over and extends the community's economic functions, the village community loses the basic traits differentiating it from other types of local community. It develops in such a way as to resemble settlements of workers engaged in large, agricultural enterprises. At the time when it is first established, and during the first period of its existence, the production co-operative temporarily strengthens or revives many of the functions of the village community, particularly its economic functions. But the co-operative creates a basis for the gradual extinction of the institution of the peasant farm, and with it the village community as a local community of a particular type.

Insurance may also be included among the village community's economic functions. Reference has been made above to the assistance rendered by the village inhabitants to families which have suffered natural disaster. The traditional village community also cares for orphans, invalids, old people, etc., when they have no family which can undertake the responsibility .

Like all local communities, the village is an administrative unit. The village authorities (in Poland the *soltys*, or headman) are charged with a number of obligations by officials at higher levels of the State administration. In addition to administrative activities which are required by regulations of the State authorities, the inhabitants of a village undertake many communal tasks. Among these are the assurance of law and order, the safeguarding of communications with other villages and other localities, and the organization of joint action in the event of disaster (fire, flood, etc). These communal functions are no different from those of other local communities. However, unlike the town, where they are regularly performed by a municipal administration which has a regular budget and personnel at its disposal, in the village these communal functions are based rather on social initiative, unpaid labour or the inhabitants' financial contributions. With the growth of villagers' needs and the breakdown of the isolation of small settlements, the scope of the village's communal activities is continually widening. As the socio-occupational structure of the village population becomes more differentiated, communal affairs come to the forefront as the concern of all the inhabitants, irrespective of their occupations. The increase of communal activity makes it difficult for it to be carried out by means of 'social labour'. More and more, specialized institutions are brought into existence to perform these functions (e.g. co-operative health centres), as well as permanent organizations (e.g. volunteer fire brigades) or periodic ones, i.e., those which remain in existence until the tasks undertaken have been accomplished (a school-building committee, a committee for village electrification, etc.). During recent years the State, or other wider social organizations, has assumed responsibility for many of these undertakings, or has contributed to financing them. The State, or other such specialized institutions, also comes to take over the village community's insurance function as well as a number of economic and cultural ones.

In the traditional village community the inhabitants' cultural needs were satisfied within its bounds. Ceremonies associated with the seasons of the year, the starting or finishing of work in the fields, the communal performance of certain tasks, linked with 'bees' (wool spinning, feather plucking, etc.), and amusements organized by 'social' societies or organizations in the village (e.g. 'circles' of rural youth), provided almost the sole occasions for entertainment and cultural life, apart from participation in church services and visits to fairs in the nearest town. The centre of cultural life was the tavern.[18] Cultural life within the village community thus constituted the basis of indigenous artistic creativity and recreational activities. Today, in most countries, the village's cultural isolation has been broken down. In the past the church and school performed a number of cultural functions in the community. Today the cinema, radio, television and the Press bring the villagers into the general current of national cultural life. The same applies to new types of village institution: People's Houses, club-rooms, reading-rooms, etc. Unlike the tavern, these are not only centres for organized participation in the cultural life of the village but above all a link with the general national culture.

The basic function of the village community is social control over the behaviour of the various families and individuals. The community establishes definite norms, moral standards and rules of conduct. In performing this function it operates as the dominant group in relation to the families composing it, and the authority with which it endows certain of the villagers is based on public recognition, on the fact that they both create this opinion and are simultaneously obedient to it. The degree of control over the conduct of individuals and the degree of intervention in their lives is enormous. Kinship and neighbourly bonds oblige the individual to observe family norms of behaviour, and ensure the effectiveness of the family's intervention. This community control complements the family's educational functions. From the day of his birth the individual is included not only in the family circle but in the village community. The child spends his time constantly in the company of a group of his peers. Together they mind the geese; then they pasture the cattle; they pass through the phases of adolescence and maturity as part of a group of the same sex. The process of socialization takes place within the family and the peer-group. Standards and values binding in the village community are inculcated. This is followed by the achievement of social adulthood, which is finally consolidated only with marriage and social acceptance as a farmer.

Thus the village community ultimately functions as a unit of social control; as the source of a binding system of standards and values; as a reference group which defines the position of the individual and of the family, and as an essential factor in the social assimilation of the younger generation.

In conclusion, the reservation must be made that this description of the village community's characteristics and of its functioning is an ideal-typical model. In reality, village communities are highly differentiated and each particular village only partially resembles the model described. But we need such a model, though it should be brought up to date, if we are to outline the main directions of change in the village community. An analysis of the different types of rural community and of the changes taking place in them requires that we now separate out the 'local village community' into villages on the one hand, and other types of rural settlements on the other.

Types of local rural community: the process of urbanization

The oldest division of local rural communities is into village and manor. Grabski distinguishes between types of villages according to the location *vis-a-vis* the manor.[19] In Poland and certain other European countries the division into village and manor has its origins in feudal society and is bound up with the persistence of the feudal division into estates of peasants and landlords. This division is not peculiar to the pre-industrial era; it appears in different forms as the division into villages and large landed estates which exist also in countries where the feudal system of social relations either never existed at all or was abolished long ago.

Two types of large-scale landed properties can be distinguished. The first is based on tenantry. Here the proprietor rents out his land either to agricultural enterprises which operate for profit and work the land commercially, or to families carrying on typical peasant farming who pay the land-owner rent in money or with part of their produce. In certain countries this type of large landed proprietorship sometimes has the character of an enterprise and the leaseholders are in fact agricultural labourers remunerated with part of the produce.[20] The second type of large estate, which was common in pre-war days in Poland and Germany, is a large-scale enterprise which often displays more or less definite features of the former *corvee* (serfdom) economy, but which is oriented to the market and designed for profit.

In the first case (excluding the rental of land to agricultural enterprises on long leases) we can scarcely speak of the estate as a separate local community. It is bound up with the village, since the leaseholders are peasant families. Only the home of the landed proprietor lies outside the village. In the other case, where the large landed property is an enterprise (a large production unit), it usually brings together a certain number of permanent agricultural labourers who live on the site and form a separate local community. Between these two types there is, of course, a whole range of intermediate types, associated with various relationships of dependence emanating from the feudal past: the size of the estate, its location, relations with the nearest village or neighbouring villages, etc.

Various types of village community can be distinguished, depending on the nature of the relations between the village and
the manor—wherever, of course, the large landed estate still exists. Nonetheless, even in countries where socialist reforms have
put an end to the existence of the class of large landed proprie-
tors, the former division into village and estate is still maintained, though its content is now different. In Poland this
division is especially important; it is a division into settlements
of workers on large State Farms which have definite characteristics of an enterprise (some production co-operatives formed
on the land of former estates and founded by former agricultural
labourers should be included in this group), and village concentrations of family peasant farms—today widely differentiated, yet
retaining the character of extended domestic economies. Production co-operatives set up on peasant lands should be included with
the villages, even if in Poland these constitute only part of the
village community as a rule, though a part which is distinguished
by its system of farming.

In other socialist countries where rural collectivization has
been completed, the division is one into two different forms of
large-scale agricultural enterprise: co-operative farms and State
Farms. The co-operative still retains a number of features of
peasant farming, while the State Farm preserves the characteristics of the former landed estate (in the organization of production, the occupational structure of the work team, the character of
production, etc.). However, these differences are diminishing, and
a fundamentally uniform structure based on the agricultural
enterprise is emerging. The former type of village community is
dying out, and the village is becoming a settlement of agricultural workers. In the future—because of the development of
communications networks and their planned extension—the village can be expected to turn into a settlement of an urban character, in which the workers of the agricultural enterprise will
dwell alongside those of other enterprises and institutions.

The differentiation of local rural communities into village and
manor (estate), and of the type of village according to the nature
of its relations with the manor, derive from the historical past.
Poland presents a very rich mosaic of types in this respect. Villages which formerly belonged to a single nobleman's estate (the
small gentry's property—gentry owning a single village); villages

subordinate to large magnates' estates; royal villages; free villages; villages of the small nobility, etc., are all different types of village community. Even today this results in different types of relations and different forms of organization, which produce variations in inter-personal relations and in norms, customs and recognized values.

The differentiation of the pre-industrial village community was intensified by industrialization. Even under feudal conditions, manufactures came into being on the basis of socage obligations: alongside the peasants, a stratum of worker-serfs developed (e.g. miners and craftsmen) employed in non-agricultural establishments.[21] As industry developed, the stratum of so-called peasant-workers increased numerically. Many villages lost their agricultural character and were transformed into settlements of workers' or artisans' settlements (primarily suburban villages and those with a comminuted land structure—groups of dwarf farms unable to support a family). In this respect the village community can be defined according to its occupational structure, the extreme types being the traditional village community—namely an aggregation of families carrying on peasant farming—and settlements where the inhabitants' occupations are of an exclusively or predominantly non-agricultural character.

Class divisions are connected with socio-occupational divisions. Villages can be distinguished where the occupational division effected by earnings outside the village and outside agriculture has led to a weakening or break-up of the social solidarity on which the village community was based, or has transformed the village community into a workers' or artisans' settlement. But there are also villages with various degrees of class differentiation into capitalists and agricultural workers (or poor peasants and kulaks), and with differing systems of class relations between the more and the less affluent families forming the village community. Both the degree of class stratification and the extent of occupational division essentially influence the compactness of the village community and its functions. The traditional village community with a less advanced division into classes has, as indicated, a correspondingly paternalistic type of inter-personal relations. The rich farmer and his poor neighbour are linked by economic ties concealed under the form of neighbourly relations, kinship, etc. Labour contributions often take the form of aid, or of mutual exchange of services (repayment by work). The poorer neighbour or day labourer is treated in a patriarchal fashion, as part of the family. More advanced class differentiation is usually based on relations of a capitalist type: the farm owner and the worker are linked by an agreement governing work and remuneration, the latter at least partly in cash.

Differentiation of villages according to class and occupational structures is associated with differences in the dominant type of production. Undoubtedly the basic features and functions of the village community are different in suburban villages—which concentrate on the production of milk and vegetables for the nearby market; in sub-alpine villages—with traditional forms of pastoral economy; in grain and livestock areas; or in villages specializing in particular crops (hops, tobacco growing, etc). The type of production trend leads to variations in agrarian structures, that is, variations in the size of the village, the density of population, the occupational structure of the village, the existence of given institutions, traditions and customs.

Another division can be made according to the degree of organization within the village. Primarily this means the degree of development of a system of economic institutions (varying forms of rural co-operation), and hence the degree of the division of labour in agricultural production, and—connected with it—the extent to which the village is organized as a production unit. As we pointed out above, the economically most cohesive type of village community is the production co-operative, which to a greater or lesser extent possesses the distinctive features of a large agricultural enterprise.

The most definitive distinction is that between villages which are located in the centre of a district and those on the periphery. As a rule, central villages are the seats of the parish and administrative authorities; they are also the service and trading centres for neighbouring villages. They are usually closer to a small town in their social character, except that the majority of the inhabitants work on peasant farms. The functions which a village performs in relation to its district naturally tend to be multiple. The parish is usually based in the larger villages, where the market place develops in front of the church, and where handicraftsmen and merchants settle. The school is located there, as well as the administrative authorities and other institutions serving the dis-

trict. In Poland, the break up of the larger rural community (the
gmina) into smaller units (the *gromada*) introduced a new differentiation.* The village, once the seat of the *gmina* but now as a
rule only the headquarters of the *gromada*, nevertheless still performs many other functions in regard to the district. The occupations of its inhabitants are also generally more diversified, with
a denser network of trading and service agencies, and often some
local industrial plants too. Such villages are sometimes elevated
to the status of the headquarters of the county administration
and become transformed into small towns or centres superior to
the *gromada*. Though they occupy a lowly status in the administrative hierarchy, nonetheless they have a high position at district
level.

Some countries have no such division into central and peripheral villages. This is the case with areas of scattered farm settlement, where it is difficult to talk of villages (sometimes linked
so as to constitute small neighbourhood groups) or, in the case
of urban-type settlements, villages which act as a service centre
for the farms. Newly settled areas often develop in this manner
(e.g. certain regions of the United States, the Dutch polders, etc.),
or where reconstruction of the agrarian system is taking place
(e.g. those areas undergoing agrarian reform in Italy). Nor does
this division exist where, because of the type of production, the
population is concentrated in large settlements of an urban type
(compactly built areas, streets, trade and service centres, etc.). In
these settlements or agricultural towns the dwelling house and
garden are often quite a considerable distance from the fields, but
the type of production does not necessitate the farmer's constant
presence on the spot.

The division into central and peripheral villages is a function
of differentiation according to distance from the town. Suburban
villages differ at every point from other village communities: they
are more numerous, more densely populated, have a more differentiated occupational and class structure, and produce a
greater variety of goods. The proximity of a town weakens the
village community's solidarity and internal economy, for many
needs (e.g. cultural ones) can now be satisfied in the town. The

* *Gmina*: the smallest unit of Polish local government up to 1954.
The *gromada*, the smallest and lowest unit from 1954 onwards, was
formed by splitting up *gminas*—*Translator*.

village community which is remote from a town is usually a more cohesive and closed group, and is, of necessity, more self-sufficient both in the economic and normative spheres, as well as being an agency of control over the behaviour of families and individuals.

The above criteria for classifying villages are seldom brought into any kind of synthesis in the literature. As a rule, one or another distinction is given priority according to the aims of the research. However, all rural sociology textbooks use the spatial disposition of the village as a criterion of division into types. The typology of the village from the standpoint of its spatial disposition has been exhaustively studied in Polish scientific, and especially ethnographic, literature,[22] which has established an abundance of such types.

In the different regions of Poland one can find almost all these basic spatial types of villages. In some western provinces (*wojewodztwo*), for instance, and wherever farm consolidation has been undertaken, one finds scattered buildings, which makes it difficult to draw the boundary between one village and another. It is even difficult to speak of a village in this case, unless the term can also be used to refer to a little town which constitutes the service centre for farms scattered over several, or even a dozen or more, kilometres. In different regions of Poland one can also point to compact villages, to villages dismembered into hamlets, colonies or homesteads, or to villages which run along a river or a road, villages located within a network of roads, etc.

The way the village is built up depends on many factors: the contours of the land, physiographical conditions, the type of production, the system of road communications, traditional custom, the degree of land consolidation, or the presence or absence of activities planned by the State. In each type, the basic features and functions of the village community vary. The dispersal of farms does not provide any basis for the emergence of a compact community. Large spatial distances weaken the social bond. Land consolidation tends to atomize the peasant community: the family assumes greater importance and it becomes more difficult for the village community to observe family life. Social control is weaker; public opinion is formed with greater difficulty and plays a diminished role. In villages fragmented into hamlets or into offshoot villages, the neighbourhood group performs the basic functions of the village community. In hamlets, norms,

ideas and opinions develop which are not always in harmony
with those of other parts of the village; different authorities are
recognized. Feelings of separateness, and even expressions of antagonism towards other neighbouring groups, are more common.
This is due to the social composition of hamlets, which are frequently inhabited by families occupying a similar social position, and a conflict between hamlets is therefore an expression of
class conflict between the poorer and richer parts of the village
(beggars and peasants, poor farmers and kulaks, etc.).

There are, of course, various types of hamlet. Apart from those
with a pronounced class character (for instance, those polarized
into agricultural workers or rich farmers), we may distinguish
(a) hamlets grouped around large farms surrounded by dwarf
farmsteads, (b) hamlets distinguished by their origin (petty nobility, a closely related family, etc.), and (c) hamlets distinguished
by type of occupation (handicrafts, factory workers, etc.). In
fragmented villages the community is a looser grouping, and
may rather be defined as aggregations of neighbourly groups.

Types of village community may thus be distinguished according to the criteria cited above:

(a)   The origin and character of relations with the manor or
      estate.
(b)   Occupational and class structure.
(c)   Type of production.
(d)   The degree to which the village is involved in production
      as a production unit, or the degree of general cohesion of
      the community and the institutionalization of its functions.
(e)   Its distance from town and the nature of the functions it
      performs in relation to other villages.
(f)   Its physical layout.

To these may be added other criteria, depending on one's heuristic purpose or the aims of one's research. Only the types most
frequently indicated are enumerated here. Nonetheless, per-
vading this multiplicity of types is a general tendency in the
changes occurring in the village community, which has been
indicated above. The influence of industrial society and its penetration into village life lead to a weakening of the differences
between the village community and other types of local community. Today the rural areas do not play a role in agricultural

production alone, nor are they inhabited only by farmers. In almost every village one can find not only farmers but also families who maintain themselves exclusively or mainly from non-agricultural employment, as well as families who draw supplementary income from such employment. Today the village, especially the suburban village, is the dwelling place of persons belonging to various occupational and professional categories, to various social classes and strata. Social, occupational and class differentiation breaks up the uniformity of social situation on which the village community has hitherto been based. Its economic functions, to an ever-growing extent, are taken over by institutions and organizations outside the village. Organizations and institutions based on local co-operatives are becoming branches, retail sales outlets and servicing points, subordinated to central organizations. In certain countries the development of production co-operatives strengthens the village community for a while, but the formation of a large agricultural enterprise obliterates its former features, and it becomes a settlement inhabited by the workers of the enterprise.

The community's cultural and educational functions are also being taken over to an ever-increasing extent by outside institutions and organizations. Its functions pass to a neighbouring group, and, in time, die out. It also ceases to be the main reference group: public opinion is formed by centres outside the village. Its effectiveness as an agency of social control also weakens: the behaviour of individuals and families more and more comes to be regarded as their private affair, or, in the event of violation of prevailing standards, as a matter for intervention by the appropriate authorities. On the other hand, the administrative functions of the village tend to increase. They are, however, more often performed by appropriate organizations endowed with responsibility for the functioning of common facilities than by the community *per se*. The tendency of the village to disintegrate, and the tendency for differences between village and town to diminish, are more or less advanced in different countries.

Much of what has been said about these tendencies may seem premature, even for Poland. Nevertheless, the general direction of change is the same. Nowhere in the world is the former village community reviving. Obviously, one can still find its characteristics here and there. One can still use the village as a basis

for the mobilization of its inhabitants, and in this way much
may be achieved. However, if such sentiments fail to find appropriate organizational expression and do not link up with the new
structure of industrial society, in the majority of cases it will be
wasted effort. Club-rooms and People's Houses, swimming pools
and sports fields will be deserted and go to ruin, for there will
be no one to bother about them. The trends are in the direction
of a greater division of labour, an increase in the importance of
formal institutions, and the incorporation of the families forming the village community into a broader society based on a
different structure. The process of urbanization of the countryside, which finds expression in the changes indicated above, is
based on the disintegration of the traditional village community
and the emergence of new local communities revealing no essential difference from urban communities.

Notes

1   A. Hillery, 'Definition of community: areas of agreement', *Rural
Sociology*, vol. xx, 1955, p. 119.
2   R. C. Buck, 'Practical applications of community research:
some preliminary considerations', *Rural Sociology*, vol. xix, 1954,
p. 294.
3   P. Sorokin and C. C. Zimmerman, *Principles of rural–urban
sociology, cit.*, pp. 13 ff.
4   E.g. E. M. Rogers, *op cit.*, p. 136.
5   Here we are speaking about large-scale agricultural enterprises. Large agricultural properties rented to peasant families do not
usually form a separate local community; one can see individual
homesteads.
6   B. Galeski and A. Wyderko, 'Poglady chlopow na przyszlosc
wsi', *cit.*
7   P. Sorokin and C. C. Zimmerman, *op. cit.*, pp. 23 ff.
8   P. Sorokin and C. C. Zimmerman, *op. cit.*, p. 17.
9   See the comparisons drawn by P. Sorokin, C. C. Zimmerman
and C. J. Galpin in *A systematic source-book of rural sociology*, Min-
neapolis, 1930.
10   K. Marx, *The 18th Brumaire of Louis-Napoléon, cit.*
11   E.g. P. Sorokin and C. C. Zimmerman, *op. cit.*, pp 49 ff.
12   Cf. P. Sorokin, C. C. Zimmerman and C. J. Galpin, *op. cit.*,
pp. 226 ff.
13   W. Grabski, 'System socjologii wsi' ('Systematic rural sociology'), *Roczniki socjologii wsi (Annals of Rural Sociology)*, vol. i,
1936, p. 79.

14   E.g. A. Romanow, 'Ludnosc miejscowa i repatrianci' ('Local population and repatriates'), *Wies wspolczesna* (*The Contemporary Village*), 1958, No. 6.
15   M. Pohoski, *Migracje z wsi do miast, cit.*, pp. 71 ff.
16   E.g. T. Lynn Smith, *Sociology of rural life, cit.*, p. 178.
17   See J. Chalasinski, *Mlode pokolenie chlopow, cit.*, p. 95.
18   See J. Burszta, *Wies i karczma* (*The village and the inn*), Warsaw, 1950.
19   W. Grabski, *op. cit.*, pp. 121 ff.
20   E.g. T. Lynn Smith, *op. cit.*, p. 284.
21   See R. Turski, *Miedzy miastem a wsia, cit.*, p. 284.
22   B. Zaborski, *O ksztaltach wsi w Polsce* (*On the forms of the village in Poland*), Cracow, 1926.

5 The social structure

Any definition of a social structure must depend, first and foremost, on the differentiation of the individual groups and categories which make up the society under consideration. Or to put it more cautiously, such differentiation is an indispensable element in every attempt at such a definition. One can take as the criterion of differentiation either one or several attributes of the units being studied; which trait or complex of traits is adopted as the basis of classification depends above all on the immediate heuristic purpose. Hence the choice of the appropriate principle must be made with reference to the end in view.

Though every definition of 'social structure' entails a specification of the units of analysis, the phrase does not cover all possible groupings within a given society. As we know, there is no general agreement on which groupings fall under this term. Some emphasize the system of inter-personal relations within the community under study; they thus consider that the term 'social structure' should be reserved exclusively for those kinds of groups which are internally united and marked off from yet other groups by the presence of a particular social bond, though this concept is variously defined by different protagonists of this standpoint. Others point rather to the system of relations within the society as a whole, regardless of whether the elements of the system are social groups (collectivities) or categories (collections) of individuals. If we adopt the first point of view, any classification according to income cannot be included under the term 'social structure', since, for example, persons with a monthly income of 1,000–1,499 zlotys are not usually linked by any system of relations, and do not, therefore, form a social group. If we adopt the second standpoint, any classification which points to inter-personal relations which are important in some way to society as a whole may be regarded as vital for the analysis of social structure and can be included among the groupings covered by this term.

Thus in order to clarify the differences between various conceptions of the social structure it is not sufficient to point to differences in the aims of analysis. Various principles of classification into groups and categories may be used, and the methods of analysis will vary according to the aim of the analysis and the theoretical standpoint adopted. Therefore the above statement concerning the connection between the principle of classification and the postulated cognitive end must be supplemented by pointing to the relationship between that principle and the adopted theoretical system. The theoretical standpoint, i.e. the system of the most general propositions concerning society, determines not only the principles underlying the classification of what is denoted by the term 'social structure' but also the ordering and the interpretation of the empirical data.

Both the definition of the social structure and the research procedure as a whole must therefore be evaluated from the viewpoint of the theoretical standpoint adopted. If a definition of social structure is criticized from some other standpoint, this is tantamount to the rejection of the theoretical standpoint which implies it. For instance, criticism of the categories Lenin introduced in his studies of the rural social structure can be undertaken only with regard to the cognitive end, interpreted one way or another, to which Lenin directed his inquiries; otherwise it is equivalent to saying that Lenin's theoretical standpoint is not shared in some respect.

The approach to the problems of rural social structure in the present study is based generally on the theoretical standpoint of Leninism. Certainly, identification with a certain standpoint also involves its interpretation. A few preliminary remarks may be in order to indicate the directions of that interpretation, at least so far as it is directly connected with the problems under consideration.

The concept of social structure

Lenin's analysis of rural social structure aimed at revealing the basic *social forces* operating, i.e. those groups or collectivities whose activity could be recognized as fundamental in determining the course—and even the feasibility—of programmes for the transformation of production relations, and, above all, of the process and outcome of the struggle for power.

Given this as the aim of analysis, it becomes of prime importance to establish the social factors determining human action, arising out of desires to change (or to maintain) existing production relations, and primarily to win (or retain) State power in order to effect this. The major social factors determining human action, can with considerable simplification, be outlined as follows:

1. Access to any universally desired value determines the possibility of access to other values of the same kind.[1] In the capitalist system of production relations the dominant factor is ownership of the means of production. If we include A's total possibilities of access to universally desired values under the term A's 'social status', we may say that in the capitalist system of production relations differentiation of social status is determined primarily via the sphere of ownership of the means of production. Or to put it less definitively, the first can be explained primarily by reference to the second. This more cautious formulation is intended, *inter alia*, to emphasize that we have in mind not absolute, but statistical determination. This reservation signifies that, strictly speaking we are referring not to individuals (persons or families) but to collectivities, although the statement may pertain to individuals if it is formulated in terms of probability.

2. The stock of many universally desired values is in practice restricted for various reasons, or else the number of positions assuring access to those values is limited in the given social system. In consequence, differentiation of social status may take on antagonistic forms, to a wider or narrower extent, indicated by the relation: 'A occupies position *p* when, and only when, B is in position non-*p*.' We assume that it is precisely this system that prevails under capitalism, above all in the sphere of ownership of the means of production. Therefore differentiation in this sphere takes the form of a scale, the extreme values of which represent antagonistic situations. Since ownership of the means of production is the main factor determining social differentiation in the capitalist system of production relations, antagonistic relationships must be seen as an intrinsic feature of that system.

3. The growth of production, brought about by a rise in the level of the productive forces, is related to the concentration of the means of production. In capitalist conditions this may be ex-

pressed as an empirically confirmed polarization of property. Growth, under capitalist conditions, is associated with the progressive polarization of society as a whole. Obviously, the growth of production can eliminate restricted access to certain universally desired goods (namely those whose restriction is associated with the level of the productive forces and not with the properties of the system). However, a change of this kind does not alter the essence of the pattern of relationships. For this antagonistic social relationship arises from the fact that restriction of the number of positions assuring access to the most fundamental value (most fundamental because it determines differentiation of social status) remains a principle of the system.

4. Where differentiation of social status takes the form of a series with the extreme expressions p and $non\text{-}p$, the direction of individuals' desires to improve their social status will conform in the aggregate with the vector $non\text{-}p—p$. Obviously, the existence of the desire to improve or to maintain one's social status will vary. These variations can be defined statistically according to their position in the social hierarchy, so we can assume that in extreme situations the dominant tendency will be either to change or to maintain the position occupied. The outcome of any particular case will be determined by many factors, above all by the properties of the system, which determine the degree of probability of success, and in which the individual's personal qualities play a greater or lesser role.

But an individual may aspire to improve, not only his own social situation, but also that of the category or group to which he belongs. To some extent such aspirations can be satisfied, above all in respect of those values whose stock has increased with the development of productive forces. However, since the system postulates the differentiation of social status as its principle, other, more far-reaching, demands can be expected to emerge. Simplification of a continuum to two polar positions[2] suggests the conclusion that individuals in the $non\text{-}p$ situation will desire to change (or eliminate) those conditions which determine this situation or from which are derived those determining forces which are so disadvantageous for them. This tendency is the stronger the greater the obstacles to the realization of the desires that the system creates. On the other hand, individuals in situation p will aim to maintain the conditions determining their status and to maintain the mechanism of determination which is so advantageous for them. Under capitalism, differentiation of social status, like the mechanism of determination itself, results primarily from the system of production relationships. The conflict between the opposing forces will thus focus on the maintenance or abolition of the capitalist system of production relations, and therefore on the conquest or retention of State power, the main instrument for realizing that end.

5. The emergence of opposed aims, which express the collective interests of those individuals who find themselves in conflicting social situations, is associated with the development of opposing rationalizations (ideologies) and of organized groups whose aim is to arouse and direct broader collective activity. The emergence of ideology signifies that collectivities of individuals in identical social situations acquire, to one degree or another, the character of social groups (they are transformed from classes 'in themselves' into classes 'for themselves'). And when they take action to promote their collective interests they begin to function as social forces.

A number of reservations must obviously be made which qualify these general and simplified proportions. However, since we are concerned only with a general characterization of the mode of interpretation we are adopting, and not with presenting the entirety of Marxist sociological theory, these reservations may be omitted. This applies also to any reservations which might be called for in attempting to apply these propositions to particular contemporary capitalist societies. Our only concern here is to define the conception of social structure; its application in interpreting the findings of empirical research will follow later.

Areas of research into social structure

Since the purpose of considering social structure is to calculate the balance of social forces, while the theoretical standpoint adopted requires examination of the interplay of these forces in a complex system of factors, our analysis must necessarily cover a very wide range. It will extend from social action *per se* to the conditions determining such action. Social structure must therefore be approached dynamically; differentiations of social status

must be studied in the process of change, as tendencies, not as
states. In empirical research a dynamic approach may suggest,
and even impose, not one but many principles of social classification into groups and categories.

1. Differentiation of social status can be examined with regard
to that quantity of values which is universally desired under given
conditions. One can also investigate the connections between different types of division in order to discover those which are specific to the given social system. Any consideration of the connections
between various series of social positions involves complex problems of social stratification and of social mobility, which we take
to mean those changes in the positions of individuals or groups
on a scale (or scales) of social differentiation specific to a given
system.

2. Another subject which might be considered is that of organized groups which aim at transforming or maintaining the given
social system, and hence primarily at conquering or retaining
State power. The aims and modes of action of these groups need
to be analysed—given such an approach—together with their
social background. Hence it is necessary to analyse systematically
the kinds of social situation which determine the emergence of
definite collective aspirations, and of ideologies and organized
groups, as well as the actual mechanism of determination. This
area of inquiry involves the question of social forces in *action*:
the transformation of collectivities into social groups and their
functioning as social forces. Marx's study *The 18th Brumaire of
Louis-Napoléon* is a classic example of this type of analysis.

3. Of fundamental significance for our analysis of social structure
is the question of changes which occur in the factors design-
ated above as the most important in the system of social determinants of human activity. Analysis of the processes shaping these
changes enables us to anticipate the growth of social forces and
the direction of their activity, as well as to understand the main
social conflicts and their consequences. In studies devoted to the
social structure of the capitalist system our basic strategy will, of
of course, be determined by this approach, via an investigation of
processes of change in the system of ownership of the means of
production, and above all of changes in the process of the concentration of capital accumulation. Such investigations must
underline any analysis of the balance of social forces. For coun-

tries where the village and agriculture are of considerable importance, such an analysis undoubtedly involves consideration of the
rural social structure.

Hence research into changes in agrarian structure, into the
accumulation of capital in agriculture, and so forth, may be regarded as pivotal in any estimation of the balance of social forces
in such countries. Lenin's works, such as *The development of
capitalism in Russia*, are classics of this kind. And Polish Marx-
ists have also devoted as much attention to these questions, notably L. Krzywicki, J. Ryng and J. Marchlewski.

The utility of the concept 'social class'

Marx uses the term 'social class' fairly loosely, and his various
definitions—which he formulated only incidentally in the process
of considering other questions—differ from one another considerably. Textbooks of Marxism–Leninism generally use Lenin's definition of class in his brochure devoted to the *Subbotniki'*,[*] the
basic determining characteristic of which is relationship to the
means of production. In the light of the system of determinants
discussed above, that definition has a number of merits, since in a
system based on private property, relationship to the means of
production is the main determinant of social status.[3] Hence a
classification which applies this characteristic as the criterion for
distinguishing groups and collectivities is basic to a consideration
of social structure—though always in combination with other
divisions.

Thus the main virtue of the textbook definition of 'class' is
that it focuses upon the most fundamental factors which determine differentiation of social status in a system based on the
private ownership of the means of production. But this basic
factor is not the only possible basis for distinguishing groups
which differ totally in respect to their social position, and is even
less so for analysing their functioning as social forces. In this respect Lenin's original definition[4] is undoubtedly more valuable.
It emphasizes the place occupied in a historically determined sys-

* 'Saturdayers': participants in voluntary, unpaid social or communal
work, in the early years of the Soviet regime, usually performed on
Saturdays—*Translator*.

tem of social production and, in addition to relationship to the means of production, includes the position in the social organization of labour.

One definition given by Marx[5] points to the role of consciousness of interests common to all the individuals in the group. Indeed, one can cite a number of different definitions of class in the works of Marx and Lenin; significantly, they all fit into the system of determinants characterized above.[6] This indicates the variety of functions the concept 'social class' performs in the Marxist–Leninist theoretical system. This multiplicity of functions makes the concept of class an extremely useful instrument for theoretical analysis, but also makes it difficult or even impossible to apply the concept directly in empirical investigations, or at least in those which use statistics.

In other words, it is impossible to distinguish a collectivity of individuals constituting a 'social class' in the full sense we have given this concept. It is only possible to apply many social divisions (including the primary one of the relation to the means of production, which determines class division in the narrower sense). Only the totality of these divisions allows us to make deductions as to the bases of class conflict and the chances of the contending sides, or, more generally, as to the balance of social forces and the prevalent trends.

In none of the numerous statistical compilations in Lenin's works on the peasant question can one find an entity which would correspond strictly with the peasant stratum or with one or another class group within it. When Lenin compiles figures of Russian peasants in groups according to the size of land cultivated, the number of horses owned, or the number of hired labourers employed, no one of these is a criterion of division into class groups, nor do all of them, taken together, embrace the whole number of persons or families constituting the total peasant stratum. Nonetheless, these compilations do provide a basis for determining the relative weight of class groups in the peasant stratum and for analysing the genesis of the Russian rural structure, which is typical of a capitalist system of production relations.

In addition to social class, we also use the term 'social stratum'. Though we use this term in three senses, it always designates groups whose identification is indispensable for analyses of social structure but which cannot be recognized as classes.

In the first sense, a social stratum is a group or community which can to some extent engage in activity aimed at achieving common interests, but which disintegrates and becomes absorbed into the basic class system, the existing social system. Most often, a stratum is a group or collectivity which—like the peasant stratum, for instance—would, in an earlier historical system, have been regarded as a social class, or even a basic class.[7] In the second sense, the term 'social stratum' is used to distinguish groups and collectivities which cannot be included among the *basic* categories of the system's structure, but whose social situation is nevertheless determined by their relationship to that structure. It is in this sense that one speaks, for instance, of the intelligentsia as a social stratum. Finally, in the third sense, the term is used to distinguish groups within a class whose social situation differs from that of the rest of the class. In this sense one can speak, for instance, of the 'labour aristocracy' as a stratum.

Leaving aside the question of the heuristic value of the concept of 'stratum' in all its three meanings (and also of the concepts of 'basic' and 'non-basic', 'antagonistic' and 'non-antagonistic' classes), we should note that, given the system of determinants outlined above, none of the social strata we have referred to can be identified with any collectivity which has been distinguished via empirical investigation.

Thus in statistical analysis one cannot, strictly speaking, study the peasant stratum or the intelligentsia; one can only investigate a group of families inhabiting a settlement recognized in official nomenclature as a village, or a group of persons running a farm of more than 0·1 or 0·5 hectares, etc. So far as the intelligentsia are concerned one can only study a collectivity of persons practising a profession which has an official nomenclature.

This gulf between theoretical constructs and the groupings used in empirical research and operationally defined appears in many contexts. Various sociological definitions of youth may be more or less useful in studies of this theme, for example, but generally speaking they are not, and probably cannot be, applied in empirical research, which generally involves specific age groups.

The relationship of theoretical constructs to operational definitions adopted—consciously or unconsciously—in empirical investigations is perhaps one of the most difficult problems of modern sociology. It is a problem of great importance, since these contructs are used to build theoretical systems which define the aim of the investigation and the principles of classification adopted, and determine the direction and the method of interpreting the facts which are collected. But even if the confrontation of theoretical constructions with empirical investigation can yield only partial verification, or—more often—necessitates modifications to the approach, the effort is still worthwhile.

These general considerations are exemplified below in our examination of changes in the rural social structure of pre-war and contemporary Poland, on the basis of contemporary empirical research, but without detailed citation of factual material or detailed description of the research methods used, since these can easily be found in various specialized publications.[8]

The accumulation of capital and class differentiation in the countryside

We shall turn to changes of rural social structure in pre-war and present-day Poland, and hence to a specific situation located in time and space. In the author's opinion, however, this topic has general relevance and is therefore formulated more broadly in terms of the mechanisms moulding rural social forces. It may be as well to start with the textbook characterization of changes in rural social structure under capitalism.

According to this picture the former peasant class, homogeneous in its basic class features, undergoes stratification with the development of capitalism. The elements of this stratification are already inherent in social differentiation within this class during the feudal era. But as long as the fundamental characteristics of this system prevail—the concentration of landed property in the hands of the feudal lords, together with peasant serfdom based on this relation to the land and the obligation of socage—differentiation within the peasant class remains a subsidiary phenomenon compared to the basic peasant–lord relationship of inequality. When the peasants acquire the land, and serfdom and socage are abolished, the socio-economic structure of the countryside starts to change in the same direction as the general structure of capitalist society. The former manorial estates are transformed into large capitalist properties, and their owners into capitalist entrepreneurs. An agricultural proletariat, employed together with already proletarianized manorial servants on the large capitalist properties, as well as a rural proletariat employed on peasant capitalist farms, emerges out of the former peasant class. The social differences between these two groups of agricultural proletariat diminish in parallel with the development of capitalist relations. Nonetheless, striking differences were evident, even in pre-war Poland, between many features of the situation of the day labourer on peasant farms (the rate and form of wages, the nature of the labour, the worker–farm-owner relation, etc., and that of the agricultural labourer on a large estate. The peasant class, i.e. owners of farms (which we distinguish from the proletariat) can be roughly divided into three categories of families. In Leninist terminology the first group is composed of the village poor, owners of very small and dwarf farms who do not possess sufficient means of production (above all, land) to assure their families' subsistence, and are compelled to seek work away from their farms, chiefly on capitalist farms. Sometimes the category of village poor[9] is split into two sub-categories: the rural semi-proletariat, where the farm is so small that its owner obtains his main means of subsistence from outside labour (by the sale of his labour-power), and small peasants whose farms are not large enough to maintain the family but which nevertheless still provide the main part of the means of subsistence, while gainful employment off the farm plays only a supplementary role.

The second group of families can, with great simplification, be distinguished as the middle peasants. Here the farm is sufficiently large to assure the family's maintenance but not large enough to require the steady employment of hired labourers. Consequently, production here depends on the labour of the family members. Economic relations with neighbours are often of a non-capitalist nature, and even when there are capitalist relationships these play no serious part in determining the family's material and social situation.

The third group consists of the village capitalists. These are peasants whose farms are so large or are so intensively cultivated that it is beyond the labour-power of the family to work them, hence they are obliged to hire labourers on a steady basis. Theoretical distinctions between different class groups in the peasant stratum make it possible to grasp the process of class stratification which takes place in the rural community. The formerly homogeneous peasant class is split into a proletarian class and a bourgeoisie. These two classes should be understood as the modal points of this process, creating a *continuum* of intermediate forms. The middle peasant, the last representative of the former peasant class (a typical petty commodity-producer) is faced, roughly speaking, with two possibilities. Either (*a*) he keeps in step with the economic requirements of the market and assures his family of a standard of living at the level recognized at the given time as fulfilling their minimum needs—in which case he must produce more and more cheaply, and hence transforms his farm into an enterprise, i.e. he takes the road to becoming a capitalist farmer—or (*b*) he falls behind, in which case he cannot stabilize this uneasy equilibrium and at any moment (usually in connection with the change of generations: dowry, family share payments, the partitioning of land) may fall from his position as an independent farmer to that of a small farmer, a semi-proletarian or proletarian-to-be.

In accordance with the above approach, changes in rural socio-economic structure consist of a process of class stratification which is analogous to that in feudal towns (e.g. the emergence of handicrafts), when the proletariat and the bourgeoisie emerged from the former peasant class and other classes. A number of intermediate groups are created in the course of this process, too, as a result of the disintegration of the former classes. These groups gradually lose the social features linking them with these classes and acquire the traits characteristic of the basic classes of capitalist society.

Along with the formation of these groups, there come into play class contradictions which divide them, based at first on early capitalist economic relations (usury, payment in labour) and later on those typical of developed capitalism (the sale of labour-power). According to the above approach, conflicting class interests lead to class struggle on the economic as well as on the political and ideological planes as the breakup of the former peasant class proceeds and as the emerging groups begin to approximate to the classes basic to capitalist society, and generate a social consciousness appropriate to their material situation.

This summary and highly simplified textbook exposition of changes in rural socio-economic structure may be regarded as a vulgarization. Without enlarging on the matter, it should be pointed out that in concrete analysis this conception need not be superficial nor schematic if qualified by certain reservations.

To begin with, it is necessary to recall that when Lenin emphasized class stratification within the village, he saw in some social situations the possibilty of winning the entire peasant stratum for the revolution, and thereby acknowledged the persisting social cohesion of this group. Wherever capitalism failed to eliminate large landed estates, and where they were not rapidly transformed into large agricultural enterprises (as in tsarist Russia or in pre-war Poland) because of the general economic backwardness of the country, former class antagonism between the large land-owners and peasants persisted side by side with the contradictions within the peasant stratum between the poor and rich peasants. In some social situations—for instance, in the struggle for agrarian reform—the proletariat could win over not only the rural poor as its ally, but also the entire peasant stratum, even if individual groups displayed a more or less active, or even a virtually passive, attitude. But the social force, in this situation, is the peasant stratum as a whole.

Therefore, in specific analysis of particular social situations— during a revolution, for instance—Lenin considered it necessary to take into account elements of the pre-capitalist structure, and in this connection saw the possibility of mobilizing the entire peasant stratum as a social force.

Thus, while stressing the importance of class divisions in the peasant stratum, Lenin saw also the limitations of this approach in some social situations, and the danger of treating the process of rural class stratification schematically.

The need to modify textbook conceptions of changes in rural socio-economic structure in specific social situations raises the following question: is it simply a matter of taking specific conditions into account, or does the whole conception require more general modification? This suggests that we need to consider the development of the process of capital formation in agriculture. Leninism does not regard agriculture as an island isolated from the operation of the economic laws of the capitalist system, especially the laws of accumulation of capital. But at the same time, it recognizes the special characteristics of this sector of the national economy, including the special way the law of capital accumulation operates and the changes it brings about in the rural socio-economic structure. A great deal has been said on this theme, especially on the specific properties of the village and agriculture. Without repeating what is generally known, a few words may be in place on other questions which have hitherto received less attention.

The peasant farm has to be treated not only as an agricultural enterprise but also as an extended unit of domestic economy. Its very foundation lies in the fact that it produces, not one specialized commodity or another, but the family's basic means of existence. As an extended domestic economy it is less subject to those economic changes characteristic of the enterprise. It can survive (though obviously only at the cost of worsening conditions of work and the family's living standards) even in a very unfavourable economic situation in which normal industrial enterprises would be forced into bankruptcy. On the other hand, in conditions of cyclical fluctuation the typical peasant farm changes more slowly into a capitalist-type enterprise. In this event, it usually passes through a 'patriarchal' phase appropriate to early capitalist relations, where the enlargement of the farm (or the intensification of production) leads to augmentation of the family labour force by hired labourers, though the production team as a whole continues to function on the pattern of the traditional peasant family. To a large extent, these family-farm characteristics account for the resistance to the operation of those economic factors which bring about changes in the structure of enterprises. The force of this resistance is strengthened by the aforementioned fact that agriculture produces the family's basic means of maintenance; farm specialization has not gone so far as in non-agricultural sectors, while market competition is not as strong, since less of the output is produced for the market.

Other economic aspects of agriculture are also of great importance—above all, the existence of ground rent. It is difficult to agree with the view[10] that ground rent generally eliminates competition on the agricultural market. But it has to be admitted that market competition usually has a weak influence on peasant farming, since the development of industry and towns—as well as the increase in the non-agricultural population (as is the case today)—raise the demand for agricultural products.

These special features of agriculture are enough to cause the process of capital accumulation to be slower than in other sections of the national economy. Uneven development under capitalism between town and country, and between industry and agriculture, naturally have repercussions in the economic sphere and exert a powerful influence on social and cultural change in the village in general, including the structure of the peasant stratum. It may also be said that in general the process of capitalist stratification occurs more slowly and does not create such differentiation in the country, as compared with the towns.

Thus in this respect social differences between town and country arise not from their divergence but from the retardation, in the village, of processes taking place in society as a whole.

However, it is not just that the process of capital accumulation occurs more slowly and in a more specific form in agriculture. For this process does not proceed separately within agriculture and outside agriculture, but in the economy as a whole. It is therefore necessary to observe not only the slower tempo of this process in the country but also the relative weakening of the position of the country and of agriculture as compared with industry and the town, and hence the different roles which these two sectors of the economy and these two social systems play in the process of change in the economy and the social structure as a whole.

If the processes of capitalist development and of capitalist accumulation are examined in the light of the fact that both country and town are parts of a social *whole* in which this process is occurring, then the scheme of changes in the village socio-economic structure outlined at the beginning of this chapter will prove inadequate for understanding these actual changes. For that scheme is limited to an examination of the analogous effects of the process of capital accumulation in town and country, whereas here the argument leads to a different proposition, namely that many of the social effects of the process of capital accumulation occurring in the village—and quite often its *basic effects*—have repercussions *not so much in the countryside as in the towns.*

This proposition becomes even more convincing when one considers changes in rural social structure. Excess labour-power freed in the village is absorbed not only locally, where it forms a rural proletariat, but also—even primarily—by the cities, where it becomes absorbed into the working class. Peasants with smallholdings do not necessarily have to seek work with their more affluent neighbours; as industry develops they can seek it primarily outside agriculture. They then come to constitute a semi-proletarian group largely outside the system of rural class relations.

Capital created in agriculture does not necessarily accumulate only in the hands of the rural bourgeoisie, but also, even mainly, in the hands of the banks, large industrial and trading corporations, and so on. Even that part of the capital which remains in the farmers' hands can be, and usually is, invested not only in agriculture but outside it.

It would appear that Marx foresaw this process of capital accumulation when he wrote: 'But in the course of the nineteenth century the feudal lords were replaced by urban usurers; the feudal obligations that went with the land was replaced by bourgeois capital. The small-holding of the peasant is now only the pretext that allows the capitalist to draw profit, interest and rent from the soil, while leaving it to the tiller of the soil himself to see how he can extract his wages.'[11]

It may be said that these words, which stress the general concept of capital accumulation, are still relevant in the twentieth century, though 'urban usurer' must now be replaced by great banking and industrial corporations. It is therefore all the more impossible to consider the problem of capital accumulation in agriculture in isolation. One cannot look for the effects of this process only in changes in the size of peasant farms, for instance. This process could occur even in a country where all the peasant farms were of identical size. For the effect of capital accumulation in the rural areas can be such that the entire peasant stratum (numerically diminishing and losing its position in society) would be transformed from a stratum of independent farmers into a stratum of cottage workers working in fact for industrial banking, or trading corporations.

Of course a situation in which the peasant stratum changed its position in society only as a complete whole would be as extreme a phenomenon as one in which it changed only its internal structure without changing its position. Both phenomena usually occur simultaneously, and their mutual proportions determine the particular type of structure. This would seem to explain why in present-day capitalism we are confronted here and there with areas of typical family economy, although this is not explicable solely in terms of the operation of this factor.

Starting from the concept of the process of capital formation as a general social process gives us a better understanding of changes in rural socio-economic structure than the above schema allows for. In view of the unevenness of capitalist development, we must mention two effects of the process of capital accumulation in the rural areas. First, it leads to class stratification analogous to that which occurs in the towns as the formerly homogeneous peasant class becomes divided into capitalists and proletarians (the problem here is to determine the direction of class polarization and not whether such groups have actually been formed). Second, within the structure of society as a whole the entire peasant stratum is reduced to the position of 'a proletarian with land'. These two undoubtedly mutually contradictory effects of the process of capital accumulation, though they derive from the same source, interlock and create a highly complex social structure. The reason is that, in addition to the social differentiation introduced into the village by capitalism, old social bonds and old forms of differentiations derived from previous times still persist. But even if this complication is ignored one can still maintain that under capitalist conditions the peasant stratum will act as a whole in certain situations.

Thus, under capitalism, the village can be seen from two different aspects: first, as a community in which a class structure emerges analogous to that in the towns, and second, as a social stratum which, with the development of capitalism, approximates to the position of the working class, and in certain countries even becomes the 'lowest social class'.

The rural socio-economic structure of a country is determined by historical conditions which define the course of capital accumu-

lation. In pre-war Poland for instance, we have to see former
class antagonisms—large land-owners v. peasants, as well as the
class conflicts of the late-capitalist type (peasants v. monopoly
capital)—as involving the entire peasant stratum in the clash of
social forces. In addition, class division within the peasant stratum must be taken into account: poor peasants and kulaks,
characteristic of the early capitalist structure based on relations
of a 'patriarchal' type (the villages in Malopolska*) and the proletariat–capitalist antagonism characteristic of the period of developed capitalism and its corresponding 'farmer' culture (the
villages of Poznan).[12]

Depending upon the time and the manner in which their industries developed, the economic policy pursued by the State,
etc., other countries display the following structures: (1) an already developed structure of the 'farmer' type, in which rural
class antagonisms are merged in the general class struggle of the
proletariat v. the bourgeoisie, (2) a structure of the 'peasant'
type, poor peasants v. kulaks, (3) a structure based on family
farms (in which case the owners are in fact 'proletarians with
land'), or some other type of structure with more or less definitely formed groups and class antagonisms. In different areas
of a given country it may be possible to find various types of
structure corresponding to specific socio-economic conditions.

There are thus not one but many types of rural socio-economic
structure. Hence the paradigm of the process of rural class stratification given in textbooks must be regarded as corresponding to
the structure of the Russian village at the end of the nineteenth
century. This is a good example of the operation of the law of
accumulation of capital in the village, but it is not an absolute.
In particular, the conclusion frequently drawn from this paradigm, that under capitalist conditions the village should simply
be regarded as a social entity in which antagonistic classes (or
groups of classes) analogous to those of the towns begin to
develop, does not correspond with reality. Even if we ignore pre-
capitalist survivals in the social structure, and the class antagonisms related to them, we have to admit that under capitalist
conditions the peasant stratum also preserves a number of features

---

* Approximately the western part of that area of Poland formerly
under Austrian domination, with Cracow as its administrative
centre—*Translator*.

as a whole and occupies a special place in the structure of society. Even when the internal class differentiation of this stratum is quite evident, in certain situations it can act as a homogeneous social force. In this connection, the question as to whether the term 'peasant class' or 'peasant stratum' is the more appropriate would appear to be badly formulated. If we ignore the emotional overtones of these terms, and consider the question in the light of the above argument, the question should rather read: 'In what social situations does the rural community still act as a class, and in which situations is it necessary to take into account, first and foremost, internal class differentiation in the countryside?'

This problem is still of serious practical importance. In pre-war Poland the failure to perceive that the peasantry did act as a class in many social situations (agrarian reform, the problem of indebtedness, etc.) prevented the Communist Party from developing broader revolutionary activity. Appraisals of social forces which saw only class struggle in the countryside yielded poor results, not because the assumption did not correspond to the realities of the time, but because it was too narrow for practical activity. In post-war conditions this scheme proved to be even less useful, for it became a question not only of too one-sided an approach but also of a failure to take into account the fundamental changes brought about by the socialist industrialization of the country.

Changes in rural social structure in the context of socialist industrialization

The previous section contrasted textbook models of change in rural social structure with actual developments in pre-war Poland. Our interpretation was supported by citations from Marx and Lenin, especially in the shape of the Leninist definition of the peasantry as a 'class estate'.[13] It is true that Lenin's definition was developed with reference to conditions in pre-revolutionary Russia, where vestiges of serfdom existed, whereas the interpretation advanced here attempts to be more general, being based on an analysis of the process of capital accumulation which shapes the social forces. But this is, in some degree, only an extension of ideas which have been developed earlier. Unfortunately, such an approach is not possible for the analysis of change in the rural social structure under conditions of socialism. The most important problem in this sphere, that of the influence of socialist industrialization on rural social structure, has not been studied to any great extent so far. True, Soviet economic literature includes many interesting studies of rural class stratification,[14] but for many reasons there seems to have been no special occasion in the Soviet Union for more thorough research into the influence of socialist industrialization on rural stratification. Agrarian Marxist work on the subject was interrupted during the collectivization period. However, such conditions no longer obtain in Poland, where the process of socialist industrialization has exerted a strong influence on the general pattern of the country's socio-economic relations and exists side by side with peasant farming, based on private ownership of the means of production, which dominates agricultural production and provides the basis for the employment and maintenance of a considerable part (over one third) of the population. Moreover, Polish science has taken stock of this situation: since the immediate post-war years extensive research into rural social structure has been carried out, and makes it possible to compare textbook models with empirical data.

Textbook models of change in rural social structure during the period of the construction of socialism do not conceive of any basic modification of the approach presented at the beginning of the previous section. They assume that class stratification in the countryside remains the same as in the pre-revolutionary period, except that with the elimination of feudal survivals those factors which supported the peasant stratum in its dual condition as both class and estate disappeared. The only corrections recognized consist of noting that the activity of the socialist regime changes the composition of social forces in the village to some extent. It strengthens the middle group numerically and links it with State economic policy; organizes the semi-proletarian elements in the village; gives them greater scope for social activity, and restricts the influence of capitalist elements. This is, however, a recognition of changes in the balance of forces, not of changes in the principles of their formation or in the overall pattern. Moreover, it assumes that the earlier pattern of rural class divisions not only persists but is constantly being renewed as long as its basis—i.e. the private ownership of the means of production—persists.

Any appraisal of social forces based on this approach leads to the acceptance of a number of propositions and principles which directly affect practical activity: the thesis, for instance, of the intensification of the class struggle in the village, the notion of collectivization as the way to freeing poor peasants from kulak exploitation, etc. Obviously, in some situations this model may correspond to the actual situation. But the question is the extent to which these propositions remain valid under conditions where the impact of socialist industrialization on the village is strong and continuous. This is a very real problem for Poland (and not only for Poland), and it is vital in formulating general hypotheses about changes in the rural social structure brought by socialism.

Without resorting to extensive citation of materials available in various publications,[9] it is worth while sketching these changes in Poland's rural social structure by drawing on empirical data. This makes possible the classification of rural families with reference to the main criteria for determining the bases of formation of social forces, and especially of the antagonistic class groups, i.e. the rural proletariat and semi-proletariat (the village poor) on the one hand, and the village capitalists on the other.

In research carried out by the IER the agricultural proletariat is taken to embrace families without land (or owning up to half a hectare of land) or other means of agricultural production, and who maintain themselves mainly by working as wage labourers on private farms. According to the 1931 census this category, at that time, constituted some 12 per cent of the total number of families living in the rural areas. In 1950 it had shrunk to about 2 per cent. According to IER research in 1952, the agricultural proletariat then constituted 2–3 per cent, but by 1957 had dropped to at best 1 per cent on a national scale; only in one area (central–eastern) did the percentage exceed the average of 1·7 per cent. Studies made in 1960, and preliminary data from the general census taken in the same year, indicate that the percentage is still falling. This very general information needs to be supplemented by an examination of other aspects of the situation of families included in this category. They are often widely dispersed and often consist of invalided soldiers, widows with children and so on (who should be under the care of institutions concerned with social welfare); their very low cultural level accounts for their social passivity.

The categories 'agricultural semi-proletariat' and 'small peasants working for neighbours' distinguished by Lenin are subsumed, in IER research, under the label 'earnings outside agriculture'. In general, it would correspond to the 'village poor', if this term is used not to indicate all 'poor' families living in the rural areas but farm families which to a greater or lesser extent maintain themselves by working for neighbours. This category covers families owning farms over half a hectare in size and working for neighbours for at least 150 days per annum.

An analysis of pre-war class relations would have to include in this category almost all the smallholding families (owning farms of $\frac{1}{2}$–3 or 4 hectares in size, according to the region). The findings of IER surveys in 1947 and 1952 were interpreted in this manner. But in the light of the large-scale employment of smallholding families in socialized enterprises and institutions, this categorization became more and more inaccurate.[15] Even if we assume that the standard of living of families which work for neighbours is similar to that of families employed in socialized institutions and enterprises (which is not the case), there is still a fundamental difference in the social situation of these two categories, for the second category, in fact, belongs outside the system of class relations in the village, whereas the situation of the first category is determined by this very system.

The IER poll of 1957 justifies the statement that the category of 'earnings outside agriculture', like that of the 'agricultural proletariat', has become quite insignificant in the Polish village. At the national level it does not exceed 1·5 per cent of the total number of rural families; only in certain central–eastern counties can one speak of a greater frequency. Those who remain in both these categories are mainly families that did not want, or were not able, to take advantage of opportunities to obtain a middle-sized farm in the western region, to move to town, or to obtain gainful employment locally (in certain counties of southern and central–eastern Poland, though, this last possibility does not exist). Furthermore, it is unlikely that people in this category will be capable of organized social activity.

The categories of 'agricultural proletariat' and 'rural semi-proletariat' together constitute a class grouping objectively opposed to the category of rural capitalists. So far, research suggests no reason for believing that the consciousness of these categories corresponds to their social situation. Their small numbers, their dispersion, their passivity, and the absence of any sign of consciousness of common interests preclude even the potential emergence of these categories as significant social forces in the village.

The category of rural capitalists is even more insignificant numerically. The IER classifies under this category families operating farms which regularly employ hired labour (the lower limit of working days is taken by convention as 150 per annum). This is considerably lower than would result from the classification made by Lenin, who considered a peasant capitalist farm one in which the number of days worked by hired labourers exceeded those contributed by members of the family. Hence the IER figure for capitalist farms can be regarded as too high, in any case, not as too low. In the course of research in 1957, even with the limit fixed so low, it was possible to single out families working capitalist-type farms in only two regions where the percentage of rural capitalists amongst the total body of rural families exceeded one per cent. Usually they operated farms of about twenty hectares, adequately equipped with draught-power (246 horses per 100 families) and with machinery, which results in quite a high level of production. Capitalist farms are obviously economically stronger than family farms, though the differences are not great.

Considering that in the pre-war period the category of rural capitalists embraced approximately 5–6 per cent of the rural families, and in 1950 was estimated to be some 4 per cent, the tendency for it to decline is obvious. A particularly severe decline has occurred in the area where the greatest development of capitalist rural stratification existed before the war: in the Poznan and Bydgoszcz provinces, where most capitalist farms went into self-liquidation or were liquidated in 1952–54. This tendency to decline is evidenced by their owners' inclination to restrict their hire of labour, either by selling part of their land or by improving the technical equipment of their farms. IER investigations do not provide enough material for an exhaustive treatment of

the question of the formation of this category's social consciousness. But undoubtedly the capitalist farmers lack the conditions
which would enable them to act as an organized social force. On
the other hand, those aspirations and views characteristic of
smallholders and small entrepreneurs in general are naturally
more strongly manifested amongst people in this category than in
others.

One important reservation is necessary at this point. The
question of class polarization of the peasant stratum cannot be
reduced to the existence of antagonistic groups of rural proletariat and semi-proletariat on the one side and village capitalists
on the other. The peasant stratum, whose existence is based on
the private ownership of means of production, is, to use Lenin's
words, 'the last capitalist class', both in respect of its social consciousness and in respect of tendencies toward polarization in-
separably associated with private ownership of means of
production.

IER research demonstrates continuing differentiation of peasant farms with respect to assets in terms of means of production,
which reflects the class situation of the peasant family. Such differentiation is difficult to express in terms of the analysis described above. In order to examine this differentiation we must
turn to the more traditional classification of peasant families into
small, medium and (with some exaggeration) large farmers—a
classification which is inadequate for a more thoroughgoing analysis of class relations.

An example of this kind of differentiation drawn from one
region (central–western Poznan and Bydgoszcz provinces) should
be sufficient to show what is meant. There, smallholding peasants (owning up to 4 hectares) form a quite numerous group,
38·5 per cent of the total farm owners. Of course, this group is
poorly equipped with the means of production: in the villages
studied, it held only some 8 per cent of the land (12·6 per cent
of total output in terms of value, and 8·4 per cent of the total
commodity production). Out of every 100 farms, 88 had no
horses, 39 did not even have a cow, and 81 owned no agricultural
machinery of any kind. These farms are of recent origin (44 per
cent came into being after 1950); they achieve low levels of production (an average total output value of about 16,000 zlotys)
and a low level of commodity production (about 35 per cent of

the total). Their poor equipment and means of production and their low production level do not assure the families of an adequate means of subsistence. In 82 out of every 100 farms of this type, at least one person was gainfully employed off the farm, and in 71 cases this included the owner himself. About 15 per cent of the total employed away from the farm were working for neighbours. In addition, other forms of class relations were observable. Some 50 per cent of the small farm owners (and 19 per cent of the total farm operators) worked for neighbours in exchange for the loan of production equipment, mainly horses. This high percentage must be taken with the reservation that the average number of days of labour services performed by families as payment for debt was only 18 per annum, while this type of transaction was chiefly entered into by neighbours who did not differ greatly in respect of the size of their farms.

Consequently, the range of relationships is much more extensive than might have been imagined from our earlier characterization of the outside income-earning group; but the basis is too slender (the number of days worked, and work for neighbours) to enable us to designate the entire group of smallholding families as 'rural poor' in the Leninist sense of the term. The relation is nonetheless sufficiently obvious to confirm the existence of elements of 'impoverishment', though it is difficult to recognize such elements as the main feature in the contemporary social position of these families. It may be assumed that under certain conditions (e.g. in the event of restricted employment opportunities outside the village and outside agriculture) the position of families in this category could constitute a basis for the formation of a group of rural poor. But under present-day conditions such a possibility does not exist.

Farmers owning 25 or more hectares constitute 1·1 per cent of the total population of the villages studied, and they cultivate 5·3 per cent of the land (3·7 per cent of total output in terms of value, and 3·9 per cent of commodity production). 83·4 per cent of these farms came into existence before 1939 and are incomparably better supplied with production equipment than the others. For example, 67 per cent in this group have three horses; 83 per cent own four or more cows; 100 per cent have complete sets of agricultural machinery (excluding tractors); the average annual output in terms of value is 149,000 zlotys (the proportion of commodity production to the total being 58 per cent). Hired labour is used on 91 per cent of the farms in this category, the number of days of such labour averaging 113 per annum.

Comparison between the situation of the families working the largest and those on the smallest farms confirms this great disparity in the possession of production equipment, and hence enables us to ascertain the degree of differentiation in social status. It follows from this that the previously discussed categories of rural capitalists and outside income-earners constitute only the most developed cases of far more wide-spread trends in rural class stratification. However, the limited crystallization of the main antagonistic groups and the gradual decline in their numbers justify our assertion that the existing differentiation of rural families is not increasing. This means that so far tendencies towards polarization are not being realized, although class stratification still continues and the conditions under which these tendencies might emerge under certain circumstances persist. So one may judge that the process of class polarization associated with private peasant farming is encountering obstacles and is not in fact manifesting itself.

The factors which have directly influenced this situation are generally known. Most important is the development of new centres of employment, which to a large extent have absorbed the former agricultural labourers and owners of smallholdings. The reduction in the supply of labour within the villages, and even shortages of labour in certain areas, have greatly restricted the hiring of labour on capitalist farms and have compelled many owners to adapt their land areas or their technical equipment to compensate for limited reserves of family labour.

The need for a market system geared to the reconstruction of the towns and the expansion of industry has greatly restricted the possibilities of development of capitalist farms (and almost eliminated competition), while the progressive distribution of burdens associated with industrialization has tended to even out disparities in the position of small and large farm owners. Factors other than economic ones have also been involved. The urban system of values has exerted a considerable influence on the village. Division into owners and hired hands is not a premise of this system. As a result, a position as a day labourer has become

unacceptable to village youth, while the career of independent
farmer (a 'boor', a 'rustic') is no longer attractive.

Many other similar factors could be mentioned, all associated
with the socialist industrialization of the country. The term
'socialist' is meant to emphasize that it is not a matter of industrialization in general. Industrialization here is based on the
socialization of the means of production, and this conditions the
kind of effect industrialization has on the rural social structure.
The former agricultural labourer living in a village, or the small
farmer who takes a job in industry, enters a different type of
social structure today.

Market relations are primarily based on the principle of planning and not on profit. Occupation is the determinant of social
position, and there is a different set of positions from which to
choose. We have mentioned here only those properties of the
social system which lead directly to significant changes in rural
social structure. In addition, other factors have also emerged in
Poland which need to be defined differently. For instance, the
elimination of some of the capitalist farms in 1951–53 was not,
as one might expect, the result of the operation of the socialist
system, and although it affected the number of such farms it did
not determine the direction of the changes under discussion.

This leads us to deduce that the process of capital accumulation is not the basis for the moulding of rural social forces
under conditions of socialist industrialization. Though the bases
of social stratification still exist, and manifestations of class conflict still appear from one country to another, the relations of
social forces in the countryside cannot be said to rest on these
elements, and policies which did not take this phenomenon into
account would prove fallacious. For instance, the directive 'Base
yourself on the village poor' must be misleading, since that
group, in the Leninist sense, is a fragmented one and incapable
of social activity. The conviction, based on the textbook approach, that the working peasants will organize production co-
operatives in order to free themselves from kulak exploitation is
also fallacious, since the conflict of the poor against the kulaks is
not at issue, and the small peasants find it much easier and
quicker to free themselves from economic dependence on their
neighbours by finding employment outside the village and
agriculture.

The continuation of a situation in which tendencies towards polarization in the countryside might emerge, given certain conditions, is one aspect of reality which corresponds to the Leninist definition of the peasantry as 'the last capitalist class'. Although there are no such tendencies today, and objective bases for the formation of conflicting social forces in the countryside no longer exist, there is still a feeling of separateness and even of the existence of opposed interests (e.g. during sales of machinery at the State Machinery Centres—POM) which, though secondary in importance, are still real social antagonisms.

A second aspect of reality which also corresponds to the Leninist definition is the type of social consciousness characteristic of petty commodity producers in general as private owners of means of production. Hence there is still a possibility of the rural population emerging as a social class which will make itself felt under certain conditions (e.g. when attempts are made to introduce mass collectivization in Poland).

The question as to whether social consciousness can be a factor favouring the formation of other social forces leads us to a more general problem. In view of the fact that under the conditions of socialist industrialization the concept of class has only limited value for the analysis of the balance of rural social forces, the question arises as to whether bases are emerging for the formation of social forces on different principles, and what role social consciousness plays in this process. Before making any conjectures on this subject we must return to our picture of the social structure of the Polish village. For the influence of socialist industrialization has not been confined to the weakening of class divisions in the village; it has also led to much deeper changes in the structural system.

One such change which catches the eye, and is confirmed by everyone who studies Polish rural problems today, is the progressive differentiation of the occupational composition of the rural population. In addition to the categories mentioned above, IER investigations distinguished further categories of families maintaining themselves by work on their own farms; those who maintain themselves partly or mainly by employment outside their own or their neighbours' farms ('peasant–workers', or 'part-time farmers', as they might be called); and families dependent exclusively on employment outside their own or their neighbours' farms (mainly in non-agricultural production) but living in the villages studied. Because of considerable regional differences, information by way of example concerning such categories will relate only to the central–western region.

In this region the last of the above-mentioned categories constitutes some 15 per cent of the total number of families living in the villages studied. In non-farm families the majority of people at work (49 per cent) are employed in State enterprises outside agriculture, i.e. in industry, building and transport. Workers in the co-operative sector are much fewer in number (8·6 per cent), as are also those in State institutions such as schools or local councils (6·8 per cent). Craftsmen working on their own account form a still smaller percentage (3·6 per cent). 10·8 per cent work in State agricultural enterprises, and the remainder (20·2 per cent) are pensioners and retired persons living in the country. It follows that a considerable proportion of the families included in this category (estimated at 60 per cent) are connected with the village only by residence.[16]

Families permanently employed outside their own and neighbours' farms, but which also draw part of their income from their own farm, are incomparably more closely linked with agriculture and the village. In the IER studies these families are divided into two categories: type Z, who draw the main part of their income from work outside the farm (these earnings exceeding the estimated income from the farm) and type RZ, for whom outside earnings are an additional source of maintenance, though the farm remains the main source. In the region under consideration the first of these two categories constitutes 14·3 per cent of the total number of families living in the villages studied, the second category 12·3 per cent. In other regions the proportions are different, but the percentage falling within these two categories jointly is not less than 25 per cent, while in southern Poland it reaches 50 per cent.

The categories Z and RZ are made up mainly of smallholding families. According to M. Dziewicka[17] (who uses a different classification by separating out peasant–workers' families which are permanently employed outside their own and neighbours' farms), this group makes up 72 per cent of the total number of the smallholding families in the region. The type of production characteristic of this last group does not differ fundamentally from other farms in the same area. The value of the means of production and the level of production per farm are somewhat lower, but the differences are small. There is a greater difference in the level of commodity production, which indicates that the worker–peasants' output is directed more to satisfying the family's consumption needs than to market requirements.

The categories Z and RZ, and the 'worker–peasants' category in the Dziewicka classification, are very heterogenous: they include both manual and white-collar workers (14·7 per cent of the total outside earners); those employed in industry (20·9 per cent), in transport and communications (13·3 per cent), in building and land drainage (11·5 per cent), in trade (3·4 per cent), administration (9·4 per cent), handicrafts (9·9 per cent) and so on. 17·1 per cent of those employed off the farm work in socialist agricultural and forestry enterprises. In the categories in question, some work in the village and others outside the village. In the villages studied in the central–western region 30 per cent work on the spot, 18 per cent travel up to 5 km to work, 32 per cent travel 5–20 km, and 14 per cent travel over 20 km.

The above data illustrate the effect of socialist industrialization on the rural social structure. The existing differentiation of rural families in respect of their links with the internal village system of relations and the changes they are undergoing justifies our reference to a process of drawing away from the peasant stratum and of moving closer to other classes and strata.

This is not a new phenomenon; it was already confirmed by Lenin.[18] Reflecting the conditions of his time, Lenin saw this as a manifestation of the operation of the law of capital accumulation, which dismembered the former peasant estate and thrust a large proportion of the smallholding families into the proletariat—above all, the industrial proletariat. Under capitalist conditions this process was thus connected with the class stratification of the rural population, and was its natural extension and consequence. The fundamental change in the nature of this process in Poland's present conditions consists, not in the circumstance that the categories in question have considerably increased numerically, but in the fact that it is a process which links the former peasant stratum with the new social structure, based on other foundations, namely the socialization of the means of production. This process indicates that socialist industrialization has not only fundamentally changed the former rural social structure but has also brought about the formation of a new structure and set in motion in this sector a process of transformation consisting of the penetration of the general social structure into the rural community.

This penetration, and the emergence of groups constituting a series (continuum) of transitional forms linking the peasant stratum with the new social structure formed on other bases, create conditions for the emergence of corresponding types of social consciousness and for the moulding of new social forces developing on different principles.

This refers, however, to that part of the rural population which has broken or weakened its connection with peasant farming. Undoubtedly this process also influences the position and the consciousness of families who derive their living exclusively from their farms. This is the most numerous category of rural families. In the region cited as an example above, it forms some 52 per cent of the total number of rural families, owns the largest share of the land and other means of production, and produces the main part of the agricultural commodities. Because of its importance this category requires separate discussion. Without giving figures—which in this case would involve far too many items—we can say that it is the most active group, both economically and socially. The possibilities for capitalist farms developing in Poland are very restricted. Hence individual farmers' economic activities do not lead to the formation of a class group of rural capitalists. But if this element is eliminated from the set of roles typical of the peasant farmer's social position, it might be suggested that the main process shaping internal social differentiation in this category in present-day Poland is the development of farming as a specialized occupation. The changes and differentiations within this group may be conceived as a series typified at the extremes by traditional peasant farming, i.e. running the farm as a domestic economy, and the farmer who engages in specialized economic activities.

These are of course ideal types (on the private peasant farm the farmer who follows an occupation can only be an ideal type), but the movement tends to be in this direction. This requires separate consideration and confirmation. Here we must be content with expressing the tendency, which is: the process of development of farming as a specialized occupation with material and legal bases, and with its own recognized values. It is necessary to relate this process also to socialist industrialization, since its aim, in essence, is to weaken (and elminate) existing social differences between country and town. In Poland this means differences between the private and socialized sectors of the economy, through the gradual economic and social transformation of the private sector; in the domain of changes in social structure it involves reducing the differences between the old structure of the rural community and the new structure of the present-day Polish town.

The question of the creation of farming as an occupation has already been discussed in chapter 2. It may, however, be stated, on the basis of the data examined here, that today the most clearly defined social division in the village is the occupational division into farmers and non-farmers. The suggestive hypothesis springs to mind that under conditions of socialist industrialization the basis for the crystallization of rural social forces is not those factors which determine social class but those which define occupational groups.[19] It may be that the terms 'social class' and 'occupational group' as understood here correspond best to 'groupings of a class nature distinguished on the basis of the criterion of the social division of labour'. This idea is especially pertinent with reference to the village, and the peasant farm undoubtedly provides a basis for the existence today of a 'class which is also an occupation' (peasant farmers). But in our conceptual framework the stress is laid upon trends toward the future, and particular importance is therefore attached to factors leading to social change.

The above hypothesis can, of course, be formulated in a more general fashion. If it is advanced with reference to changes in the social structure of the Polish countryside, where, after all, differentiation still prevails in respect of the ownership of means of production, it applies all the more with reference to the town, or, more precisely, to socialist society in general. This idea may be formulated as follows: as a result of the socialization of the main means of production and the creation of a socialist type of national economy, the process of capital accumulation does not lay the basis for the formation of social forces on class lines. Even in those branches of the economy which in one country or another have not yet been socialized—like agriculture in Poland, for instance—the process of capital concentration is not, generally speaking, the basic factor shaping the social structure. On the contrary, even while retaining older economic features, these branches are themselves determined by processes occurring in the national economy as a whole. If division by occupation can be recognized as the basis for the shaping of the social struc-ture under the conditions of socialism, it may be presumed that with the development of socialist industrialization the old struc-ture will give way to a new one, even in the village, where the old class structure still survives.

Of course, this hypothesis is an imprecise one. Definition of terms and the formulation of empirically verifiable propositions are matters for further inquiry in various fields of sociology. In the field of rural social structure such inquiries are being pursued. For the moment, there are more questons than answers in this field. This chapter has attempted to formulate certain of these questions, to indicate the difficulties involved in applying theo-retical constructs to the study of empirical data, and has sug-gested changes needed in those constructs. Obviously this is a highly controversial subject. The problem of passing from the language of empirical research to that of the theoretical con-structs which the interpreter uses remains one of the most diffi-cult in present-day sociology. But if one cannot cross by a solid bridge, one has to resort to an unstable gangplank.

Notes

1   We exclude here, of course, personal idiosyncrasies, since, al-though they have undoubted significance, analysis of mass phenomena requires that we use a type of analysis such as that developed later in this chapter.

2   The simplification of the continuum to two polar positions is justified in the light of section 3.

3   We should note that the adequacy of a classification based on this principle for analysing the structure of socialist societies is a controversial matter. It is questionable, *inter alia,* whether these dif-ferences, which still remain in such societies with regard to ownership of the means of production (whether general property or group property), can be regarded (in view of distinct trends towards their abolition) as a central factor determining differentiation of social

position. It is therefore doubtful whether a classification based on this principle is of greater value in analysing social forces in a socialist society than one based on other criteria (e.g. occupational divisions, rural–urban differences, differences in access to power, etc.).

4   V. I. Lenin, 'A great beginning', *Selected works*, vol. 3, Moscow 1967, pp. 242 ff.

5   K. Marx, *The 18th Brumaire of Louis-Napoleon*, cit.

6   Obviously, these definitions can be linked so as to form a coherent system. See, for example, the attempt at a systematization of the Marxist theory of classes by J. Hochfeld in his *Studja o marksistowskiej teorii spoleczenstwa* (*Studies in the Marxist theory of society*), Warsaw, 1963.

7   The term 'intermediate class' is used in the same sense as 'social stratum', in distinction from 'basic class', which, in a given system, occupies one of the polar positions in the process of social differentiation going on within the system.

8   Cf. *Spoleczno-ekonomiczna struktura wsi . . ., cit.*; B. Galeski, 'Spoleczna struktura . . .'; A. Szemberg, *Przemiany struktury agrarnej . . . , cit.*; M. Dziewicka, *Chlopi-robotnicy, cit.*, etc.

9   V. I. Lenin, 'The agrarian programme of Russian social democracy', *Selected works*, vol. 3, Moscow and Leningrad, 1934.

10   See, for instance, W. Stys, *Wspolzaleznosc rozwoju rodziny chlopskiej, cit.*

11   K. Marx, *The 18th Brumaire of Louis-Napoleon, cit.*, pp. 177–8.

12   For a fuller discussion of this question see B. Galeski, 'J. Ryng o spoleczno-ekonomicznej strukturze wsi' ('J. Ryng on the socio-economic structure of the village'), *Ekonomista*, 1959, No. 1.

13   V. I. Lenin, 'The agrarian programme of Russian social democracy', *cit.*

14   For instance, studies by Krytzman, Gaister, Uzhanski, etc.

15   J. Tepicht drew attention to this in, for example, 'Przemiany wsi Rzeszowskiej' ('Changes in Rzeszow village'), *Zagadnienia ekonomiki rolnej* (*Problems of Agricultural Economics*), 1952, No. 1.

16   For fuller data see J. Przychodzen, 'Struktura spoleczno-zawodowa ludnosci bezrolnej na wsi' ('The socio-occupational structure of the non-agricultural rural population'), *Zagadnienia ekonomiki rolnej*, 1962, No. 6, and 1963, No. 1.

17   *Chlopi-robotnicy, cit.*

18   *The development of capitalism in Russia, cit.*

19   This idea is more commonly expressed today. For example, at a symposium devoted to changes in rural social structure where the main paper was presented by the present writer, it was put forward by Professor J. Chalasinski.

6 From peasant class to stratum of farmers

The occupational structure and the class structure

The family model of the organization of production contains two basic elements: control of the means of production, i.e. the land and implements, and control of labour, i.e. the complex of activities which consist in utilizing those means in order to obtain given products. We shall see how the 'social' organization of production constitutes a transformation which leads on to a specialized mode of farming. Both these elements develop in two different, though closely related, ways (and without this dual transformation production could not be achieved): (1) the system of ownership of the means of production, and (2) the system through which labour is organized.

1. Within the family production unit a particular mode of allocation of the means of production already exists, taking the form of differential participation by the various members of the family in production decisions and in decisions concerning the use of implements and the product of the family's labour. Differentiation within the family production unit leads to a more complex division of labour; that is, production becomes organized on a 'social' scale, entailing a division of labour between families. Since over the course of time family control derives from a basis in family (i.e. private) ownership, differentiation in control over the means of production is determined mainly by differentiation of ownership. This differentiated system of ownership is the basis for the formation of a class system in society (see chapter 5).

The concentration of property creates the conditions for its socialization. With the socialization of wealth comes the problem of socializing control and management, which cannot be ignored when considering the formation of class structure in a socialist society, but which goes beyond the scope of this work. It is sufficient to assert here that the transformation of family control of the means of production into a differentiated system of social control provides a basis for the formation of a class system.

2. Within the family production unit there also develops a certain differentiation in the way members of the family participate in production activities (the division of labour). This differentiation is itself closely linked to differentiation in the control of the means of production. Both are determined by the positions which the various members occupy in the family. This division of labour within the family, together with the emergence of production on a 'social' scale, develops into an occupational structure.

As has been pointed out already, it is not that family control of the means of production and family production itself are eliminated. The systems of control of the means of production and control of labour are formed outside agriculture, which remains the domain of the family mode of organizing production; with industrialization these systems become dominant in society as a whole. Family control and operation of the means of production becomes just one of the elements of the social organization of labour and the system of property. As far as the formation of the occupational structure is concerned, we should point out that its basis lies not only in production activities or those directly associated with production (e.g. the organization of production) but also in activities outside the sphere of material production, which have their analogues in family activities (e.g. education). Where there is no equivalent, it is because these activities are associated with an increasing range of culturally accepted material wants and the operation of social institutions. Consequently, occupations not associated with production are 'free' from direct connections with the control of the means of production and are ignored in considering the relationship between occupation and social class for the time being.

Thus the relationship between occupation and class structure depends upon the fact that both have their basis in the production process, which we view as the combination of two elements: labour and the means of production. Since the means of production can be monopolized much more easily than can production activities, in societies differentiated with regard to ownership and activities possession of the means of production is the chief determinant of the individual's social situation and the basis of the formation of social alignments.

To a great extent, the fact that the differential social situation of individuals and families is based on ownership of the means of

production is largely obliterated by the strict relationship between social class and occupation. Occupational groups are
formed above all within the framework of social classes. Managerial and organizational activities are closely associated with control of the means of production, and are an integral part of these
social roles. When ownership is the basis of control these activities
can be performed not by the owner but by special personnel, for
ownership allows the constant possibility of control and, if necessary, the power to change the directing personnel. Although
managerial and organizational activity in the production sphere
and in the wider system of organization of society (the State ap-
paratus) do not have to be directly linked with ownership of the
means of production—which makes possible control in both
spheres, since monopolization of the means of production is the
main determinant of the hierarchy of social positions—occupational groups based on these activities are drawn primarily from
the class of owners of the means of production. Conversely,
labourers are usually recruited from the ranks of non-owners of
the means of production, or from the peasant stratum, whose most
notable feature is the domination of the family model—a family
which produces and controls its means of production. This relationship between class and occupation—that is, the emergence
of occupational groupings distinguished on the basis of the division of labour within the class framework—is generally recognized. Hence the importance of research into the occupational
hierarchy for the analysis of class structure.

There is also another relationship—a negative one—which is
less often noticed, namely class differentiation *within* occupations, most often in the pre-industrial period. As an example we
may cite any group of handicraftsmen, for instance tailors. A
tailor employed in a large factory, one who works at home, the
owner of a small tailoring shop, and one running a large enterprise—these undoubtedly represent class divisions within the occupation. Such relationships arise particularly among classes
which are undergoing polarization within a newly emerging class
structure.

The two types of relationship between class and occupation
(occupational differentiation within the class, and class differentiation within the occupation) are characteristic of the capitalistic
model in a very simplified and traditional form. As well as these

relationships, yet another pattern develops which is worth special consideration as far as socialist society is concerned. This is the specialization of many spheres of activity, e.g. the growth of co-operative and political spheres which bring occupational groups into existence in order to direct the means of production. This is particularly important under socialist conditions, for although differentiation based on ownership ceases to exist, a more or less pronounced differentiation does arise, depending on the particular mode of organizing the control of the means of production in various socialist societies. The question arises—and we cannot answer it here—whether certain occupational groups do not acquire the features of a social class under such conditions.

The problem raised previously of the formation of social alignments resting on occupational groupings can now be examined in the light of the relationships between class and occupation discussed above. Since classes are occupationally differentiated internally, it is easy to see that class-consciousness emerges with the awareness of common interests within the occupational group. This process, referred to often by Marx and by almost every socialist theorist, manifests itself not only in the shaping of class-consciousness but also in the activity from which this consciousness derives—in the economic struggle which is the basis of the political struggle. Obviously, not every occupational organization is a factor in the formation of social alignments—not even occupations directly involved in the production process, or organizations of owners of the means of production. Organizations also exist which are based on the so-called 'share in management', as well as occupational groupings which cut across the class barriers dividing the individuals composing them. 'Corporations' in which, for instance, the factory owner and the workers, the porter and the director participate, are used by capitalist States to hamper the formation of social forces; they represent a definite technique of manipulating social forces rather than a base for their consolidation.

Differences between occupational organizations based on class and those based on other principles (participation in management, ties between producers and consumers, etc.) is only one aspect of the problem under consideration. That problem is whether occupation can be the basis of the formation of social alignments of forces made up of groups or collectivities which aim at transforming existing production relations. A further problem, especially important as far as the practical task of directing social change in the Polish countryside is concerned, emerges when we look more closely at the process of specialization of the farmer's labour, such as that developing in Poland today.

The specialization of farming in contemporary Poland

The decline of the family mode of production and the emergence of a specialized mode of production is an historical process reaching back to the beginnings of human society, a process which, despite deviations, has undoubtedly been proceeding in one direction. The pace quickens in capitalist conditions, with the development of industry and the formation of a world economic system based on the market. The family producing on its own and for itself is now to be found only in agriculture, although here too, with the influence of the market, one can no longer speak of self-sufficient family farming. Although in most countries such self-sufficient family farming belongs to the past, since it has now become part of a nation-wide organization of production (like the large landed estates much earlier), nevertheless the main features of family farming have been largely preserved. The swifter tempo of transformation and the new directions it takes have come about only in the present epoch, when industrial production has become the main form of production in the overall society, and urbanism the main feature of contemporary culture.

The problem of occupational specialization in farm work requires a rather broad approach, and although the present work is mainly concerned with private farmers and the members of their families on the farm, the broader subjects of changes in village occupational structure and the emergence of new occupations connected with agricultural production need to be considered.

Under capitalist conditions the process of specialization in farming is closely tied to the process of class differentiation among the peasant stratum. The division of the peasant family's production activities into tasks performed by individuals or teams within the enterprise and activities performed by specialized enterprises, whether based on the family or not, occurs as a consequence of the concentration of ownership and monopolization of the agricultural means of production. This process—best analysed and most carefully researched in Marxist literature[1]—takes the form of the emergence of capitalist agricultural enterprises, principally on the former large landed estates. In capitalist agricultural enterprise the list of agricultural occupations embraces a large number of items, though still incomparably fewer than in any branch of industry. The emergence of capitalist agricultural enterprises takes place mainly in two ways:

1. By an increase in the area farmed. This is associated with a comparatively low level of production technique and the absence of clearly defined specialization.
2. By an increase in the level of production with the size of farm basically unchanged, in certain instances even with a reduced area (since this is a way of specialization which in some cases does not require a large area of land) and an increase in the input of abstract labour.

Obviously, these two ways may be interconnected and in many countries recently a rapid increase in large, mechanized and specialized farms, for instance, can be observed. Both these avenues of emergence of the capitalist agricultural enterprise have been developing lately on an even wider scale, in the form of enterprises which service farms. These first came into existence many years ago, chiefly in the form of co-operatives founded by the owners of farms which were small both in size and in level of production, and based mainly on family labour. They were first and foremost trading enterprises providing loans, loaning machinery, transport organizations and industrial enterprises for the provision of seed, fodder, seed potatoes, etc., the processing of milk, fruit, etc., as well as enterprises hiring out machinery or providing mechanized equipment for the farms (whether operated by the farmer or by personnel employed by the enterprise), etc. In certain branches of production they organized agricultural production itself and organized the farmers within a single production unit which, though loosely organized, still had a quite definite structure.[2] Recently the further emergence of economic institutions of this type has been noticeable in certain branches of agricultural production: the linking together of various economic activities within a single concern associated with a group of specialized agricultural enterprises. This organization supplies the raw materials needed for production, as well as machinery and implements, sometimes credit too; it may also be a customer and processor of produce; at times it also acts as the distributor. Hence this is a definite type of production association linking together a number of production units, especially good peasant farms, which are brought together as a single enterprise with a very wide-ranging set of production and service functions, and which, in consequence, are subordinated to the control of the enterprise. In this system of 'vertical consolidation' the farm owner becomes one of the links in the organization of the production process, and in fact plays the part of an employee with a particular occupational role in the given enterprise. There are obviously differences (advantageous and disadvantageous) between this kind of farmer and the hired wage worker. But the differences appear to be declining, while the degree of specialization in farming and of class differentiation of the peasant stratum are more advanced than ever before.

We have indicated the various ways in which the process of commercialization of farming works in capitalist conditions. This process has to be viewed against the wider background of occupational changes in the rural areas. The occupational structure of the non-agricultural rural population primarily includes groups of trades followed in urban industrial establishments. These include industrial workers, miners, building workers travelling to work in the towns, manual and non-manual workers in urban institutions, etc., all of whom live in the country. Second, the rural areas are inhabited by people belonging to occupational groups which directly service the production needs of the farms, as well as the increasingly diverse needs of the rural population generally, performing functions connected with the village as a place of residence, a nodal point in the communications network. The difficulty of distinguishing these two groups[3] is the cause of many problems in statistical analyses. It is nevertheless useful to do so, for it points to two factors moulding the occupational structure of the rural population. One is the flight from agricultural work. The other is the economic development of agriculture and its incorporation within the country's economic system, side by side with the growth of the village inhabitants' requirements and their desire to obtain the basic benefits available to urban inhabitants, which today are considered to be the minimum standard of living. Although we speak of the inhabitants' desires and needs it is often not so much these as activity on the part of the authorities, of social organizations or enterprises interested in extending their clientele that is the key factor.

Among these members of occupational groups already listed, who constitute an increasingly large proportion of the rural occupational structure, we have to include people owning land and running farms who turn to other occupations. Groups of part-time farmers, peasant handicraftsmen, peasant officials, etc., are not new phenomena. They have become numerous in every country lately. The numerical growth of these groups—an outcome of the general process of industrialization and urbanization —is one manifestation of the exodus from the small peasant farm and of the search for standards of living it does not provide and values it cannot provide (e.g. a specialized occupation). But it is not an irreversible exodus, whether it be due to lack of qualifications or to emerging or foreseen difficulties in adapting to the urban milieu and the desire to ensure the possibility of returning to the land in the event of failure. The emergence of farmers with dual occupations is often a result of the occupational independence of married couples: the wife takes over all the work of running the farm, for instance, while the husband takes a job away from it. It is possible to speak of dual occupation because the identification of the farm and the household makes it inevitable that the husband must work off the farm if he is to perform some of his agricultural production activities, since these are also 'domestic' activities.

Certain changes in the occupational structure of the rural population are caused by restrictions in the range of activities performed by the family. Certain facilities falling within the sphere of the home and the farm (baking bread, processing agricultural produce) and to some extent, too, educational and cultural functions are separated from the range of activities performed by the peasant family and taken over by institutions and service points, by people who undertake these activities as a specialized occupation.

In summary, the process of specialization in farming can be seen (1) in changes in the occupational structure of the rural population, including, among other things, the emergence of occupations which are based on activities traditionally performed

by the peasant family; (2) in the emergence of large or highly
productive farms based on a paid and occupationally differentiated team; (3) in the growth of specialization and of commodity
production, farms being increasingly organized via a system of
enterprises (trading, credit, processing, the servicing of agricultural production, etc.) within a large production aggregate with
varying degrees of organizational cohesiveness.

Thus the penetration of the commercial model into village life
and into agriculture is many-sided: through the restriction of the
range of activities performed by the farm family in all spheres;
through the separating out, within the peasant farm, of the functions of a producing unit and those of a domestic economic unit;
through the inclusion of the labour of specialized producers in a
complex of activities performed and directed within a larger production whole. With the penetration of the commercial model the
separation of the producers from ownership and control of the
means of production begins; in capitalist countries, this leads to
class polarization among the rural population.

All these manifestations of the commercialization of the
farmer's labour can be found in Poland, although the tempo of
the process differs and one has to take a different view of the
changes in class structure among the rural population which
result.

In 1960 about 32 per cent of the rural population were non-
agricultural residents (in 1931 about 20 per cent), while the 'dual
occupation' category constituted about 15 per cent (in the USA
the non-agricultural population constitutes about 60 per cent of
the rural residents). As noted above, it is difficult to divide the
non-agricultural population into one group functionally linked
with the village and with agriculture, and another connected with
the town and industry. Perhaps some guideline is provided by
the fact that among the non-farm-owning population, an estimated 45 per cent give the country as their place of work (including persons employed as hired labourers in agriculture[4]). The
occupational structure of the non-agricultural population employed in the rural areas varies greatly today. Besides traditional
occupations (teachers, priests, village craftsmen) there are those
which take over activities formerly performed by the peasant
family (bakeries, small establishments for agricultural produce
and food processing), as well as occupations associated with mech-

anization and increased sophistication:[5] the repair of motor-cycles, radio and television sets, the permanent personnel of village cinemas, etc.).

But it is a striking fact that even in a region of large-scale capital investment, where the influence of industry and the town on the village is already strong, the Plock district, 54 per cent of the farms still regularly or sometimes bake their own bread, 20 per cent process their own ham, etc., and 28 per cent make their own butter.[6] Thus the process of freeing the peasant family from activities which have long since been performed by other occupational groups does not occur as rapidly as changes in conditions which open up such possibilities.

A second factor in the specialization of farming work which has penetrated the sphere of agricultural production itself and has served to diminish the participation of the family unit in farming is the formation of various kinds of agricultural enterprise based on occupationally differentiated personnel.

In Poland almost the only type of large agricultural enterprise is the socialized type, such as the State Farms, run by industry, e.g. the industrialized stock-fattening centres, production co-operatives, farms run by dairy and market gardening co-operatives and Agricultural Circles, farms attached to agricultural schools and scientific institutions. The extent of their importance to agriculture is revealed by the fact that they account for more than 10 per cent of gross output and some 15 per cent of commodity production.

In 1960 370,000 persons were employed in socialized agriculture, or about 5.7 per cent of all those engaged in agriculture. (The figure for that segment of the population gainfully employed in individual farming was 6,108,000.) 4,500 of those engaged in socialized agriculture had higher educational qualifications, 6,500 had secondary vocational education and 10,000 had basic vocational training. The number of persons with vocational education engaged in individual farming is not known. Investigations by the IER, for instance in the Plock area, provide a picture which is fairly typical of central Poland; there the percentage of individual farm owners with no agricultural education, not even a course of instruction, was over 90 per cent.

The large socialized farm in Poland today shows a relatively minor advance in specialization of farming work, if occupational

qualifications can be taken as an index. The basic feature of a
specialized occupation—the exchange of individual for social
labour—is not uniformly present in the many different varieties
of this type of enterprise. People employed on State Farms undoubtedly follow definite vocations. However, the degree of education in agricultural occupations is relatively low if the large
proportion of unskilled labourers who can be put to various
tasks is taken into account. In addition, limited but persistent
forms of payment in kind, and older large-estate patterns of organization may still be observed (the whole family is often employed), and the retention here and there of *corvee* services,[7]
workers' individual plots, etc. All this is evidence of the low level
of development of the process of labour-specialization, and above
all of persisting landed-estate patterns of organizing farming.
These are the basic reasons why occupations associated with this
type of farm are not very attractive.[8] Of course, the situation will
change as the State Farms are modernized and go over to industrial forms of labour organization.

Although work on State Farms is not very attractive, this type
of work is relatively more popular than work on production
co-operatives. It is more frequently recognized as a type of employment with good prospects, and among certain groups of individual farmers the transfer of land to a State Farm, and transfer to
working on a State Farm, is recognized as a convenient solution
to economic problems.[9]

Production co-operatives undoubtedly make it possible also for
the commercial model of production to penetrate agriculture.
Certain of them, the more specialized, already work with occupationally differentiated teams. But the pattern of production
co-operatives which has been dominant so far necessitates their
being treated as associations of producing families. A considerable
part of the product is shared out among the families and used to
satisfy their immediate needs. The basis of the family's maintenance—sometimes the main part—is derived from the private plot.
So the families associated in a production co-operative (formally,
membership of a co-operative is on an individual, not a family
basis, but it is in fact an association of families) derive their means
of support from (1) the private individual plot, which it works
itself, and (2) the common farm, which it works together with the
other families. The extent to which the organization of the pro-

duction co-operative is tied into the organization of production in society as a whole is determined by the marketability of the co-operative's product, and also by the amount of output from private plots, which may be considerable. Thus the occupational situation of production co-operative members, and the state of the process of labour specialization, are not much better than those of families farming individually. Here, *inter alia*, is one source of the low popularity of the production co-operatives (in 1961 there were 1,534 such co-operatives, involving 14,000 families). The emergence of collective agricultural enterprises obviously opens up possibilities of extending the commercial pattern of agricultural production, but as yet this process has not gone far. In passing it should be noted that administrative acceleration of the process (for instance, by legislative restrictions on private plots) has a rather detrimental effect, both on the development of the co-operative and on the general level of agricultural production.

The increase in the number of State Farms and production co-operatives, and their improvement, is undoubtedly the way in which the commercial model of production (which in Polish conditions is bound up with the socialization of property) will penetrate agriculture. This also applies to some extent to the system of control of the means of production (workers' self-government in the State Farms and the principles governing the functioning of production co-operatives).

Another way which is new in Polish conditions is through the formation of a system of enterprises servicing the peasant farms and partially taking over certain production and other economic activities which were traditionally performed by the family itself. This system is now widely developed. In 1961 there were 2,678 trading co-operatives in the rural areas, with 3,692,000 members; 1,471 savings and loan co-operatives, with 2,065,000 members; 659 dairy co-operatives, with 774,000 members; 136 market gardening co-operatives, with 196,000 members; and numerous labour, craft, building, medical and similar co-operatives at work in the rural areas. The most important element in this system at present is the Agricultural Circle. In 1961 there were 25,000 of these, together with 13,000 Circles of Rural Housewives, a joint total of 907,000 members. The Agricultural Circles are very closely involved in agricultural production and dispose of considerable funds (some seven million zlotys from the Fund for Agricultural Development in 1961) and possess as well a large pool of machinery (14,000 tractors). Further elements in this system are the State Machinery Centres (4,500 tractors, 36,000 workers), and other State enterprises such as sugar refineries, retting works, starch works and distilleries, which all base their production activities on direct contact with the farmers by means of contractual agreements. (In 1961 some 600,000 hectares of arable land were involved in contractual cultivation.)

The term 'system of enterprises', in relation to the above data, is used in the sense of an indicator of growth, for so far they have been simply enterprises operating in various branches of agriculture, and greatly interested in extending their activities so as to become centres linking up the peasant farms with which they are in contact into a compact production whole. In recent years notions about the 'vertical consolidation' of agriculture, especially a State investment system,[10] have been canvassed, and experiments in this direction have occurred. If such a system develops, it may well accelerate greatly the penetration of the commercial model of production organization into agriculture.

The general schema outlined above of the ways in which commercial models of production can be introduced into agriculture is meant only to provide an orientation to the central problems of agricultural modernization. Studies now being carried out of the types of organization operating in agriculture will possibly provide a more satisfactory analysis.

Studies are also being made of another aspect of this same process, namely changes occurring in peasant farming. Here the process of specialization of labour is characterized mainly by the development of entrepreneurial elements, as an example of which may be cited the following indicators (obtained by research in Plock province).[11] Some 80 per cent of the farms studied (2,910 families, living in four *gromadas*) are specialized in one way or another, mainly in livestock breeding; in 86 per cent of the farms commodity production accounts for 50 per cent of the final product (in 44 per cent, commodity production amounts to over 75 per cent of the total). Contractual production covers 55 per cent of vegetable output in terms of value, and 18 per cent of the animal products. (Ninety per cent of the farmers are covered by contract agreements.) Nevertheless, 92 per cent of the farmers have had no agricultural education, and the farms are run on the traditional lines of the family economy. Of the children aged between 7 and 14, 36·6 per cent help regularly on the farm. Older children (over 14) who work on the farm, of course, receive no regular remuneration; only 6·4 per cent receive regular allowances for personal expenses, while 16·6 per cent get allowances irregularly, whenever the parents deem it necessary. Sixty-four per cent of the families also perform particular tasks in the household (activities such as produce processing, baking bread, etc., which were mentioned above).

Some figures illustrating commonly known phenomena provide a very general picture of the degree of development in the specialization of farm work entailed in changes in agriculture. In the Plock villages the system of enterprises servicing the peasant farms was not so well developed as to make a thorough study of their prevalence in agricultural production possible. Fifteen per cent of the farmers made use of the services of the Agricultural Circle, chiefly with regard to machinery. Both this situation and others indicated by facts given above will be more thoroughly analysed in a separate work to be based on the poll conducted by the IER in 1962. For the moment, our concern is simply to indicate the nature of this set of problems and to provide very general background information. Moreover, the specialization of farming work has been dealt with from only one point of view, namely that of the formation of a system of agricultural enterprises and the rather slow transformation of the peasant farm type of agriculture.

In pointing to this aspect of the problem, it should be observed that although the process of commercialization is taking a course analogous to that followed in capitalist countries, one fundamental difference does exist. This difference arises from the fact that in Poland the possibility of capitalist enterprises coming into being is practically nil. Consequently in Poland this process does not lead to the increasing differentiation in the system of ownership of the means of production and the formation of a class structure based on a division into rural capitalists and proletarians.

Hence the penetration of the commercial mode of production into the village is not associated with class polarization based on differentiation in the system of ownership. The same complex of determinants which in capitalist countries gives rise

to new occupations and to classes, operates in favour of the
farmer in Polish conditions. But if differentiation on the basis
of ownership of the means of production is not the basis of the
formation of social alignments in present-day Polish rural society, does occupation provide such a basis?

In the light of the picture of the process we outlined above,
the answer would seem to be in the negative. It might be expected that the moulding of the system of enterprises in agriculture will in time lead to the emergence of new production
entities in which at first the peasant farm will be an element,
but which will eventually yield to an organizationally more
compact type of enterprise corresponding to that of industry.
The motivating forces are economic institutions: the State and
co-operative enterprises, i.e. people who by their specialized
work are involved in the development of the enterprise and are
interested in extending its range of operation. But it is difficult
to treat them as a social force, in the sense given the term in
chapter 5.

However, the primary motivating force is the activity of
farmers. They themselves make the decision to join production
co-operatives or to transfer their land to State Farms. They conclude contractual and labour agreements with the Machinery
Centre and the Agricultural Circle; they invest in the trading
co-operatives and in Agricultural Circles for the purchase of
machinery. They themselves also have to decide whether to establish closer contacts with this or that enterprise, whether to
subordinate themselves to the enterprise's production plans and
to decisions of the management, and, finally, they themselves
will have to decide whether to exchange the position of co-
producer for that of worker. These decisions do not necessarily
call for faith in a great idea and in the happiness of future
generations. Rather, they are often the result of sober calculation or even of taking advantage of offers and propositions
which bring them direct and palpable benefits.

Even if the formation of occupational groups in agriculture
is looked at only from the point of view of the need to undertake the decisions indicated above, studies of the process of
specialization of farm work cannot be restricted to objective
changes in peasant farming and in agriculture as a whole. It is
also necessary to investigate the farmers' way of thinking about

questions affecting their farms, especially about contacts between the farm and enterprises in the process of formation or which already function. It is necessary to investigate how farmers see the difference between their vocation and those of other people, what associations the term 'occupation' has for them, and whether they regard a specialized occupation or the transformation of farm work into such an occupation as something desirable. Furthermore, we have to study the determinants of their occupational activity, and the basis of authority in the village: the extent to which they are successful or wealthy farmers, with special qualifications and attitudes to agricultural science, the extent to which they take advantage of the opportunities open to them of increasing their knowledge and encouraging their children to follow the same path. Finally, farmers' views on the future of agriculture are important, especially their ideas of what modern agriculture ought to look like if it is to give the farmer a position of equality with other vocations.

The answers to these questions would make it possible to formulate definite views on the prospects not only for the specialization of farm work but also for the socialization of the agricultural means of production. They would also throw light on likely patterns of social alignment based on occupation. The development of such social alignments depends not only upon individual peasant families becoming involved in the system of socialized agricultural enterprises now developing, but also perhaps upon the type of occupational ideology being formed: a consciousness of the necessity for change towards definite goals and a sense of the need for organized activity if these goals are to be reached. If the results of research were to confirm these hypotheses, occupation might not only become the basis of the formation of social alignments via class–occupational relationships—and thus not only as a 'school' of class thinking—but might also turn into an independent social force, which, in Polish conditions (where changes in rural social structure do not provide any basis for the growth of social alignments of a class nature), would make it possible to see occupation as the source of a system of forces grounded in those same determinants which in other social systems bring into being social classes and occupations. The arguments developed above, however, based on the study of 'objective' change, cannot provide us with answers to these questions.

Notes

1   K Kautsky, *The agrarian question*; V. I. Lenin, *The development of capitalism in Russia, cit.*
2   See L. Krzywicki, *Kwestja rolna* (*The agrarian question*), Warsaw, 1903.
3   R. Turski, *Miedzy miastem a wsia, cit.*
4   J. Przychodzen, 'Struktura spoleczno-zawodowa . . .', *cit.*
5   See R. Turski, *op. cit.*
6   In 1961 the IER Workshop on Rural Social Structure studied thirty villages in the Plock area.
7   Studies carried out by J. Poniatowski for the Committee on Social Agronomy of the Institute of Philosophy and Sociology of the Polish Academy of Sciences.
8   See W. Wesolowski and A. Sarapata, 'Hierarchie zawodow i stanowisk' ('Hierarchies of occupations and positions'), *Studia socjologiczne* (*Sociological Studies*), 1961, No. 2.
9   L. M. Szwengrub's research in six villages of Gniezno county.
10   J. Tepicht, *Doswiadczenia i perspektywy rolnictwa, cit.*
11   The Plock villages can be taken as typical of central Poland.

7 Determinants of rural social change: sociological problems of the contemporary Polish village

An understanding of the social differences which mark the village off from the urban world is fundamental to any sociological analysis of rural society as a separate branch of social science. The interpretation of those differences is not only the basis of its theory but also provides a basis for defining its scope as well as defining the position of rural sociology *vis-a-vis* sociology generally. This point of departure for rural sociology raises a question, which, though it has a rather nineteenth century flavour, is still being discussed today. Put simply, the question is: can the known differences be treated as differences in rural society so great as to constitute a fundamentally different social system—i.e. a society which, though not necessarily closed, functions and changes according to its own principles—or can these differences be explained simply in terms of the historical backwardness of the village as compared with the town?[1] Are these differences, therefore, to put it even more simply, just differences in *tempo*, or differences in the sources and the direction of change as well?

A general definition of rural sociology is involved here. Either we recognize it as an independent science with its own body of theory, its own terminology and its own methods, or—to put the point in extreme form—we restrict it to the description of social phenomena observed in environments conventionally isolated and defined as 'rural'.

Observation of contemporary change in the village, particularly changes connected with the growth of industrialization and urbanization, throws new light on this question, which we have raised in very general form. In certain countries many older social differences between the village and the town no longer exist;[2] while the indications are that those which we regard today as most characteristic will disappear in the future.

The issues in rural sociology mentioned in the Introduction are not, however, so attractive that rural social change is studied

solely out of theoretical interest. Practical considerations play a
much bigger and more direct role. The village and agriculture
are the objects of activity on the part of central institutions which
direct the economic and social life of their countries, and their
activities lead to many extremely difficult problems which have
to be solved. Observation of social change in the village and in
agriculture is vital both for evaluating the effects of operations
already undertaken and for planning future ones. Naturally,
rural sociology has to deal with a different social reality in each
country, and different answers will emerge from asking different
questions. Rural sociology formulates its research problems in
various ways, depending on the nature of the social forces whose
interests are realized by the circles which run the country, on
their objectives, and on the social situation in which the activity
of these circles is both co-determinant and an element. For all
these reasons, this summary presentation of contemporary rural
change refers to today's Polish village. The analogies which come
to mind, however, suggest that the phenomena under discussion
are of a wider relevance; so that some may seem as typical of the
present era in general, while others pertain only to countries in
which individual peasant farms exist. Yet others apply only to
these socialist countries where the general policy of the State
includes, to one degree or another, the notion of the abolition of
contradictions between country and town.

    In this chapter, we will develop and bring together some of
the themes discussed in earlier chapters and examine the nature
of the changes taking place in rural society. Let us begin with
an institution usually neglected in rural sociology, namely the
peasant farm.

The peasant farm and farming as an occupation

We have seen that in its traditional form—not yet, in Poland,
a thing of the past—the peasant farm differs from other production establishments not only in what is produced but also in
how it is produced, who produces it, and for whom. Commodities produced elsewhere are destined to be consumed by society
generally and must be accepted by it (by being either purchased,
or acquired in other ways). But the products of peasant farming

are only partially subject to this mechanism, for a considerable proportion of them—incomparably more than in any other production unit—is destined to be consumed by the family working the farm, and is hence not subject to 'acceptance' by society in the sense used here. Thus the peasant farm, to a large extent, eludes the broader social mechanisms which almost totally determine the operations of other economic institutions. The fact that the peasant farm produces foodstuffs (the basic means of existence), and the complexity of the production process (biological processes), make it possible for these differences to persist, though not as a decisive factor. For the distinctive features of peasant farming cannot be reduced to a difference in the character of the product alone, nor to differences in the technology of production; they are *social* differences.

In its traditional form, therefore, the peasant farm is a *combination of domestic economy unit and an enterprise* (a production unit producing commodities). Further, it is both of these at one and the same time, and neither commercial considerations (as certain economists believe) nor consumption considerations alone, as Chayanov considered to be the case,[3] fully explain its functioning. This feature cannot be found to any important extent in other kinds of production unit. The place of production may also be the producer's dwelling place (handicrafts, cottage industry); the product may, to one extent or another, be consumed by the owner and his family. Payment may be in kind (on large farms). But all these phenomena (which are actually uncommon nowadays) still do not adequately define the peculiar identification of the domestic economy with the enterprise. This combination occurs only when a considerable part of the farm's products are consumed by the producer and his family themselves; when, in consequence, the path from production to realization does not have to pass in some way through the mechanism of social acceptance, and when productive labour largely follows the patterns which obtain in the domestic economy. Making use of an exaggerated analogy, it can be said that productive labour on the peasant farm is of the same order as that of a woman who prepares meals for her family.

Hence, the domestic economy functions on different principles from those of the enterprise. Profitability and other economic categories which are vital to the operation of an enterprise cannot be meaningfully applied, or are not of decisive importance. To state that the traditional peasant farm combines the features of a domestic economy with those of an enterprise is to say that it functions on the basis of two different, and in certain respects opposed, principles. Although it is not compelled to do so, it must at the same time fulfil many of the demands of economic rationalization. In many respects it is dependent on, and in other respects independent of, broader economic mechanisms. One can illustrate this in many ways. For instance, the argument that horses are not profitable on small farms is not decisive in situations where ownership of a horse is a condition of high status. On a small farm a tractor is also unprofitable, but the farmer may buy it for convenience or, for example, in order to stimulate the interest of his son in the farm. On the other hand, one can cite many examples which show that peasant farming reacts to market stimuli, though not always in a manner as economically rational as other production units. Yet so far as the traditional peasant farmer is concerned one cannot say that he will always be governed in matters affecting his farm by those economic considerations which are viewed as decisive by managers in every other kind of production enterprise. Of course, we do not deny the utility of economic analyses of peasant farming. On the contrary, they are indispensable for many purposes—to get some idea of the input–output ratio in the national economy for instance, which after all includes peasant agriculture. They are also important for the understanding of peasant farming. But we do not consider that this kind of analysis fully explains the principles of its functioning (even as far as the production aspect alone is concerned).

The most superficial glance at peasant farming reveals the need for sociological analysis. For many problems, e.g. the now fundamental one of technical progress in the village, such an analysis is indispensable. An agronomist who is not familiar with sociology—and the agronomists of the future are not so trained in Polish educational institutions—may, as Mendras writes,[4] spend a long time persuading a farmer to introduce two more productive cows instead of four less productive ones. His arguments will remain ineffective if one element of village prestige is associated with ownership and not with the contribution the cows make in terms of production. In this kind of situation sociological analysis of the rural system of prestige would be at least as necessary as research into profitability.

However, the characteristics of peasant farming raise considerably wider sociological problems, such as the nature of farming as an occupation. The difficulties of applying this term to peasant labour on the traditional farm have often been pointed out. Naturally, the point is not whether this labour can or cannot be defined as 'pursuit of an occupation'—that depends on one's definition of the term. The question is whether the obvious differences between the farmer's occupation and all others are reducible not so much to the techniques involved in farming but to the social relationships involved. As noted above, the peasant farmer, or, more precisely, the peasant family, works to a large extent directly for itself. Everybody else works for society, and obtains his means of existence from society through the operation of extant social mechanisms. This results from the social division of labour, and the concept of 'occupation' involves the individual's relationship to society. The peasant farmer's work lies partly outside this social mechanism, for he himself creates the basic means of existence for himself and his family. So it is not related to society to the same extent as work in other specializations. The peasant's production activity seems largely to have retained certain features of undifferentiated family production from which, perhaps, various specific occupations have become separated at various times. Hence it is difficult to use the phrase 'specialized occupation' in its everyday meaning, and one peasant's remark, 'I have no particular occupation, I'm on the farm', must be regarded as characteristic.

The nature of farm work on the traditional peasant farm raises further problems. Here the farmer is the owner. But ownership is a category originating from another system, at least as it is specified in lists of occupations. In traditional peasant farming, 'farmer' and 'husbandman' (owner) are synonyms, and it is not possible to separate these two social roles. Two examples may be cited which may afford a better understanding of these difficulties, which are by no means simply terminological.

The first is that of preparation for the occupation of farmer. On the traditional peasant farm this occurs in the course of the child's socialization within the family. The child assimilates occupational habits and skills together with all the 'wisdom of life' with which the parents endeavour to endow it. The father's authority is simultaneously that of the craftsman, while the actual acquisition of knowledge to a large extent takes the form of occupational apprenticeship.[5] Perhaps this is the origin of the fact that the farming system dominant in the village has behind it, like moral norms, the force of social compulsion. This makes the diffusion of new methods difficult, for they are only thinly spread, even though they are obviously the most rational, and this inhibits the discarding of accepted methods even when they have ceased to be efficient. The future peasant farmer achieves his occupational position via the family: marriage and then inheritance of the farm are the factors which determine whether and when he will become an independent farmer. In this system of preparation for occupations in traditional peasant farming there is no place for the agricultural school. The agricultural school, like other schools (apart from the lowest classes of the primary school), is the road to the world, not to the farm.[6] A poll conducted among pupils who finished agricultural school in Poland showed that only an insignificant proportion (some 4 per cent) saw their future in terms of returning to their father's farm.[7] So even in Poland, where the need for vocational training seems to be widely recognized in the villages, and widely advocated,[8] the occupation of farmer still retains its traditional features.

Another example in this sphere is the question of occupational prestige and advancement. As a rule, the owner of a small farm is not recognized as a 'good farmer',[9] and the view is also widespread that in general he could not be a good farmer. The rungs of the ladder of the occupational hierarchy are largely determined by the size of the farm. In this respect peasant farmers display characteristics resembling such categories as *rentiers* or owners of enterprises, with whom they can be classified as constituting a specific category within the occupational system.

Sociological analysis of farming as an occupation, together with analysis of the peasant farm, is of major relevance for policy in present-day Poland. The diminished social status of farming as an occupation; the feeble contribution of the agricultural school towards raising the level of skill typical of most agricultural producers (owners of individual peasant farms); the barriers obstructing the penetration of technical progress within the village; the role of the Agricultural Circles as organizations of innovators—these are only some of the problems calling for sociological analysis of farming as an occupation. Such an analysis would be most helpful in thinking about the future of the village and of agriculture. Which leads us back to the question of social change.

The characteristics of the traditional peasant farm and of farming as an occupation, if the term 'occupation' be allowed, refer only to characteristics often neglected in the literature (or at least presented in them in a different way), and relate to the dominant type of farm in the contemporary Polish countryside (roughly 75 per cent of owners of individual peasant farms[10]). This type is naturally an ideal construction. In reality we have to deal with varying degrees of persistence of traditional characteristics on particular farms, and in particular regions and categories. Differentiation of this kind reflects the processes of change which have been occurring.

Since we have accepted that the peasant farm is a combination of both domestic economy and enterprise, then, logically, we need to concentrate above all on changes in the relative weight of these two elements. The first striking fact is the growth of the entrepreneurial component. Changes in this direction have been proceeding for a long time and have been noted again and again.[11] Now, however, the rate of change has accelerated considerably. Intensified social division of labour has separated off particular branches of agricultural activity from peasant farming (recently, for instance, egg and poultry production); specialization has increased, as well the share of 'social' labour in peasant farming; marketable output has grown, as has rationalization in many countries as a result of administrative action. All these indicators make empirical confirmation of this process possible. It has also been demonstrated for Poland, particularly in recent years.[12] The above indicators suggest that the process is taking place not only on the peasant farms, but also in relation to the social aspects of farming as an occupation.

But it is also necessary to point to a different—indeed, opposite—direction of change. At present this is only a theoretical possibility, though it has already begun to occur in reality. Analysis of the so-called 'peasant–workers' who are quite numerous in many countries today,[13] has revealed that many of them develop as a result of the certain features of domestic economy, in that they begin with the cultivation of kitchen gardens geared solely to meeting the family's consumption needs. Other indicators, particularly the much lower proportion of commodity production on part-time farms, point in the same direction.[14] This development is also associated with changes in the pattern of labour, namely, the farm owner is employed outside agriculture, and hence has a definitely non-agricultural occupation. The significance of this development is considerable, since the number of peasant–workers' holdings in Poland has been estimated at approximately one million, and it is thus not a question of a splinter group but of a mass phenomenon. (We shall examine these problems below.)

The intensification of the entrepreneurial elements in traditional peasant farming raises the questions of the sources and social consequences of the farmers' occupational activity, as well as the direction of change. The rapid growth of industrial enterprises, the increase in their technical complexity and in the productivity of labour, the rationalization of their structure, etc., have in the past been attributed to the central influence of competition. Enterprises which reduced production costs and rationalized production gained additional profit; those left behind in this race for technical modernization and economic rationalization went bankrupt. But in traditional peasant farming these factors were never so important. To a large extent, peasant farming was not linked to wider economic mechanisms, notably the market, and was less susceptible to the effects of competition than industrial enterprises. Even under difficult economic conditions (such as a fall in prices) it could survive without going bankrupt. The growth of the market for agricultural products, arising out of increased industrialization and urbanization, strengthens the influence of market stimuli but weakens competition to such an extent that in Poland this factor has ceased to play any serious role.

But the development of industry has an even greater significance, for by making new goods available it stimulates the farmer's wants both as producer (entrepreneur) and as consumer, and thus encourages him to broaden his production and market contacts. Migration is also of great importance, both as a result of the exodus of labour, which necessitates modernization of the farm, and through the extension of contacts between the peasant family, i.e. the village and the 'world'. The development of transport and mass communications also works in this direction. Moreover, the development of industry, and, more broadly, the general economic development of the country, lead to the penetration of the system of industrial production into fields hitherto unaffected by it. Social division of labour is thus extended, and in consequence there is a narrowing of specialization in peasant farming and in farming as an occupation. Finally, an important part is played by the increased demands made on the farmer, for instance a minimum of agricultural education, prohibitions on the partition of farms, etc.

In examining the stimuli motivating the farmer's occupational activity, very little attention has hitherto been paid to the mode of operation of the peasant farm. To a large extent it functions like the household economy, but there are also forces working towards modernization. The needs which have to be satisfied, as established by prevailing cultural norms, involve both individual and family obligations. Both as producer and consumer, the farmer has to deal not with an anonymous society but to a large extent with himself. There is no one to shelter behind, nor are there any social mechanisms which release him from his personal responsibility. But since the work must be done, anything which makes it easier will be attractive in the last resort, despite the initial resistances mentioned above. The introduction of improvements—agricultural machinery, for example—is a factor changing the traditional peasant farm in the direction of becoming an enterprise. The farm gains from improvements which represent social labour for society. But when improvements are introduced they change both the production possibilities and the producer's attitude. In the language of cybernetics one can say that, especially lately, intensification of the entrepreneurial elements in peasant farming resembles a feed-back mechanism. As a result, the traditional peasant farm, in which incentives to commercial activity are limited, becomes transformed into an enterprise when other stimuli come into play on a larger scale—in so far, of course, as the general economic system of the given country allows these stimuli to operate at all.

In connection with the farmer's motivation, attention is sometimes drawn to his 'attachment to the patrimony' or to the importance of 'ownership'. Without denying the significance of feelings of attachment to values inherited from the previous generation (the land), one should point out that mass migration from village to town warns us not to over-estimate the significance of this factor. Ownership is not always connected with the presence of such sentiments, and these in their turn do not always derive from ownership. To restrict the sources of motivation solely to the explanation that farmers are usually owners of the land is surely an over-simplification; in general, motivation cannot be reduced to the operation of a single factor.

The intensification of entrepreneurial features within the traditional peasant farm has far-reaching consequences. The characteristics of the farmer's occupation change; technical, biological and economic knowledge (and consequently the agricultural school) become important, first as an ideal and then as a normal standard. Contacts with the urban world increase and, with the penetration of new values, the farm is drawn into orbit of the wider society outside the family and the village, etc. These changes in their turn influence the intensification of the entrepreneurial features. Each of these developments has been the subject of specialized sociological analyses. Among the various problems which arise we draw attention to one which is closely bound up with the future, namely the limits of the process of transforming the peasant farm into an enterprise.

Economic categories become important in this process. The central social agencies directing economic life evaluate farming in terms of these categories; for society in general the main question is that of increases in the prices of agricultural products, and in many countries the need to subsidize agriculture. These categories also become important for the farmer-entrepreneur, since he is troubled by increases in production costs arising from the need to increase investment in order to ensure higher output. But thinking about the agricultural enterprise even in economic terms inevitably involves consideration of the greater effectiveness of specialized teams, of the economic exploitation of machinery, etc., i.e. the characteristic features of the rational, large-scale enterprise.

Must a large-scale, rational agricultural enterprise rid itself of the main characteristics of traditional peasant farming, namely the family character of labour? This does occur when it becomes a large capitalist enterprise based on hired labour, usually specialized in what it produces and linked to an industrial enterprise. In large-scale capitalist agricultural enterprises the complete separation of the domestic economy from the farm takes place, and a split between the dual social roles of the peasant farmer's activity (as owner, and at times administrator, and as worker carrying out specialized tasks) occurs. The sociological features of a farm of this kind are not much different from those of non-agricultural enterprises. There has been much discussion in Western literature lately of large family farms. Examples are cited of the possibilities of large farms (of 100 hectares, for instance), completely mechanized and based only on family labour. Usually these references are of the nature of publicity material, and it is difficult to see how such farms actually operate. However, it may be worth while drawing attention to two questions. First, farms of this kind are usually composed of a group of more or less specialized enterprises, usually employing a large labour force and using a large stock of machinery. They are often co-operatives, with the result that the members are usually the farmers and not hired personnel. Such enterprises carry on very varied activities, including field labour; they engage in a number of activities, such as stock-rearing, sorting and packing, transport and marketing. They thus take over a considerable part of the work previously performed by the family. Obviously, this system is more or less well developed from one country to another. The completely developed form is the exception, but so are 'large family farms'. It is difficult, however, to imagine agriculture without such a system in many countries. In this case, it would seem that what is entailed is the complete separation of the domestic economy from the enterprise, and of the occupational role of the peasant farmer from the vocational and social aspects which it still retains today: the roles of owner, production organizer, merchant, technician with various kinds of skills, tractor driver, transport worker, etc.

But it is not only economic mechanisms which are working in this direction. The transformation of the peasant farm into an enterprise, and its increase in size or in degree of specialization and volume of production, leave little room for family life, if the family really wishes to run the farm by itself, and even if it avails itself to some extent of the services of specialized enterprises. With mechanization, rational organization and other

features of the contemporary enterprise come other values accepted in the urban milieu: occupational specialization, free
time, forms of recreation, the urban way of life. It would seem
that on a large peasant family farm the interests of the enterprise
and those of the domestic economy come into conflict. This clash
is not resolved by the present-day level of mechanization, especially since the limits of profitability grow narrower with the
growth of entrepreneurial features. Sociological analysis reveals
the existence of these phenomena not only in the capitalist
world, where they are more easily visible, but also in Poland.
Some particularly interesting material is supplied by description
of extreme cases, i.e. farms in which the intensification of entrepreneurial features has gone furthest.[15]

The possibility of capitalist farms, or co-operatives with capitalist features, coming into existence are practically nil in Poland.
In socialist countries the basic form of the large farm is the
collective peasant farm, the production co-operative. However,
this form, at least in the shape it has usually taken up to now,
has not proved very popular in Poland.[16] Of course, one cannot
treat the production co-operatives model as static, and important
changes are occurring in them in all socialist countries, where
ways of modernizing them are being studied. The reasons for
their low popularity among Polish farmers may lie not only in
the fact that the farm violates the principles of the traditional
peasant farm and its way of life, but also in the fact that it does
not provide the advantages connected with industrial life and
life in town, which constitute the recognized pattern of modernity. Until now the production co-operative has retained many of
the features of the traditional peasant farm: its comprehensive-
ness, its connection with the household economy through the
complicated institution of personal garden plots, the absence of
rigid occupational specialization and of a rational organizational structure, and the absence of the division of responsibility
and specialization of tasks which are typical of the enterprise.
It has also retained many of the disadvantages of peasant farming, for instance the lack of regular earnings, of insurance against
old age, of social security, and so on; it does not bring the
peasant farmer within the orbit of the wider society as is the
case with other occupations. Nor is the peasant farmer any
longer independent of outside labour.

The retention of these traditional features of peasant farming was intended to facilitate farmers' acceptance of co-operatives. Co-operative regulations stressed 'educational' tasks, but irrespective of type the co-operative has emerged as a large, multi-family peasant farm, in principle embracing the entire village. Perhaps changes now occurring will lead to the emergence of completely different types which the farmer might accept as being 'modern'. And instead of thinking in terms of one single 'educational' road, it might be better to envisage the organization of specialized enterprises based on permanent, qualified personnel, taking over various kinds of activity hitherto combined in peasant farming as a generalized occupation. This will depend on the balance of forces as between tradition and 'modernity' in the Polish village, and on the meanings which peasant farmers associate with 'modernity'. So far these matters have scarcely been studied.

The design of a model for the agricultural enterprise of the future is obviously a practical question. Sociological analysis of changes in peasant farming and in farming as an occupation, of the peasant farmer's views on his conditions of work and his vocation, and of the functioning of production co-operatives in Poland (not undertaken so far) could give us a fuller knowledge of the changes taking place as social differentiation between country and town develops, and could help lay the empirical foundations of future plans for the village and for agriculture. Analysis of the changes occurring in the second basic institution of village life, the peasant family, will lead us to the same problems from a somewhat different angle.

The peasant family: family–neighbour bonds

We have devoted more space to the changes occurring in peasant farming because they are rarely analysed by sociologists, and works dealing with this area of study seldom go beyond a stereotyped compilation of economic data. The same holds true for the study of farming as an occupation. Only in recent years have preliminary explorations of this area begun to appear in Poland. These questions undoubtedly require sociological analysis of economic situations and their relationship to social consciousness, and hence suggest an approach which links up various

branches of knowledge—mainly rural sociology and agricultural
economics. This is perhaps why they do not enjoy much success.
The situation is different as far as the rural family, or, more
precisely, the peasant family, is concerned. There are numerous
studies of the family in general in the world literature, and undoubtedly these help us in studying the rural family. Moreover,
these works have not only contributed to theory but have also
accumulated considerable substantive information. No broad
and systematic analysis of changes in the mode of life of the
traditional peasant family was undertaken in Poland after the
war. Although we possess quite sophisticated theoretical analyses
of the traditional family, empirical data[17] are far more meagre
than data on changes in peasant farming. Here we will discuss,
in more extended fashion than is usual, those problems of the
peasant family which are most definitely related to the central
theoretical issues in rural sociology and which seem to be the
most crucial in operational thinking about the future of the
Polish village.

Rural sociology is interested primarily in those differences between the rural and urban family which are associated with
other social differences between town and country, and which
provide us with a better understanding or explanation of the
distinctive features of the village as a separate social system with
its own dynamics. Among these differences, listed in almost every
textbook of rural sociology, and penetratingly illuminated in
the well known work by Thomas and Znaniecki,[18] one in particular should be singled out which could prove especially useful
in studying change in the village. This is the family's links with
the farm (discussed above, in the form of the proposition that
the traditional peasant farm is a combination of domestic economy and enterprise), and the link between the family and farming as an occupation, based on the family's participation in
productive labour and the way in which the family operates as
an institution.

A traditional feature of the peasant family is the identification
of its interests with the farm. The farm is the basis of the family's
maintenance, its insurance for the future and the basis of its
prestige. It is the common good of the family, a heritage passed
down from generation to generation. The replacement of both
parents and the future succession of their children is central, as

well as the labour contribution of all members of the family. The farm requires the solidarity of the family if they are to work it as a heritage and exploit it for their common good. The family are the farm's production team; a person's position in the family determines his obligations towards the farm, the allocation of tasks and the privileges associated with different work rules. The rhythm of the farm sets the rhythm of family life. In the traditional peasant family the combined interests of farm and family have a decisive influence on the destinies of its members: the child's opportunities of education, its chances of being sent to earn a living in the outside world, its choice of marriage partner, are all looked at from the point of view of protecting those interests.

Contemporary social changes in this kind of family and its mode of life are bringing about a blurring of the features which differentiate it from the urban family (as pointed out above in discussing the peasant farm). The growth of entrepreneurial characteristics eventually causes a weakening of the family's productive functions as well as the solidarity of the family farm, although, in our view, for a time it can also lead to a hypertrophy of these functions to the detriment of others. Of course, these changes are not one-way: the family farm depends on society also, and the sources of change lie mainly outside village life and derive from the general development of society, particularly the development of industrialization and urbanization. These developments penetrate into the entire system through one channel or another.

The changes are of many kinds. With the intensification of entrepreneurial features on the peasant farm, commercial attitudes towards farming develop.[19] Specialization in farm work weakens its family character. The introduction of improvements makes the existing division of labour out of date. Young people's earnings off the farm increase their independence and hence weaken family solidarity. Mass emigration to the town, even if it only amounts to the 'disposable' labour-power[20] of the villages, takes away not only those who should go (from the viewpoint of the interests of family and farm) but also those who ought to remain. The widening of the peasant family's contacts with the outside world opens the way for the penetration of new values, and makes new patterns of life originating in the town almost obligatory. This is most visible in the attitudes of young people, who almost universally want to take up skilled occupations, to acquire training and qualifications in jobs with opportunities of advancement, the right to holidays and recreation—all the benefits which modern technology makes possible. Marriage based on romantic love and aspirations towards a private life, impossible in rural society, also become attractive.[21]

When we refer to patterns of change in the peasant farm and family we do not mean that the basic characteristics of the traditional peasant family no longer exist in Poland. They are still fairly universal, and regard for the farm and the family is the most frequent motivation for the youth to remain in the village.[22] The criteria governing choice of marriage partner are certainly formulated differently in the statements people make today as compared to twenty-five years ago. However, if we examine which farms present-day couples come from it soon becomes apparent that no very definite changes have occurred so far.[23] Entrepreneurial features in peasant farming and specialization in farm work are not developing fast enough[24] to indicate any very marked weakening of the family's production functions. More obvious changes have occurred in the form of demand for higher living standards and more sophisticated cultural facilities: in the general spread of urban life styles; and in a decline in the family's educational functions. The latter is perhaps due less to the growth in importance of the school than to tendency of young people to work in the towns and to urban influence generally. Although the typical traditional peasant family is still common in the Polish village, it appears to be on the decline, since changes both in Poland and in the rest of the world all tend in the same general direction.

In discussing changes in the structure and functioning of the peasant family, it is impossible to ignore one of its principal characteristics which used to be emphasized by sociologists studying rural life but which is now definitely dying out. We refer to the multi-generation peasant family. The fact that the peasant family was usually a large one determined many of its other traditional features, but above all it provided a basis for a sense of the continuity of the farm as the central element in the cultural heritage passed down from generation to generation.[25]

The peasant family in its multi-generation form is becoming

a thing of the past everywhere in the world, including Poland. In Poland the present-day peasant family usually consists of parents and children—a nuclear family—and does not differ greatly in composition from its urban counterpart. Its average size is four persons, and there are now very few multi-family domestic economies.[26] As a rule, when young people marry today they leave the paternal farm and establish independent farms and households. The decay of the multi-generation family weakens its other traditional features and loosens wider family–neighbour bonds.

Sociological analyses of the rural local community attach a great deal of importance to family–neighbour bonds. Often the villages originate from a single family,[27] and the village is either treated as a large family or defined as a family–neighbour group.[28] Undoubtedly, to a large extent ties of kinship and neighbourliness did constitute the basis of the village as a primary group which exercised strong influence over individual families. The importance of the village as a group went further than this, however. Village life was characterized by its homogeneity: the priest and the teacher, as well as the squire and his servants, were all outsiders and no part of the peasant stratum; they belonged to other estates and classes. So were the few representatives of non-agricultural professions resident in the village. Handicrafts and trades were usually followed by members of the village only as a sideline. The existence of the village community and the social consciousness associated with it—a sense of separateness and a feeling of solidarity—undoubtedly made it difficult for capitalist forms of development to occur, and for class differentiation and class antagonisms to emerge, even though traditional solidarity of this kind was not enough to prevent such developments taking place.

The notion of the village as an extended peasant family, then, has its roots in the past. The village complemented the family, particularly in those areas in which the family was not self-sufficient. Help with production; mutual aid in the event of natural disasters or family catastrophes; the performance of certain economic activities—often based on common ownership (e.g. communal forests and common pasture), or common operations which benefited everybody (road building, land improvement, etc.); the maintenance of law and order; the performance

of wider cultural and social functions; and the exercise, via
public opinion, of social control over individual families and
persons—all these village functions, which develop out of family
functions, make the village a coherent, largely self-sufficient entity in relation to the outside world. Because of these activities
on the part of the village as a primary group, co-operation in
its various forms was a necessity. The model of the production
co-operative is also based on these functions today, since to a
great extent it follows the principles on which the large peasant
family was based.

But the village as a primary group is also, in its turn, affected
by changes occurring in the peasant family. Village cohesion is
weakened by the effects of wider social forces, by the influence of
the town and of industry, and by changes occurring in peasant
farming and within the peasant stratum. Even economic relations between the rich and poor farmers—which at first have
the character of patronage[29]—begin to take the form of relationship between employer and employee, and of a relation between
things rather than between human beings. Personal authority
tends to be replaced by specialist and functional authority. The
development of the farm as an enterprise leads to its articulation
with the outside world, with the market. Rational farming requires agricultural consolidation, but consolidation disintegrates
the village, transfers its original functions to neighbours, and in
the long run individualizes the farm. The development of the
market and of industry links village families to their place of
work or creates possibilities of employment outside the village.
The development of mass communications and of transport
leads to the general diffusion of urban cultural patterns. Internal sources of change are therefore reinforced by the influence of
industry and the town, which in recent years have become
dominant.

Migration from village to town, the settlement of the Western
Territories, and the growth of earnings outside the village have
had a particularly strong influence in Poland. One can no longer
say that the village constitutes a single social estate. Formerly,
landless peasants who lived in the villages did not constitute a
separate group. Today not only have their numbers increased
but the majority work outside the village and agriculture, and
belong to other social strata and classes.[30] The same can be said

of the majority of the peasants working smallholdings, except that they form a marginal category, in between two social strata and milieux.

The village has thus become a place of residence for people following various occupations and belonging to different social strata. This differentiation is only partly (in Poland only very slightly) a function of the internal needs of the rural community. It is much more due to urban influences, even the direct penetration of the town into the village. This makes it difficult today to demarcate the boundaries between village and town precisely: in the case of those areas which have been most strongly subject to the influences of urbanization and industrialization one can even speak of the emergence of local aggregations of an 'urban–rural' character. Certain features peculiar to Poland are intensifying this process. Mass migration from village to town, which strengthens mutual contacts, urbanizes the village but also 'ruralizes' the town. Improved communications facilitate the use of large urban centres as sources of supply and as places of amusement for villagers within the ever-extending orbit of the towns. The trend towards the depopulation of the small towns, which in many respects worsens the economic, cultural and even administrative services available to the village as compared with the larger urban centre, is a further factor peculiar to Poland which tends to make the village increasingly a 'suburban' place. The small towns also change their functions or go into decline, and their suburbs grow larger. The village changes its character in terms of land use: it is no longer exclusively an agricultural area, but becomes a residential and recreational area for the urban population.[31]

One could go on multiplying these observations. They are all evidence of the unidirectionality of change, of the weakening of the traditional local village community and the blurring of fundamental social differences between town and country.

Like changes in the structure and functioning of the peasant farm, changes in the rural family and the village as a group based on the family and on neighbourhood raise many theoretical and practical problems. In the light of these changes, rural sociology's traditional concern with the nature of the differences between country and town begins to look like an issue of diminishing importance. In Poland today it is virtually impossible to

point to any distinctive set of characteristics typical of the traditional peasant family. The family has undergone changes either
in the nature of the values recognized by their members or in
behaviour. Changes in the structure and functioning of the peasant family are part of the entirety of changes in village life,
which they help to intensify and extend. Older definitions of the
village also appear to be largely out of date.[32] It is doubtful, too,
whether village life, including the peasant family and the village
as a primary group, can be analysed any longer as a social system functioning according to its own peculiar principles. Phenomena occurring in the village can no longer be completely
explained on the basis of assumptions of this kind. To a large
extent, then, theories based on such assumptions are becoming
useless.

The question that now arises is the source of these changes:
to what extent do they derive from the operation of processes
internal to the village, and to what degree can they be explained
as due to the influence of the town? The root of the present-day
crisis in the family, and other contemporary problems of general
sociology, might be understood better against the background of
the crisis of the village. An approach of this kind would locate
rural sociological research within broader theoretical perspectives. However, even these tentative and very summary descriptions of the changes within the areas of social life embraced by
rural sociology indicate the scientific attractiveness of research
into the unusually rich problems of the peasant family and the
village community, and suggest also the profitability of pursuing
inquiries along the lines of the reciprocal influence operating
between village and town.

Practical problems which call for research because of their
significance for the future of the Polish village are equally interesting from a purely sociological point of view. The present-
day model of the production co-operative is based on the traditional peasant family, which is its basic element, while the
family's connection with the large collective farm subordinates
the family to the farm's organizational structure and to the
methods of operation laid down in the collective farm's rules.
The present-day model of the production co-operative is also
based on the traditional village community, which, through co-
operation, is revived as a cohesive unity. The suggestion that

we look at collectivization against the background of the village as a primary group makes sense in the light of these assumptions.[33]

In view of these changes, however, the relevance of a model based on the traditional family and village must be questioned. The contemporary Polish village differs considerably from the Russian village of half a century ago. Research can show us the extent to which one can still find traditional traits in Poland. It is not sufficient to show that they are still present in behaviour: the important question is the extent to which they are accepted. Production co-operatives cannot be assumed to be popular, especially among young people. They can become more popular only by evincing changes which would represent 'modernity', i.e. which would provide the values associated today with urban life, which are generally also desired in the village.

Thus the question of changes in the peasant family and in the village community are again bound up with the unresolved problem of the model of the large agricultural enterprise, which not only has to be economically more rational than the peasant farm, but must also be 'modern', i.e. stand for the way of life the rural population aspires to. This also raises the question of the nature of the village community. For the traditional family–neighbour group is no longer the only theoretically possible model, and thinking in these terms cannot lead to effective action if this traditional entity has largely ceased to exist in Poland. Such problems involve consideration not only of appropriate models but also of ways in which such models ought to be realized and what social forces are needed in order to bring them into existence.

The peasant stratum and changes among the peasantry

The main issues arising from changes in the social structure have been discussed in detail in chapter 5. To get these changes into perspective, we need to recapitulate briefly the observations we made there. In analyses of the class structure of capitalist society, delineation of the peasant stratum has always produced many difficulties. On the one hand, peasants have been differentiated by such clear and distinctive social characteristics that it was difficult to deny the existence of a separate peasant stratum. On the other, in the face of distinct differences between town and country the application of a uniform structural scheme was bound to be artificial. Marxism regards the peasant stratum as intermediate between the basic classes of capitalists and workers. It was considered that the operation of economic forces within capitalism leads to progressive polarization so as to give rise to two opposed classes, so that the village, like the town, would thus undergo a division into capitalists and proletarians.

With economic development, this polarization came about swiftly in some countries, more slowly in others. In the villages it took the form not so much of the emergence of a division into capitalists and workers but rather of emigration from the village, adding to the growing urban working class and the concentration of profits accruing from agriculture in the hands of *urban* capitalists. In countries where industrialization occurred later and in highly concentrated form, and where (as in pre-war Poland) large estates were preserved, these changes gave rise to a number of other features. Above all, the older class division into village and manor was preserved; the estates were transformed into capitalist agricultural enterprises and capitalist relations developed as between village and manor. Second, because of the concentration of capital mainly outside the rural areas, the position of the peasant stratum as a whole in the social structure and class system changed in accordance with the growing importance of the town and industry. Under these conditions other factors besides polarization came into play in Poland, and helped to preserve the unity of the peasant stratum. For these reasons it is not possible to treat the village and the town as communities in which a parallel and similar development of class polarization has taken place. Rather, it is necessary to treat the village as a separate entity in the general social system of classes and strata. All these changes took place more slowly in the village—changes both in the nature of peasant farming and in respect of relations between town and country which, under Polish conditions, determined the position of the peasant community as a whole.

Yet, despite these specifically Polish features, class changes were of a similar kind in both the country and the town. In capitalist countries at the present time the village is being transformed more or less rapidly from a synonym for the peasant

stratum into a community in which one finds the same patterns
of class and occupational differentiation emerging that one finds
finally developed in the towns, though on a different scale.[34]

Under present-day conditions in Poland the direction of
change in rural society differs from that in capitalist countries.
In the latter the division into owners and workers (agricultural
capitalists and agricultural proletariat) mirrors the class structure of the urban population; in Poland, however, the capitalist
class is almost non-existent in the towns, and, in general, ownership or non-ownership of the means of production no longer
differentiates people to any serious extent, nor does it constitute
the axis of social inequality. But in the Polish village differentiation with respect to ownership of means of production still
persists, despite its limited extent. This differentiation is part
of the pattern of economic relations between neighbours, or, in
more developed form, those entailed in the hiring of labour.
Under the influence of fundamental structural changes, however, both differentiation according to ownership of means of
production, and the extent of class domination, have been considerably restricted. Agrarian reform and the settlement of the
Western Territories, mass migration from village to town, the
broad possibilities open to the landless population of employment outside private enterprise—and especially outside the village and agriculture—have greatly limited the number of those
who can be regarded as rural proletariat, or 'village poor' in the
Leninist sense.[35] There has also been a reduction in the number
of owners of capitalist farms.

An important role has been played in this by the class policy
of the State, although general economic forces also played their
part (shortage of labour in the villages) as well as general social
factors such as the social position of the village day labourer,
which led to a rise in the price of day labour and thus made
hiring labour less profitable, more troublesome and even something to be avoided out of regard for public opinion. The difficulties of hiring labour for peasant farms to some extent stimulated the revival of institutions peculiar to the traditional village (e.g. loan repayment in the form of labour). But, according
to data collected in 1959, the importance of hired labour and
of repayment in labour (125 days in one group of farms of over
25 hectares in size, in areas of most advanced capitalist develop-

ment) plus a continuing decline in the hiring of labour (observations made in 1962) do not suggest that there is any significant
development of class relations, despite their evident presence.
Of course, individual farms continue to be differentiated with
regard to their economic strength; hence, potentially, class differences do exist and may revive under certain economic and
social conditions (for instance, when exodus into the towns is
restricted), while conflicting interests between small and large
owners, though not so sharp today, may reappear under certain
conditions.

These qualifications aside, class divisions in the peasant stratum, in terms of the categories introduced by Lenin,[36] are of
rather marginal importance, while class contradictions based on
this division cannot be regarded today as the main source of
contemporary alignments in the countryside. Although class divisions are not a myth and although one can point to actual rural
capitalists and proletarians, those who conceive of the future of
the village in terms of a class struggle 'between the poor and the
kulaks', and who believe that this struggle will lead to collectivization, draw no support for their views from our knowledge of
actual conditions today. The most numerous social categories in
the Polish village today are (1) peasant owners of family farms,
and (2) the highly diversified category of 'peasant–workers', i.e.
families living in the village and in varying degrees combining
work on a farm with regular employment outside the village
and outside agriculture. Thus differentiation along the village–
town axis has become the dominant division in the peasant stratum, and in Poland this differentiation is *not* associated with
the class divisions to which Lenin pointed in his works on the
pre-revolutionary Russian village[37] with regard to changes in the
urban class structure or with regard to rural change.

The changes we have noted suggest a number of areas for
sociological research. In what does the peasant stratum consist
today, in view of the existence of a full continuum of intermediate categories between peasant farmer and town dweller?
What are the social characteristics of the peasant stratum and
what are the major types of family within rural society? What,
in consequence, is the overall direction of change, since so many
factors are involved, some maintaining and even reinforcing the
cohesion of the stratum, others weakening it?

These questions, to which answers are already largely available on the basis of research material,[38] are important in defining 'social forces' in the sense of human collectivities which occupy roughly identical life situations, and hence undertake activities in ways common to all of them. Analysis of 'social forces' in this sense, of course, may be undertaken from many different aspects: it is thus possible to consider young people or the members of one organization or another as a 'social force'. The results of research lead to the conclusion that the most important analysis is that of socio-occupational divisions, linking vocational and class (strata) differences. Obviously, this requires analysis both of the groups within which these divisions occur (territorial groups, groups linked by common origin, etc.) and of groups which express the interests of one or another socio-occupational category (political and professional organizations, or the organs of government). Examining the system of social forces in this way, we come back to the categories already mentioned as the most numerous in the village today, namely family farmers and 'peasant–workers'.

Because of marked differentiation among 'peasant–workers'[39] it is difficult to analyse this category as a social force. However, it cannot be left out when considering the future of the village. It would seem that, apart from problems arising from their new vocations, peasant–workers are also concerned about being near their place of work, about freeing themselves from the burdens imposed by farming (by renting or selling their land, etc.), and about the development of the village as a residential settlement. This can be interpreted as an interest in the urbanization of the village; in its transformation into a rural–urban community. This is the attitude towards the village on the part of what today is one of the most numerous categories of the rural population and one which is fast becoming a social force, though in Poland we still cannot definitely say what part the peasant–workers will ultimately play in social change.

The basic orientations of peasants running family farms are obvious enough. As well as having similar interests in rural urbanization they wish to lighten their labour and to increase the income they derive from their agricultural holdings, to raise the social prestige of the farmer's occupation, to model their family life on that of the towns and thus to extend the family's functions in areas other than production. In order to lighten their labour and increase their income, peasant farmers undertake a number of joint activities, primarily through co-operative institutions.

Rural co-operation is nothing new. It first emerged in the nineteenth century, with the growth of entrepreneurial elements in peasant farming, and the resultant increase of mutual dependence and increase in the possibilities of utilizing wider economic structures. Originally, rural co-operation was a social movement; it rallied farmers around an ideology, to which its economic functions were subordinated. Nowadays the literature uses the phrase 'the institutionalization of rural co-operation'.[40] The co-operative is acquiring features characteristic of the enterprise, is subject to special economic requirements, and is beginning to lose those attributes of a social movement which used to make it difficult for the co-operative movement to perform its economic functions adequately. The permanent staff, which is committed to the rural co-operative and to its development, is the most significant element operating within it today. At membership meetings the farmer represents the interests not of the co-operative but of his farm; if it does not benefit him personally he is not particularly interested in whether the enterprise he works in is of a co-operative, private or State character.[41] His only concern is that it should be efficiently profitable. Today the rural co-operative, in all its various forms, is to a large extent, not a social movement but an enterprise. Its importance for the future of the village lies not so much in the fact that it teaches the smallholder to relinquish his private property in favour of the co-operative ideal as in the fact that, in lightening the burden of work for the smallholder, it gradually takes over agricultural production as a whole. In capitalist countries co-operation is at present taking over production functions only to a small extent; it mainly embraces other branches of the farmer's activity. Nevertheless, its share in production is increasing, although Krzywicki's vision of the whole of agricultural production being organized by the co-operative has not come about.[42]

Trading, savings and similar co-operatives in Poland have to a large extent been institutionalized. There are also the organizations known as Agricultural Circles, to which great hopes are attached. When it began (in 1957) this type of organization was

—and still is to a large extent—a genuine social movement, bringing together those individuals most immediately involved with farming, notably peasants running medium-size farms.[43] At present, while remaining a socio-occupational movement, the organization also performs other functions: it manages millions of zlotys from the Fund for the Development of Agriculture, arranges various official matters, carries on educational activity, encourages farmers to develop a sense of pride in being a farmer, initiates such enterprises as machinery centres and ensures their appropriate (i.e. economically rational) operation. Thus it has various bases of activity, and operates on at least three principles: those of a socio-occupational movement, an administrative agency and an enterprise. At this stage it is difficult to determine which of the three principles these organizations will finally settle upon, and equally difficult to foresee what role they will play in shaping the future of the village.

In our opinion, Agricultural Circles are most likely to develop as an enterprise, or group of enterprises, based on a permanent staff and on up-to-date techniques, performing a number of specialized production services and taking over various branches of agricultural production. Poland has already had much interesting experience in this direction; for instance, the attempts of dairy co-operatives to organize cattle-breeding, and plans for bringing into operation dairy farms based on contracts with specialized feed-growing farms organized by co-operative enterprises or by the POM (State Machine Stations). A sociological analysis of these experiences, in which new types of relationship between these enterprises and the village are being developed, could contribute much to the subject under discussion.

Problems discussed above in connection with the system of class relations in the village and in connection with rural co-operation may all be related to the basic theoretical problems of rural sociology, namely the dynamics, consequences and directions of contemporary social change in the rural areas; and to these practical problems of the optimal forms of development for the village and for agriculture in the future.

We have discussed the theoretical and practical problems confronting rural sociology here by surveying social change in the village. To a large extent this survey has been based on research findings. However, on the whole it is not so much a generalization

of the result of research as a general hypothesis whose verification
or rejection requires much further research. Such research, until
now, has been inadequate, considering its scientific interest and
the practical significance of these problems in Poland.

Notes

1   H. Kotter, *Landbevolkerung im sozialen Wandel* (*Rural popula-
tions and social change*), Cologne, 1958.
2   W. Abel, 'Stadt–Land–Beziehungen' ('Town–country relationships'), *Dorfuntersuchungen* (*Village study*) 162, special issue of
Berichte uber Landwirtschaft (*Reports on the Rural Economy*), Ham-
burg, 1955.
3   A. V. Chayanov, 'O diferentsiatsii krestianstkovo khozyaistva'
('On differentiation in peasant farming'), *Puti sel'skoyo khozyaistva*
(*The Roads of Rural Economy*), Moscow, 1927, No. 5/23, p. 109. For
a fuller discussion of the character of peasant farming see also the
earlier chapters of the present work.
4   H. Mendras, *Les Paysans et lo modernisation de l'agriculture,*
cit., p. 15.
5   K. Dobrowolski, 'Chlopska kultura tradycyjna', *cit.,* p. 32.
6   J. Chalasinski, *Mlode pokolenie chlopow, cit.,* vol. iv, chapter 1.
7   T. Hunek, 'Mlodziez technikow rolniczych o sobie i o rolnictwie'
('Young people in agricultural technical schools and their views concerning themselves and agriculture'), *Wies wspolczesna* (*The Contemporary Village*), 1960, No. 6.
8   In *Rolnicy o swoim gospodarstwie* (*Farmers on the subject of
their farms*), a questionnaire issued by the Public Opinion Poll Centre
(OBOP) in 1960, 72 per cent recognized the need for vocational training. See also B. Galeski and A. Wyderko, 'Poglady chlopow na
przyszlosc wsi', *cit.,* and D. Galaj, 'Poglady chlopow wsi Bochen na
perspektywy rozwoju gospodarstw chlopskich' ('Peasants of Bochnia
village on the prospects of development in peasant farming'), *Wies
wspolczesna,* 1961, No. 4.
9   Replies to the question 'Can the owner of a small farm be a
good farmer?' in a questionnaire concerning the modernization of agriculture sent out by the IER Workshop on Rural Social Structure in
1960.
10   On the basis of an OBOP poll.
11   L. Krzywicki, *Kwestja rolna, cit.*
12   In a number of IER investigations, e.g. *Wyniki rachunkowosci
w indywidualnych gospodarstwach chlopskich za poszczegolne lata*
(*Results of cost accounting on individual peasant farms in particular
years*).
13   H. Latii, *L'Evolution du revenu agricole* (*The evolution of agricultural incomes*), Paris, 1967, p. 98.

14   Studies carried out by M. Dziewicka of the IER. See, for example, 'Stosunek chlopow-robotnikow . . .', cit.
15   Research by D. Galaj in the village of Bochnia. See, for example, *Kultura i spoleczenstwo (Culture and Society)*, 1960, No. 4.
16   All the OBOP rural opinion polls and all studies of rural areas by other agencies point in the same direction.
17   E.g. studies by M. Trawinska-Kwasniewska and D. Markowska. See, for example, the former's 'Zmiany w rodzinie wiejskiej' ('Changes in the rural family'), *Wies wspolczesna*, 1961, No. 5.
18   W. L. Thomas and F. Znaniecki, *The Polish peasant, cit.*, p. 70.
19   A. L. Bertrand, *Rural sociology*, New York, 1957, p. 196.
20   M. Pohoski, 'Wychodzstwo do miasta a obszar gospodarstwa i rozmiary' ('Migration to the town, size of farm and size of family'), *Wies wspolczesna*, 1960, No. 9.
21   According to research by E. Jagiello-Lysiowa. See, for example, 'O czym marzy mlodziez', cit.
22   A. Sianko, 'Mlodzi rolnicy o swoim zawodzie', cit.
23   Studies carried out by the IER. See, for example, B. Galeski, 'Uwagi o spolecznym zroznicowaniu warstwy chlopskiej', cit.
24   See the questionnaire *Rolnicy o swoim gospodarstwie, cit.*
25   W. L. Thomas and F. Znaniecki, *op. cit.*
26   Cf. research by M. Latuch and M. Pohoski, *Spoleczno-ekonomiczna struktura wsi, cit.*
27   W. Grabski, 'System socjologii wsi', cit.
28   K. Duda-Dziewierz, *Wies Malopolska a emigracja amerykanska (The Malopolska village and emigration to America)*, Warsaw, 1938.
29   S. Czarnowski, *Podloze ruchu chlopskiego (Foundations of the peasant movement), Dziela (Works)*, vol. 2, Warsaw, 1956, p. 167.
30   J. Przychodzen, 'Struktura spoleczno-zawodowa', cit.
31   H. Kotter, *op. cit.*
32   H. Hoftrommer, 'The relationship of rural sociology to other fields of sociological specialization', *Rural Sociology*, vol. xxv, 1960, p. 175.
33   W. Bienkowski, 'Z zagadnien socjologii i metodyki wsi' ('On the sociological problems and methods of village reconstruction'), *Kultura i spoleczenstwo*, 1960, No. 3.
34   B. Galeski, *Zmiany spoleczno-ekonomicznej struktury wsi w Polsce Ludowej (Changes in the socio-economic structure of the village in People's Poland)*, Warsaw, 1961.
35   B. Galeski, 'Podzial ludnosci wiejskiej na kategorie spoleczne' ('The division of the rural population into social categories'), *Wies wspolczesna*, 1961, No. 3.
36   V. I. Lenin, 'Draft theses on the agrarian question', *Selected works*, vol. 2, part 2, Moscow, 1951.
37   V. I. Lenin, *The development of capitalism in Russia, cit.*
38   *Spoleczno-ekonomiczna struktura wsi, cit.*
39   This term [*chlopi-robotnicy*] was introduced into Polish agrarian literature by J. Tepicht, 'Przemiany wsi Rzeszowskiej', cit.

40   F. Abma and J. H. W. Lijfering, 'Instytutionalizacja organizacji rolniczych w Hollandii' ('The institutionalization of agricultral organizations in Holland'), *Wies wspolczesna*, 1957, No. 1.
41   O. Grande, 'Sociological problems of rural co-operation', a paper presented to the fourth World Congress of Sociology at Stresa.
42   L. Krzywicki, *op. cit.*
43   A. Romanow, 'Czlonkowie kolek rolniczych' ('The membership of Agricultural Circles'), *Wies wspolczesna*, 1961, No. 2.

8 Prerequisites for the transformation of the peasant farm

The existence of individual peasant farms within a system based on the socialization of the means of production in Poland has stimulated a consideration of ways of changing this situation, which is so out of harmony with socialist thinking.

Since the earlier ideas about rural change have been questioned, rethinking of the problem was necessarily directed to a search for different concepts and the testing of many propositions formerly regarded as unquestionable. The fact that these ideas no longer form the basis of current practice and have to some extent lost their political sharpness has allowed considerable freedom of expression on the subject. Less protected by the authority of dogma,[1] and less exposed to dogmatic condemnation, these views have been subjected to empirical and logical control. As a result, they are backed up by fuller and more painstaking documentation, and are formulated in moderate terms, modified by many qualifications.

Although the methods of transformation canvassed differ considerably, agrarian policy would seem to call for a many-pronged approach, in which the adoption of any given strategy does not exclude other courses of action, but rather is complementary. No single strategy, though each may bring many benefits, can solve every problem. In turn, agrarian policy, thanks to moderation in everyday practice and in formulating ultimate goals, promises to make it possible to implement each of the suggested proposals while not committing itself totally in favour of any one of them. In short-run terms, a policy of this kind recommends itself. But it does not answer the important question: 'What will happen tomorrow?' For, obviously, actual practice cannot be either as moderate or as precisely measured as papers read at academic meetings. In discussing the transformation of peasant farming, we have to get down to fundamentals.

In contrast to these clear (sometimes exaggerated) differences between various proposed courses of action, there is obvious agree-

ment on the basic premises, though these are less clearly formulated. One might think that everyone was convinced that individual peasant farming should give way to highly productive
(large-scale) State or co-operative agricultural enterprises. Yet
there is dissension regarding the actual working out of the principle, with differing views of the developmental prospects for
peasant farming and inadequate clarification of the ultimate
objectives.

Basically the idea that peasant farming should disappear from
the scene can be advocated both by those who think it necessary
to abolish peasant farming as quickly as possible and by those
who want to bring about the modernization of farming and the
development of closer ties with the national economy, as the best
strategy for change. Since very generally accepted assumptions (as
formulated above, or in more extreme forms) lend themselves to
contradictory interpretations, it becomes necessary to consider
them in more detail. It is especially necessary to consider:

1. Whether, when, in what conditions, and also for whom,
    large farms are economically more advantageous than peas-
    ant farms.
2. What socially important ends the transformation of peasant
    farming serves, and whether such a transformation is in
    fact called for.
3. Whether those whom it directly affects, i.e. the peasant
    farmers, are interested in this transformation.

It is answers to these questions that should govern the strategies
developed for the transformation of peasant farming which is
taking place all over the world today.

The economic advantages of large farms

The economic consequences of replacing peasant family farms by
large farms, whether State or co-operative, requires consideration
of at least two factors: changes in the size of the farm, and changes
in the nature of ownership (property relations). With respect to
the first, let us consider, for example, replacing 100 ten-hectare
farms by one of a thousand hectares. If the well established and
generally recognized relationship between output and input for

a given area is accepted as correct,[2] then the effect of this change will be a diminution of input per unit of output (especially labour inputs). It will also lend to a decline in both gross and net production per unit of land.

Assessment of the benefits arising from such an operation depends on the point of view adopted. From the viewpoint of the private entrepreneur such a change can be regarded as beneficial. If we assume that he uses the profits from the ten-hectare farms in order to finance investment in them (including the investment of labour), then the organization of a large farm might well be more profitable, since the *effectiveness* of the investment essentially determines (or co-determines) the magnitude of profit.[3] In addition the private producer could reckon on an increase in profit in connection with the anticipated rise in prices (if others follow the same path) as a result of a decline in production.

This does not apply when the State acts as entrepreneur, since it is not one farm, or even a single section of the economy, that is involved, but the entire national economy. If the level of production in the State as a whole is insufficient or barely sufficient to satisfy demand, because it would not be possible to increase the area under cultivation, such a step would be unprofitable. For a reduction in agricultural production necessarily leads to a diminution in the supply of food (through increases in prices, increased difficulties in obtaining basic agricultural products, or because of diminished allocations—depending on the system of commodity distribution). And this would undoubtedly have a detrimental influence on the efficiency of labour in all branches of the national economy, not to mention the social consequences of such a step. These consequences can be avoided. Change can be beneficial if losses accruing from a decline in agricultural output are compensated for by more effective employment in non-agricultural sectors of labour released from agriculture. The resultant increase in production would enable the shortage of food stuffs to be covered by purchases on foreign markets. For countries exporting foodstuffs and looking for agricultural self-sufficiency (countries which are unable to import from abroad), the change in question can be viewed as beneficial only if there is a surplus of agricultural products. The necessity of increasing the effectiveness of input per output unit would then surely depend upon the need for adaptation to low market prices, and would in any case yield higher profit without disadvantageous economic effects.

Of course, as a general entrepreneur the State can undertake the reconstruction of agriculture indicated above even though it may be economically unprofitable in the light of previous considerations. In that case it may be a matter of attaining important non-economic goals, or it may come about as a result of pressure from agricultural producers. (These questions will be followed up later.) It is worth noting just one instance of this kind. In an economically backward and isolated country the State authorities may come to the conclusion that the replacement of small peasant farms by large State Farms (or co-operatives, still subject to State authority) may render the attainment of certain especially important goals possible, for instance, national defence or industrialization.[4] This case is not strictly related to our foregoing considerations, because it is not primarily the economic advantages of large-scale farming that are the source of capital accumulation but the power of the State to reduce consumption by stricter regulations. It is difficult to estimate how far such a step is necessary, and its efficacy in achieving the hypothesized end is dubious (a moderate increase in levies on private producers would possibly yield better results). However, its negative implications are obvious: the worsening, for an indefinite period, of the state and the efficiency of the economy.

There are many different views on the economic necessity for agricultural reconstruction. For instance, a shortage of labour supply in agriculture may lead to its more effective exploitation in other branches of the economy and increased imports of foodstuffs, or it may be linked with a consumption-reducing type of industrialization, involving low productivity of labour. The necessity of carefully managing areas where for one reason or another peasant farming does not exist (e.g. desert lands requiring costly and complex investment which only a State organization could afford) does not affect the above reasoning.

In conclusion, the replacement of peasant farming by large farms may be economically beneficial for the State in its role as a general entrepreneur when there is either surplus food production or the possibility of more effective exploitation of labour-power outside agriculture which would allow foodstuffs from abroad to be profitably imported. (Even under these conditions the profitability of such a change is not certain.) It will not be economically beneficial if it does not increase the effectiveness of investments as a result of converting to large farms.

Agricultural transformation involves not only the replacement of small by large farms but also the conversion of private farms into State or co-operative agricultural enterprises. The owners of private farms of any size are motivated to maximize income from their investments. It might be reasonable to assume that this attitude to production existed also in State, and even more in co-operative, agricultural enterprises. But so far the model of the socialist enterprise, as well as the system of relations between producers, distributors and consumers, have not stimulated such attitudes. Among other things this is probably due to the fact that production per hectare on Polish State Farms is not only lower than that of peasant farms but also more expensive. On State Farms, a product valued at 100 zlotys requires a high material and general investment that is not compensated for by the saving in labour, even if the cost of a day's labour on a peasant farm is calculated according to the rates fixed for State Farms.[5] Comparison of Polish State Farms with peasant farms, and with large and small farms generally, is of course of limited value, since they operate under varying soil, climatic and other conditions. In any case, the producers' attitude has such an influence on the effects of economic activity that the proposition that large farms are economically more rational must be qualified by the statement that this is so as long as they are subject to market stimuli and are run according to the profit principle.

The above assumption (based on generally recognized assumptions) that replacing 100 ten-hectare farms by one of a thousand hectares lowers input per unit of output but also reduces output per unit of area, requires one further remark and a related reservation. The higher labour expenditure on a small farm is sometimes achieved by overwork on the part of the family. At the same time, if we confine ourselves to the peasant farm (and, if the hypothesis to be tested holds true, to an analysis of peasant farms of various sizes) then it must be stated that a small farm does not involve more labour by a family (per member over 14 years of age) than a large one. On the contrary, a family puts in the same or even less labour on a smaller area.[6] It is not the overwork of the family on a larger peasant farm but the different

production structure, giving a rational balance as between area
and available labour resources, that accounts for the relatively
higher output value per hectare. This being so, it should be re-
iterated that the most profitable form of farming under given
conditions is determined by the relation of labour supply to area.
Second (and here we make a reservation), it is worthwhile considering whether for particular kinds of agricultural production
there are differences between optimum size of farm, volume of
output per hectare and the effectiveness of investment. It is possible that a different size of farm is most profitable for different
branches of agricultural production and that, in certain branches,
the large farm may require less investment to yield the same
level of output per hectare. This would not modify the argument
with regard to the replacement of peasant farms by large ones,
but it would indicate the need to consider particular kinds of
specialization in organizing large farms.

Although it is possible to question both facets of the assumption, we continue to use it. If it is sound and the argument based
on it correct, then we must conclude that under Polish conditions
the immediate replacement of peasant farms by a system of large
State or co-operative farms cannot be regarded as economically
advantageous.

No special study is needed to confirm the inadequacy of the
volume of Polish agricultural production available for export
and for the satisfaction of the population's consumption needs.
No State can regard a reduction in consumption as advantageous, but in a socialist State it is, furthermore, ideologically unacceptable. It is not desirable even as a transitional step, and
only under conditions of extreme necessity could such a desperate measure be considered. The satisfaction of wants in regard
to food supplies is a recognized necessity. This necessity is recognized as all the more compelling because the market equilibrium
is disturbed, and in the consumer's interests it is desirable to
maintain prices at their present level. There is no intention of
giving up the export of agricultural produce, and it is desirable
to reduce and even eliminate the import of grain. The achievement of these ends undoubtedly depends on increased output.
As long as this is so, replacement of peasant farms by large
ones cannot be regarded as economically profitable, for it would
produce results contrary to those desired.

The task of Polish agriculture is the greatest and swiftest possible growth of production given available investment, not a reduction of investment in general. There is no country-wide shortage of agricultural labour. Over the period 1950 to 1960 there was a slight rise in the rural population (from 15 to $15\frac{1}{4}$ millions), while the agricultural population (taking agriculture as the main source of maintenance as the basis, and so excluding peasant–workers) fell slightly (from 11,597,000 to 11,205,000). Migration from village to town absorbed 46 per cent of those born in the rural areas over the years 1951–60 (61 per cent over the entire period 1946–60). Shifts from agriculture to other branches of the national economy (including peasant–worker farming among those who left agriculture) embraced a percentage estimated to be close to the birth rate.[7] It follows from this that—apart from local situations requiring local solutions—the need is not so much to curb the exodus from agriculture as, on the contrary, to encourage it. And if peasant–worker farming is considered undesirable, it is necessary to steer more of the exodus from agriculture towards the towns. The problem of farms without heirs, which is closely associated with the problem of labour supply, has also given unwarranted concern. The confirmed tendency towards the fragmentation of farms would justify the deduction that there are more potential heirs than farmers. Indeed, for that matter, the transitory phenomenon of a certain number of farms without successors is found in all countries, and the proportion for Poland, stabilized between three and four per cent, is not at all disturbing.[8]

If the agricultural labour supply does not necessitate the replacement of individual peasant farms by large-scale ones, then such a step would mean the removal from agriculture of persons who would consequently be left without an occupation. The number of persons, apart from the natural population increase, who would need to be shifted from agriculture is estimated at $2\frac{1}{2}$–3 millions.[9] These people would have to be assured of work outside agriculture and housing outside the village (if they became peasant–worker farmers they could not be included in the reorganization) as well as correspondingly increased food resources (the average consumption of an urban inhabitant is higher than that of villagers). It is doubtful whether such a measure could be carried through, and it might well cause unemployment in the Polish economy, not to mention a fall in consumption. At present the assurance of the availability of jobs for young people entering the labour market is problematical in both town and country. As long as there is no provision in the employment structure for this, the difficulty will remain of assuring work for those who must leave agriculture and of effectively utilizing redundant manpower unable to leave the countryside.

To sum up: the premises on which the argument that large farms are economically more profitable than small ones is based are the relation of volume of production to demand and of numbers employed in agriculture to area. Both a shortage of labour and a surplus of foodstuffs make large-scale farming inevitable. Both phenomena (usually interconnected) are the result of economic growth and the general development of civilization. In Poland there is neither a shortage of labour nor a surplus of food. Until now the State, acting in a marketing capacity, has viewed the replacement of peasant farms by large farms as being neither necessary nor economically advantageous. It is not a step to be taken lightly, since it would seriously weaken the entire national economy.

However, economic necessity is not the sole motivating force, and economic gain is not the only socially desirable objective, though both these elements must always be taken into consideration when making decisions. Hence the question of supplanting the peasant family farms by large agricultural enterprises has to be looked at more broadly, in the light of the fundamental aims of socialism.

The fundamental aims of socialism

The socialization of the means of production is not, and never was, an end in itself in the pronouncements of the founders of Marxism. It is the means of eliminating the social sources of antagonisms which capitalism could not abolish and of achieving aims unattainable under capitalism. The more far-reaching aim is to overcome alienation in all its forms. This is a phenomenon found extensively under capitalist conditions, although it is not associated only with that system. As we now realize, socialization of the means of production *per se* does not eliminate all forms of alienation, nor do we yet know how that aim might be achieved. A consideration of the transformation of peasant family farming (perhaps the least alienating of occupations) from this point of view would be extraordinarily interesting, but the necessary data are lacking. For this reason we shall confine ourselves to a consideration of those basic aims of socialism which were not mentioned above, or which are already part of our contemporary aims.

A basic and primary aim of socialism is the abolition of exploitation and the realization of the principle 'To each according to his labour'. In its strict, scientific sense—not diluted into colloquial meanings too imprecise for any consideration of how the aim in question might be realized—the term 'exploitation' signifies a situation in which ownership of the means of production enables one man to appropriate the results of another's labour. It should be borne in mind that under capitalism the object of exploitation is not only the proletariat but also the small commodity producer: the peasant and the handicraftsman, as well as families running small service and trading establishments. Elimination of exploitation, in the sense of the term adopted here, requires the abolition of capitalist private property (that is, socialization of capitalist enterprises). The whole of society, according to socialist economic theory, appropriates the surplus product. The fruits of the producer's labour are then divided into two parts: one part is at the producer's personal disposal, the other put into circulation to satisfy collective needs. Family (commodity) forms of production in certain branches of the economy are also amenable to socialization. For the producer's remuneration can take the form not only of wages (as in the case of employees of socialized enterprises) but also of family income obtained by means of exchange (all small commodity producers) and even the form of direct distribution of the articles produced, wherever the nature of the product makes this possible (the peasant family's income in kind). The part going into the social fund can take the form of the enterprises profit, taxes and levies.

Non-capitalist, family ownership of the means of production has a number of features in common with capitalist property, which it preceded. Enterprises carried on by the family may develop into small capitalist businesses operating with hired labour when a market exists. In a twofold sense, peasant family property has been a buttress of capitalist ownership. First, labour-power released from the rural areas and the surplus value created by the peasant families were absorbed by the capitalist economic system; second, a capitalist structure arose within the peasant economy which caused it to disintegrate. Although both processes sprang from the same source, they were mutually competitive, and in particular the first tended to restrict the second. While the socialization of capitalist property abolished the first process, it did not eliminate the bases of the second, and it was even to be expected that the appropriation by capitalist enterprises of the profits of peasant families would reinforce tendencies towards rural class stratification. Yet that did not happen.

Abolition of capitalist property entails the socialization of the basic elements in the national economy. As a result the socialist State becomes able effectively to control small-scale production and determine the direction of its development. The socialized economy absorbs both the labour-power released from the family farms and the surplus products they produce. The family farm becomes subordinate to the whole socialist economy and becomes a factor in its overall development. As Polish experience demonstrates, tendencies in the direction of capitalist stratification can thus be effectively mastered. Smallholder families are no longer compelled to go to work on capitalist farms, because work can be found in socialized enterprises. The stability of the market, under State control, the progressive elimination of compulsory deliveries and the increased cost of hired labour are effective brakes upon the transformation of small family property into capitalist property.

A capitalist career becomes less attractive as positions within socialist society are increasingly valued. This does not imply the elimination of the differentiation of small producers, for the latter arises out of the variety of conditions of production in relation to the market. With this differentiation of the small producers emerge not only tendencies towards class stratification but also countervailing ones. For instance, research into changes in rural social structure[10] have confirmed that the process of proletarianization is effectively counteracted by the stronger process of freeing oneself from the necessity of working for a richer neighbour. The weakening of small capitalist farms checks their development. As a result, tendencies towards class stratification are insufficient to lead to a renewal of the capitalist structure; elements of this structure are, on the contrary, already vestigial in Poland today. Moreover, the peasant family's social situation, i.e. its access to desired values (income, prestige, education, authority), is no longer determined exclusively by the extent of its ownership of means of production. Today this factor is steadily losing its importance.

Thus the socialization of capitalist property not only enabled the exploitation of peasant families by capitalist enterprises to be abolished but also turned the peasant family farm into a factor in the development of the national economy. It has made control over tendencies towards rural class stratification possible by introducing to the village the socialist principle 'To each according to his labour'; it has assured large-scale penetration of a structure appropriate to socialist society—one which does not make ownership of the means of production the key factor determining the social situation of peasant families.

It must be mentioned in passing that premature liquidation (or partial liquidation) of small family trading and handicraft enterprises and service establishments would not contribute to the realization of the aims of socialism. Rather it would create difficulties in satisfying the population's needs, would make the functioning of the entire economy problematic, and would condemn many socially useful spheres of activity to a semi-legal vegetative state, thus creating favourable conditions for an extension of economic crime.

If the abolition of peasant farming is considered in terms of realizing the fundamental aims of socialism (the abolition of exploitation and the introduction of the principle 'To each according to his labour'), then the conclusion follows that these aims are not incompatible with the retention of the family form of production. The scale on which these aims can be achieved depends on the degree of development of the economy. The family form of production is a vital element in this development of the economy. The family form of production is a vital element in this development as long as it is economically advantageous. The elimination of fundamental social differences between town and country is another far-reaching aim of socialism. It is an aim which cannot be realized at this stage. However, resolutions do not determine social processes and trends, and social aspirations can only facilitate or hinder their maturation. The desire to abolish basic social differences already exists and, moreover, is already creating urgent practical problems. The general reluctance on the part of young people to remain in the village and in agriculture, for instance, entails a search for means of making rural life more attractive to them.

Differences between town and country involve complexes of characteristics which may be regarded as constituting different social systems. No matter how these systems are defined, these differences are fundamental. These differences between town and country can be found as far as the conditions of life and systems of inter-personal relations in urban and rural communities are concerned (differences of milieu); in respect of work, and particularly non-agricultural occupational differences; or with regard to social relations as between the peasant family and workers in concentrated and socialized production (class differences). Instead of considering all these aspects (which are closely interlinked) it will be more convenient to discuss those particular differences which are at present the cause of the peasant population's sense of being discriminated against.

First and foremost are differences in income. In every country, peasant families have lower incomes than those maintaining themselves through labour outside agriculture. Under capitalist conditions, attempts by the peasant population to increase their income are opposed by enterprises interested solely in appropriating the maximum share of the goods the farmers produce. Under socialist conditions (in accordance with the principle 'To each according to his labour') the peasant population's smaller share of distributed income corresponds with its smaller share in the income produced. Since the basic premise of this situation is the lower productivity of labour in agriculture, creation of large farms in which labour productivity might be higher would make it possible to increase the income of the agricultural producers. But it is not always possible or desirable to increase their share. It depends on whether the general income increases, remains unchanged or falls. Moreover, income must be considered not only in terms of value but also in a substantive form. If the farmers were to produce less food than is necessary to meet the population's needs, an increase in their income would involve a decided fall in the real income of other social groups; and if the State intervened to counteract this trend (by freezing prices or by stricter control of consumption), there would be a more or less proportionate drop in the real income of the entire population. Hence any increase in the farming population's income resulting from a rise in the productivity of its labour is limited by the level of output which would satisfy the population's need for foodstuffs. The economic interests of the State also influence the possibility of raising the producer's income. This does not mean that it is impossible to reduce the differences between the incomes of the peasant and the non-agricultural population as long as peasant farms are not replaced by large ones. Nor would the creation of large farms of itself guarantee the equalization of incomes. Under modern technical conditions labour productivity is increasing on family farms. While a single peasant farm is not in a position to purchase machinery and installations, these can be made available to a group of farms, for instance in the form of a co-operative. Large farms make for an increase in farmer's incomes only if their high labour productivity is really guaranteed by sufficient technical equipment and sound organization of labour which assures, *inter alia,* the interest of the producers in the results of their production.

Next, the conditions of labour in agriculture must be considered. They are generally recognized as being arduous because of the considerable physical effort involved, together with the long working day and the difficult environmental conditions (work in the open air, often in unpleasant weather, etc.). Difficult working conditions exist in all branches of agriculture. On the whole they are harder on peasant than on large-scale farms, although the peasant's freedom to organize his own activities is some compensation. It is easier to suffer hardship if it is self-imposed, as all social reformers well know.

In addition, working conditions in agriculture are unattractive because in the main the work is unskilled and non-prestigious. There is no formal career structure which would act as a mechanism of social advance. Although this is true to a large extent of the differences between the large-scale farm and the non-agricultural enterprises on the other. On the peasant farm,

labour is expended as a family obligation rather than as a re-
quirement of an occupational role. Hence there is a basic contradiction between the peasant family's productive functions and
its non-productive ones, which leads, *inter alia*, to the overload-
ing of the children with work, an under-utilization of cultural
facilities, a shortage of free time, and lack of independence for
young people as long as they remain on their father's farm.

By separating work from family life, large farms provide better conditions for the producers, and—especially important—
assure them a position in society of whatever status, based on
occupational role. State Farms are more advanced in this respect than collectives, which are closer to the family farm pattern
of production but have lost a major part of the latter's attractiveness. Yet even State Farms are less attractive than non-agricultural enterprises. Replacement of peasant farms by large-scale
farms does not guarantee any equalization of working conditions
as between agriculture and non-agricultural occupations. Socialized agriculture will appeal to those unable to obtain non-
agricultural work as the most favourable alternative.

Abolition of the distinctions between town and country must
involve a consideration of living conditions in rural and urban
settlements. Rural settlements, as a result of the nature of production and smallness of population, are composed of groups
of relatively few families, which are only slightly differentiated
both occupationally and functionally. As close-knit groups they
exercise stricter social control over the behaviour of individuals
and families. Their relative cultural isolation limits the possibilities of attaining the way of life typically associated with
urban and industrial centres. This includes education, medical
care, services and cultural amusements, as well as wider social
horizons for the individual, for whom cultural and political involvement now becomes national in scale. The small size of the
village (or rural settlement) and patterns of living this entails
are to a large extent dictated by the nature of agricultural production (notably the wide spatial distributions agriculture imposes), and thus cannot be changed simply by transforming the
peasant farm into a large farm.

However, a change of this kind is not irrelevant to the issue
under discussion. For the large farm not only reduces the number of producers per unit of space but also permits a looser as-

sociation between the dwelling place and the place of work. These partly opposed features of large-scale farming can have various consequences, depending upon the degree of development of the means of transport and communication (in the broadest sense of the word), which counteract the social isolation of the village. In conditions of low economic and technical development, resulting in poor communications and transport networks, large farms, by forming smaller concentrations of people, expose their workers all the more to the restrictions of rural life. Where the level of development is high, easier connections between the place of work and the home make it possible for employees on a large farm to choose the location of their home as they wish without risking social isolation. The decisive factor, therefore, is the general development of a country's economy and civilization. The organizational form of agriculture constitutes not an independent but a dependent variable, although it is undoubtedly important in shaping the type of settlement and the nature of its interpersonal relations.

The socialization of capitalist property provided the basis for policies aimed at achieving the fundamental aims, both immediate and long-term, of socialism. These processes, subjectively expressed in the aspirations of the people, find objective expression in the development of the socialist economy. The peasant family farm does not prevent the realization of the basic aims of socialism in so far as they can be objectively realized. Family forms of production undergo certain transformations in the course of adapting to the contemporary aspirations of the rural population, brought about by the development of socialist economy. This is a complex process, and the emergence of large farms is only one of its elements, not its sole prerequisite. The large farm becomes indispensable to the realization of the basic aims of socialism only when other prerequisites exist—above all, economic ones. The abolition of peasant farming, and the introduction of a system of large-scale farming before the full range of necessary prerequisites exist, would make the achievement of the fundamental aims of socialism more difficult. Among these prerequisites are a high general level of economic and social development and a high level of agricultural development, an economic system capable of producing the maximum

ratio of output to input, and the interest of the producers in
these changes. Since this last factor is as important as the economic factor, and has a fundamental influence on what is
achieved, it must be discussed more fully.

The aspirations of the peasantry

The peasant population's attitude to the transformation of
agriculture is of such basic importance that economic activity
which is perfectly rational from the point of view of the State
may not be viable if it is not given support at the grass roots.
On the other hand, if it stimulates the initiative and activity of
the peasant families, then even mistakes or so-called 'objective
difficulties' will not thwart success.

As we showed above, family production, particularly in agriculture, has the advantage of giving the producer a sense of
independence in making decisions over a wide area. One may
say that family production is relatively the least alienated form.
Nonetheless, those who remain on the peasant farm consider
themselves under-privileged. Farm work is an unattractive way
of earning a living. This is shown by migration, although this
can be regarded as a deliberate choice of alternative modes of
life only to a limited extent (the number who migrate corresponds to the number who have to leave because they cannot
make a living in agriculture); it is shown especially by statements to this effect, which are almost universal. But young
people in the rural areas leave large farms to an equal or even
greater extent. Such farms would appear to be just as unattractive, then. As already pointed out, the reason they are unattractive is either that they do not assure any greater access to certain
desired goods than do peasant farms (at least at present), or that
even if they do assure access to certain of these goods (better
working conditions) they do not compensate for the loss of other
advantages of the family farm.

It would be wrong to conclude that the peasants are 'anti-
socialists'. All the fundamental aims of socialism—the abolition
of exploitation, the implementation of the principle of distribution of the social product according to one's labour contribution, the abolition or weakening of the basic distinctions

between town and country—can attract peasant support, especially that of young people in the countryside. For to a large extent they coincide with their own aspirations. As we saw above, the abolition of peasant family farming today would not advance these aims but, on the contrary, would delay them. There is thus no reason why the peasants should advocate such a step.

It should be observed in passing that no amount of special privileges granted to employees on large farms would cause peasants to change their attitude to collectivization. For instance, the benefits which the State grants to members of production co-operatives—much lower taxes, retirement pensions, social security, etc.—do not succeed in making these co-operatives more attractive. For the State either has insufficient resources to make such benefits available to all agricultural producers (in which case collectivization will not change the situation) or it has the resources but is reluctant to dispense such benefits freely (in which case one cannot expect that this will not still be the case after collectivization).

The only real inducement might be that the producer needs to expend less labour, and the work itself can be lighter on a large farm. But, as is well known, most people, whether in town or country, do not, for the most part, wish to work less but rather to achieve more (higher material benefits, higher status, etc.), and are prepared to give their all to gain these things. So a decrease in the amount of working time is not in itself a sufficient inducement, particularly when unsatisfied wants remain. One strong argument in favour of large-scale farming might be the rise in output achieved, but in fact this has not so far been greater on large farms, and there is no reason to expect that it should be so.

The fact that there are no reports of large-scale farming winning support among the peasantry does not mean that they are not conscious of the limitations of peasant farming. This is clearly expressed among young people who have to remain on the farm as a sense of being under-privileged. Socialist ideology has some effect in stimulating these feelings and in suggesting alternative models of social relations in the village. But the development of industrial society itself leads to the diffusion of precisely those values (not easily obtained, if at all, under conditions of peasant family farming). Since large-scale farming does not guarantee immediate access to those values, people's wants do not focus on such things. However, they might become more significant if means were found through which the peasant farm could adapt to industrial society—even at the cost of losing certain of its advantages.

Therefore any innovation which aims at increasing the importance of labour as the factor determining the individual's situation and restricting the influence of class can count on peasant support—e.g. all innovations which reduce differences between working conditions in agriculture and in other kinds of work, differences between living conditions in town and country, or which increase the farmers' income, professional prestige, etc.

While it may be impossible to introduce these innovations into the individual peasant farm, they could be adopted by groups of farmers. The activating factor might be a group of producers (various forms of rural co-operatives) or organizations of purchasers of agricultural produce (State or co-operative institutions storing or processing agricultural produce). These enterprises, whether interested in acquiring a certain quantity of products of given quality or simply in selling their services, organize the agricultural producers to the extent required by their objectives.

So one can scarcely expect the large farm, in its present form, to attract peasant families. It will undoubtedly grow more attractive as it becomes economically more rational. But because the large farm is not attractive, this does not mean that the peasant farm is. Peasant families strive to realize values which are difficult or impossible to achieve within the limits of their farms, whilst preserving this form of production unchanged. They will adapt the family type of production to industrial society in any form which guarantees them the maximum achievement of the values they desire. Rural transformation can thus be seen as a process which is being gradually achieved, in various ways, while the creation of mechanisms linking the peasant farm with industrial society will come about to the extent that the model of the large farm proves attractive to the peasant. These are not mutually contradictory processes but aspects of a single process of development, under conditions where the entire national economy is undergoing rapid change.

The transformation of peasant farming

The elements specified above involve the interconnection of economic and social development. To be effective, policy aimed at raising agricultural production must be based both on the development of those industries supplying agriculture with the necessary technical resources, and on raising the level of rural demand. It is obvious that industrial enterprises, as well as service and trading institutions, will fulfil this function as long as the market network ensures the necessary price incentives. The development of industry, and of non-agricultural spheres generally, especially services—which do not call for large investments—will assure employment opportunities for that section of rural youth for whom there will not be room on the parental farm. Moreover, migration may be expected to create new jobs. These factors should make possible a rational basis for large-scale farming and increasing its attractiveness as a place of work. The development of farming based on social ownership of the means of production will make it possible effectively to check tendencies to rural class stratification, to eliminate vestigial forms of exploitation which still exist, and to extend the values appropriate to a society of workers on the basis of the key principle 'To each according to his labour'. State economic institutions which provide assistance to peasant farms and organize their contacts with industrial society, and which also bring small peasant farms together into larger units, are necessary for the achievement of broader access to the desired goods, particularly if increased output is to be achieved. These institutions, coming into existence because of demand on the part of the producers (various forms of rural co-operative, including its most widespread form, the Agricultural Circles) as well as from the socialized economy (contracting, large-scale co-operatives, the agricultural industry, State enterprises servicing peasant agriculture, credit organizations), will doubtless evolve organizationally in accordance with gradual increases in their functions. They will become the basis of a new type of agricultural enterprise, emerging from a pattern of production which is no longer based on the family. A new form of highly productive agricultural production (no doubt much of it on large-scale farms), organized in connection with peasant farming, will gradually take over the peasant's land and, with the existing large farms reshaped in the course of economic development, create the agriculture of the future.

This is a vision of a long and protracted process. At some point, perhaps, peasant families may decide to combine their holdings so as to create co-operatives which will take over the production functions now performed by the family. Such a decision, if taken voluntarily in order to improve their working conditions, would be an important step towards agricultural development. Even so, as we have shown, there is a gradual movement towards the take-over of the functions of the peasant farms by the socialized economy and the integration of the agricultural producer into urban industrial society. With the loss of its economic functions, the peasant farm as a legal–organizational institution could disappear. But this is not inevitable; such assumptions are not needed, and such predictions cannot be made with certainty. However, our concern is not to predict the organizational characteristics of agriculture in the future but to analyse the factors which will play a significant role in its development.

The predictions outlined above do not rest on the supposition that people will do other than simply aim to achieve their own wishes. The achievement of higher agricultural production is in the interests of society as a whole (and therefore of the State) as well as in those of agricultural producers. Peasants do not need to be persuaded to recognize their own interests, and we need not suppose that there is any problem here. The major obstacle to development will be the production and distribution of the prerequisites for increased production.

It is in the interest of all to establish State or co-operative organizations to act as distribution centres, mobilizing producers and marketing quality controlled goods. In many instances public investment is necessary. The determining criteria for the establishment of such systems must necessarily be proven efficiency and greater profitability than that which an independent entrepreneur can achieve. If marketing institutions cannot maximize profits under ideal conditions (e.g. when the milk producer wishes to sell and urban consumers are keen to buy), then it is obvious that the principles they operate under must be thoroughly reviewed. This proposition might seem obvious enough but, if not observed, can lead to serious shortfalls in agricultural production. For if the demand for foodstuffs remains unsatisfied, if the agricultural producer does not know how to sell his produce, and if his own demand is not enlarged through the desire for new industrial products, then he has no incentive to increase production, and even if he does his demands will still not be satisfied.

If we can arrive at a sound model for the economy which would ensure the efficient operation of production, trading and service enterprises, levels of agricultural output which would fully cope with demand could be achieved in a comparatively short time. Further, the development of these enterprises— especially those undertaking new functions or functions previously poorly executed—will ensure that the movement of population out of agriculture increases. As we have shown, this will create the prerequisites for the development of large farms, not because they are ideal but because they are imposed by economic development.

The development of forms linking the peasant farm with industrial society comes about in the same way. Various kinds of enterprise which, however, do not require extensive investment are called for in economic development. These are (a) enterprises hiring out machinery, (b) those carrying out given production tasks on peasant farms jointly with the peasant families, (c) enterprises providing the means of production or credit, or which buy the produce via large-scale contracting activities, (d) those processing peasant produce, and (e) enterprises creating new employment opportunities in the countryside and linking the peasant families with the system of industrial society.

Not all these forms will be created at once, for not all will be profitable at once. But, by foreseeing demand, State and co-operative organizations can take the initiative and, by anticipating the main directions of technical and organizational progress in agriculture, make possible the achievement of the desired direction of development.

It is more advantageous from the agricultural producer's point of view to hire machinery (if, of course, this is possible at the time he needs it, and if the price is appropriately adjusted) than to lay out money on its purchase and then use it only a few days in the year. It is also advantageous to be assured of an outlet for the disposal of his produce. An agreement with an enterprise which will take over the trouble of arranging for fertilizers or fodder, which will supply him with suitable material to start with and expert advice during production, which will see to transport and sales, is preferable to a situation where he has to do all this himself at his own risk. If the producer's role becomes restricted to a particular type of work, and if it becomes more profitable to have other functions taken care of by other kinds of enterprise, then he will not regard the transfer of these activities to specialized enterprises as unthinkable. Indeed, it may appear very sensible, especially if the enterprise is a co-operative which the producer knows well from having taken part in its activities and having benefited from them.

Thus in order to achieve his goals the producer comes to specialize in a definite type of activity, and after some success in that branch specialization may decide to shift to a large-scale agricultural enterprise, not from ideological but from entirely self-interested considerations.

The result is that family forms of production are transformed where activity is aimed at increasing agricultural production— in a situation where increased productivity is ensured, either because the producers have an interest in the outcome of the farming operations, or because production is based on socialized forms of organization. As far as agriculture is concerned, these activities make it necessary to create various State—or, more often, co-operative—enterprises. Such enterprises, as one element in the general socialized economy, increasingly take on the social character of agrobusinesses.[11] In other words, in the course of its natural adaptation to industrial society, peasant farming undergoes a transformation which is in the interests of the producers and which results primarily from their own activity.

The process outlined above brings together elements of both an investment system[12] and a general contracting system,[13] or represents in general the vertical consolidation of agriculture under socialist conditions. Integration does not come about only in this way, for in the course of development horizontal forms also emerge. The emergence of enterprises servicing peasant farms and then passing over to independent production has been widely canvassed, and concrete examples of such solutions have been given.[14] Industrial stock fattening enterprises, the breeding of calves, co-operative fodder-producing farms, etc., are types of enterprise of this kind, geared to co-operation with peasant farms but also independent agricultural enterprises in their own right, often taking the form of producer co-operatives, which already operate over a wide field.

The emergence of new co-operative and State agricultural enterprises which take over the functions of peasant farming in various ways necessarily involves the transformation of existing large-scale farms. What is needed is a model of the enterprise which would enable existing large farms to realize their inherent potential. The need for a model of the rational enterprise has been pointed out many times. If it has not been discussed in more detail this is because the question requires fuller and separate consideration. However, in general it may be said that, so far, the best way of interesting employees in minimizing investment or maximizing output is via profit-sharing schemes. The question of how the enterprise can most effectively achieve a profit within the framework of the general regulations protecting the interest of the owner, i.e. the State, and the consumer cannot be dealt with here. Obviously, it may be easier to stimulate independence in decision-making, as well as interest in ensuring a profit on the part of the members (or a lower price for the product, or cheaper cost of services) within co-operative enterprises. And although up to now co-operative farms have not been very popular, they can be as rationally organized as State Farms.

Some comment on the concept of production co-operatives is called for. They are a kind of compromise, for they retain elements of family production (or even originated as aggregates of small family farms) which then become linked with a system based on the social ownership of the means of production. They retain neither the advantages of peasant farming nor introduce the advantages of industrial-type enterprise. The system of vertical consolidation of agriculture is also based on the principle of linking peasant farming with the socialized economy. But because the compromise is achieved at market level it combines the virtues of both forms, and this gives it a sounder basis. One may expect the co-operative agricultural enterprises of the future to be more specialized and more uniformly organized than those already in existence, since for a long time they will continue to be based on the peasant farm, although it will not form an element of the internal organization. Under these circumstances the model of the consumer co-operative may well prove more relevant than that of the present production co-operative. Nor is there any reason why future co-operatives should be identified with the village as a local community. It is likely, rather, that rural settlements will be concentrations of employees and members of various agricultural and non-agricultural co-operatives and State enterprises, who will, perhaps, additionally cultivate small individual plots for their own benefit.

A consideration of the prerequisites for the transformation of peasant farming leads to the inevitable conclusion that the decisive factor is the development of industrial society. Rural society is gradually transformed because of the predominance of the non-agricultural sector. This process is furthest advanced in highly industrialized countries where peasant property has been transformed and allocated a subsidiary role in the capitalist economy. In socialist countries, where capitalist property has been taken over for the benefit of society and where ownership of means of production does not determine differences in social status—i.e. in the conditions of a workers' society in which the main principle is distribution of the social product according to one's labour contribution—the peasant farm, in the course of economic development, becomes converted into one based on the socialization of the means of production. The truly transforming factor, however, is the development of industrial society; the level of economic development determines the extent of the transformation. Socialism first emerged in countries where the development of industrial society was retarded. It is all the more necessary, therefore, to visualize the transformation process as a long-term one. For that matter, it has not been completed anywhere in the world. Collectivization, too, has not abolished family forms of agricultural production: in the shape of personal plots, these are still a very necessary element in the national economy. The abolition of peasant farming in favour of large farms, then, will not accelerate either economic development or the achievement of the aims of socialism. On the contrary, it will delay them. The real transformation will occur over an extended period of economic and social development. Special reorganization, in the form of 'collectivization' or 'State Farm-ization' is undesirable, as are propaganda campaigns which serve only to undermine the producer's pride in the value of his labour. Transformation requires the development of the forces of production, rationalization of the form of the socialist enterprise, and rationalization of the entire national economy. It requires a policy aiming at an increase in production and an extension of socialist principles of income distribution. Implementation of such a policy is possible because the socialization of capitalist property has created the basis for controlling the development of the entire national economy and determining the direction of that development. The faster this development proceeds—and this depends at least as much on objective conditions as on the adoption of a dynamic model for economic growth—the sooner will the transformation of peasant farming be achieved.

Notes

1   The most important views are contained in the symposium *O socialistyczny rozwoj wsi* (*On the socialist development of the village*), Warsaw, 1964.

2   See A. Brzoza, 'Indywidualna gospodarka chlopska', *cit.*, pp. 20 ff.

3   'An increase in the productivity of labour is an end in itself only for the capitalist, since it reacts directly on his profit'—M. Kalecki, contribution to the plenary meeting of Department Five of the Polish Academy of Sciences. See *Dalsze uwagi o kierunkach perspektyw rozwoju rolnictwa* (*Further observations on the prospects for agricultural development*), Warsaw, 1964.

4   Cf. M. Mieszczankowski, 'Stopniowa socjalizacja rolnictwa polskiego' ('The gradual socialization of Polish agriculture') in *O socjalistyczny rozwoj wsi, cit.*, p. 478.

5   Cf. T. Rychlik, 'Problemy rozwoju panstwowych gospodarstw rolnych' ('Problems of the development of State Farms') in *O socjalistyczny rozwoj wsi, cit.*, p. 216. The rate for a day's work is taken as 50 zlotys in accordance with the calculations of the IER.

6   A. Brzoza, *op. cit.*, p. 19.
7   M. Pohoski, *Migracje z wsi do miast, cit.*, p. 53.
8   M. Pohoski, *op. cit.*, pp. 97–8.
9   J. Okuniewski estimates the needs of the large farms of the future at 3–3½ million persons, whereas at present over 6 millions are employed in peasant farming. See his 'Revolucja techniczna w rolnictwie i jago tendencje rozwojowe' ('The technical revolution in agriculture and the direction of its development') in *O socjalistyczny rozwoj wsi, cit.*, p. 268.
10   B. Galeski, 'Stabilizacja i zmiany spolecznej struktury wsi' ('Stability and change in the social structure of the village'), *Zycie gospodarcze (Economic Life)*, 1965, No. 12 (705).
11   J. H. Davis and R. A. Goldberg, *A concept of agrobusiness*, Boston, Mass., 1957.
12   J. Tepicht, *Doswiadczenia i perspektywy rolnictwa, cit.*
13   H. Cholaj, 'Ustrojowe i produkcyjne znaczenie systemu nakladu i kontraktacji' ('The structural and production significance of an investment and contractation system') in *O socjalistyczny rozwoj wsi, cit.*, p. 431.
14   M. Urban, *Mozliwosci i kierunki rozwoju gospodarki drobnotowarowej w rolnictwie (Possibilities and trends of development in small commodity economics in agriculture)*, pp. 419 ff.

Index